WHOSE LIFE
ARE YOU LIVING?

WHOSE LIFE ARE YOU LIVING?

Finding and Living Your Unique Purpose in Christ

CURT P. MARTIN

Copyrighted Material

Whose Life Are You Living?
Finding and Living Your Unique Purpose in Christ

Copyright © 2023 by Curt P. Martin.
All Rights Reserved.

No part of this publication may be reproduced, stored in a retrieval system or transmitted, in any form or by any means—electronic, mechanical, photocopying, recording, or otherwise—without prior written permission from the publisher, except for the inclusion of brief quotations in a review.

For information about this title or to order other books and/or electronic media, contact the publisher:

Curt P. Martin
curtpmartin.com
cpmartjoy@gmail.com

ISBNs:
979-8-9883326-0-2 (softcover)
979-8-9883326-1-9 (eBook)

Printed in the United States of America

All scripture is from the NKJ version of the Bible
unless otherwise noted.

Cover and Interior Design: 1106 Design

To Joanne

God has done many incredible things to show me how much He cares about every aspect of my life. Among all of these, you are His greatest earthly blessing. Our journey together has always been centered in Him as He has guided us through all stages of life, and we grow individually and collectively in His kingdom purposes. Living for Christ with you is a great honor. He knew how much I needed your faithfulness to Him, your unconditional love, and our mutual commitment to our marriage in Christ. Loving you as much as you deserve has been beyond my reach, but I have always trusted in Christ to continue to transform me and to fill in where I fall short.

The Christian Life is to be an Incredible Journey of Walking with the Best Father Ever—Your Loving Heavenly Father. (This is the "reminder picture" God provided for my use.)

It Is Not About What You Can Do But What Christ's Spirit Is Doing Both in and Through You.

TABLE OF CONTENTS

PART ONE: *Christ's Invitation*

1. Your Choice: Christ's Incredible Life in His Spirit or Your Imitation — 3

PART TWO: *Only Christ Knows the Real You. Do You Know Who You Are in Christ?*

2. Whose Life Are You Living? Whose Life Do You Choose to Live? — 21

PART THREE: *Solid Foundations Are Essential for Truly Living Christ's Life. How Strong Are Your Cornerstones?*

3. Nothing Can Change the Depth of Christ's Love for You — 39
4. Your Salvation: Real or Club Membership? — 51
5. Know God Through His Revelation. How Do You See Him? — 63
6. Seeing Yourself With God's Eyes — 77
7. True Christian Faith Is the Gift of God — 87
8. Prayer: Intimacy and Kingdom Impact — 107
9. An Initial Look at How God Wired You — 135

PART FOUR: *Mature in Christ, and Experience the Life He Designed for You*

10.	You Are God's Unique Masterpiece	147
11.	Unique Life Journeys Significantly Impact Kingdom Missions	159
12.	The Spiritual Man and the Natural Man	169
13.	God's Revelation vs. Mankind's Head Knowledge	185
14.	Always Ask, "What Is God's Truth?" and Stand on It Alone	197
15.	If We Live in the Spirit, Let Us Also Walk in the Spirit	211
16.	The Fruit of the Spirit and the Gifts of the Spirit	229
17.	The Spirit Realm and Spiritual Warfare	255
18.	The Kingdom of God Is Not in Word but in Power	269
19.	Our Kingdom Missions Define Our Spiritual-Warfare Roles	281
20.	The Resurrection of the Lion of Judah in Christ's Church	303
21.	Breaking Free: Christ's Victory Over Strongholds and Bondages	335

PART FIVE: *Putting It All Together: Embracing and Living As Christ's Masterpiece*

22.	Accepting and Embracing the Real You—God's Unique Masterpiece	347
23.	Identify Christ's Vision, Mission, and Plans for Your Life	357
24.	This Christian Life Is Not a Game	373
25.	Put on God's Mantle, Go, and Truly Live!	385

About the Author	391

PART ONE

CHRIST'S INVITATION

CHAPTER 1

Your Choice: Christ's Incredible Life in His Spirit or Your Imitation

Gal 2:20
I have been crucified with Christ; it is no longer I who live, but Christ lives in me;

Gal 5:25
If we live in the Spirit, let us also walk in the Spirit

Eph 2:10
For we are His workmanship (masterpiece), created in Christ Jesus for good works, which God prepared beforehand that we should walk in them.

Christ's Invitation

Wherever we are in our journey with Christ or our search for truth and meaningful life, Christ is inviting us to walk with Him through this book's biblical adventure. He calls us to "Come and See" who He truly is, who we truly are to be in Christ, and how He always has more of both Himself and His unique kingdom purpose for us to embrace. He builds this journey on His unconditional love and the understanding that we are to be intentional about continuously choosing whose life we will live—His unique masterpiece or our broken imitation. This book is loving *with an edge.* Just as competitive athletes continue to sharpen their abilities, God always desires to develop us for deepening impact in His kingdom. We learn to *truly live* so that nothing of His unique masterpiece design is left caged within as we transition from this life to heaven.

The Incredible Life of Walking Your Unique Journey with God

What does it really mean to live the unique and incredible life that God designed? And how might that life be different from the average Christian's life? God awakens us to His specific purposes and kingdom missions. These become our primary focus. The important priorities of family, work, friendship, etc., take on greater meaning and are approached much more effectively. Accordingly, we become, as the Apostle Paul described in the book of Ephesians: "God's masterpiece." We are transformed through God's specific journey as we learn to "walk in the Spirit" instead of in our own efforts.

What will it really mean to "walk in the Spirit" as God commands in Galatians? And what will it be like as this walk transforms us? We will learn to live as God designed, where it is "no longer I who live, but Christ lives in me." It will then be the Spirit of God residing within, who not only transforms us but also accomplishes His purposes in and through us in His power. We will learn to no longer attempt anything for Him by operating in our own efforts, our flesh, as we gladly surrender everything and place ourselves completely under the authority of His Spirit. Our futile attempts at trying to "act like Christ" will be set aside and replaced by the victorious life of His Spirit. As we explore this life biblically, we will learn the wonderful freedom of turning from comfortable and safe Christianity to God's masterpiece life in Christ, and we will truly live.

The idea of God's Spirit living and working both *in and through us* is often misunderstood. God's Spirit is always engaged in both activities when we are living under the Spirit's authority and obeying His voice. Many Christians understand at least part of this concept. Our Father's desire is for us to continuously grow in this Spirit-led life (Gal 2:20 and 5:25) so that it is *always* His Spirit, not our flesh, which is flowing through us to achieve His will. As we learn the incredible difference between walking in the Spirit and walking in the flesh, He reveals when we have taken charge, and we gladly return control. Walking in the Spirit is living under the control of God's Spirit and operating in His power; this glorifies God. Walking in our flesh results from living in our own initiative, skills, and power; scripture teaches that this is detrimental to God's purposes.

Walking in God's Spirit provides us with not only greater knowledge of Him but also greater knowledge of who He created us to be and of how we may live uniquely for Him. We learn to ask ourselves if we are utilizing our time and resources to express our faith in every aspect of our lives in ways that are aligned with God's unique missions vs. supporting our own initiatives. We honor God's differences in ourselves and others because each of us is unique in Christ and has unique kingdom missions.

As we walk with Him, our loving Father provides us with the freedom of setting down the burden of trying to please Him, which is a burden He never intended. We learn to thrive in the incredible freedom of knowing that when we are walking in His Spirit, we are always *Being* who He designed. As these Spirit-led moments build upon each other (even though we sometimes fail as part of learning), we are *Being and Becoming* who we are yet to *Be* in the future. It cannot be otherwise unless we rebel. We *are* His masterpieces as we walk under the authority of His Spirit. God lovingly guides and develops us through victories and mistakes. When our hearts are truly focused on Him, mistakes become opportunities for growth, and our loving Father views them as such. As a simple analogy, an eagle that is raised in a healthy environment does not have to try to be an eagle. It *is one* and is naturally maturing in all the skills and behaviors that are appropriate for age and environment. We are much more complex, and we have choices that include saying "No" to God and deciding to *Be and Become* less than He designed. But the analogy holds if we have chosen a truly healthy walk with God and are intentional about each moment being lived in His Spirit.

As our Father teaches us to walk in the Spirit, we will be in unity with His Church. He frees us from trying to fit in with incorrect expectations in mankind's church and secular cultures, and we become more effective in both.

Living His way is not easy. Many in our families, cultures, and churches will not understand us and will pressure us to conform to their expectations, even when we are fully obedient to Christ. However, this life eclipses all lesser attempts. Every aspect of life is better than it ever could have been if we were doing it in our own strength.

Regardless of where we are in our walk with God, our journey with Him through this book will result in growth. We will understand and thrive in the enormous differences between simply trying to be what others (including religion) want us to be and walking in Christ's Spirit to *be* the kingdom masterpieces He created.

How to Gain the Most from Your Journey through This Book

The most effective way to experience this book is to walk through each chapter under the leadership of God's Spirit, where each time we pick it up, we surrender our will and ask for His revelations of both the biblical content that He has for us and the specific actions we are to take *under His transforming power*. Accordingly, as we set aside our efforts at *trying to act like Christ* and learn to walk in His Spirit, we will be both *Being and Becoming* His masterpiece. We come alive as He provides His freedom of living solely for Him in His power. His Spirit reveals what we are able to accept at the present stage of our journey. Each chapter ends with an application session. Its purpose is to help us have meaningful interactions with the Spirit so that we internalize all He has for us and permit Him to put it into action. Skimming through chapters for head-knowledge, without taking intimate time with God's Spirit, will rob us of much or all that He intends to reveal. Please embrace these application times. He will go well beyond the words in this book as He personalizes the Bible's truths in each chapter.

This book does not present formulas, rules to follow, or religious behaviors that you are to copy in your own strength and will. You will find biblical truths, thoughts, and examples about how God's truths bring you into the fullness of life in Christ. Biblical truths and lifestyles are presented that you are asked to consider/validate through the Bible and your intimate walk with His Spirit. Return to this book as He leads. Each time, He will reveal new biblical truths and steps for your life, those that you will then be ready to live. Enjoy walking with Him as He does the work of transformation and accomplishing His will through you. This walk is not a mental journey that relies on natural intelligence or physical gifts. It is a spiritual journey where God's communications are from His Holy Spirit to your spirit, and you learn to enjoy surrendering control of your life to God's Spirit. He is your source. He is your wisdom, knowledge, skill, and power.

Building Our Life on Biblical Truths

Each chapter presents truths that are foundations for learning to live as God designed. Many will not be new, but we believe new energy will be found in all chapters. It is important to engage each biblical truth with God's Spirit and an open heart. The following are foundational truths for learning to thrive in God's masterpiece plan.

First: God loves you just as you are and delights in walking with you right where you are, at a pace that is right for you! He loves you completely, and there is nothing that you have ever done or ever will do that can change the depth of His love for you.

Second: Salvation must be real and have resulted from a life-transforming encounter with the living Christ. Some have claimed salvation based on prevalent religious deceptions. We will evaluate these. This is not judgmental. You and God process this together, as only you and He can confirm your situation.

Third: After salvation, we have free will and face daily choices. We are saved from sin, *but for what purpose: God's or our own?* What direction will we follow: God's will and plan for our life, our own, or confusing expectations generated by others, including the church? Are we going to walk in His Spirit or in our own efforts? We learn the joy of dynamically choosing *Whose Life Are We Living?*

Fourth: The Bible teaches that it is the inerrant word of God, inspired by His Spirit. Only the Spirit can reveal this biblical truth and plant it in our hearts. Secular beliefs have infiltrated the church as pride and self-focus attempt to deny this central truth and replace it with mankind's vacillating interpretations.

Fifth: We are spiritual beings who have natural bodies, not natural beings who happen to have a spirit. God designed us to live under the authority of the Holy Spirit as He works through our spirit. Our flesh (mind, will, and emotions) is merely an instrument for touching the natural and spiritual realms for His purposes. It is not to be in control.

Sixth: We are to "Walk in the Spirit" as the Bible teaches. When we are saved and follow the Spirit in this way, we always walk in God's process of *Being* and *Becoming* the masterpieces God created. The Christian life is not about trying through our own power but about *Being and Becoming through the work of God's Spirit. If we do not learn this, we miss much of His masterpiece life.* Satan has created much confusion and division regarding God's design of this foundation of Christian life, because he recognizes how vitally important it is and seeks to rob Christians of the wonder and power of God's design. We learn to not let either the excesses or denials of individuals or churches rob us of this biblical life that God commands and provides.

Seventh: The *Revelation* of God's Spirit to our spirits is God's source of meaningful transformation and communication of wisdom, knowledge, and understanding. His revelation is to come ahead of the head-knowledge that is accumulated by the natural person (mind, will, emotions, and body.)

Eighth: We are to intentionally build deepening and personal relationships with God through each moment of every day. Our relationship truly blossoms when we walk with Him in the truths of the Bible that come through revelation, prayer, and faith.

Ninth: In the most positive and life-giving sense, we learn that our Christian life is not a game. Thriving Christians are always engaged in some level of spiritual warfare. God designs our kingdom missions as integral parts of His kingdom plans.

Tenth: We are unique in design, missions, and life-journeys. These unique journeys prepare and empower us for specific kingdom roles.

The Book's Flow

This book is presented in five parts that follow natural steps toward biblical spiritual life and maturity. They present God's foundations for truly living in a deeply personal and empowered relationship with Christ. Each chapter helps answer the question, "Whose Life Are You Living?" This chapter includes Part One, *The Invitation*.

Part Two helps us understand that, regardless of where we are in our Christian walk, we are living portions of our life for past and present audiences, instead of living solely for God. We are asked to permit Him to have full control and authority over our life, as we embrace the lifelong journey of living daily as His masterpiece. When we drift into performing for others, we will learn to enjoy His patient reminders as His Spirit lovingly asks, "Whose Life Are You Living?"

Part Three develops the basic cornerstones for building life in Christ. If we do not understand and believe these truths, we are engaging the Christian life without God's solid foundation and are like a racehorse that pursues its purpose while hobbled and partially blindfolded. In order to truly live for God, our salvation is to be firmly established; we are to know Him as He says He is; we are to view ourself as He sees and loves us, and we are to grow in understanding His truths about Faith and Prayer. As we confirm our biblical positions in these foundations, we are able to take off any hobbles and blindfolds that have constrained us and walk in His light. This Part ends by presenting the first portions of the jigsaw puzzle of who we are and how we are wired in Christ.

Part Four presents additional Bible truths that are necessary for embracing the journey of maturing into our masterpiece identity. Step by step, the futile, Carnal Christian life is cast aside, and the spiritual life is realized, though it is never perfected on this Earth.

Part Five helps pull all of this together so that we may more fully engage the journey of living in the unique specifics of who we are in Christ. We develop an improved understanding of His unique missions and plans for engaging life in and through us. This is a beginning, as God always stretches us beyond your natural capabilities. He does not limit purpose and missions to the obvious.

> *As we trust fully in Christ and Walk in His Spirit, He transforms us into the Unique Masterpiece He Designed. In This Way we truly live and eventually leave this Earth with none of His masterpiece life left caged within.*

BACKGROUND: GOD'S PREPARATION FOR THIS BOOK?

Do Not Compromise Your True Identity in Christ

Although I did not know it, God's passion for people's lives (and therefore this book) began to impact me through my earliest struggles regarding understanding who I was and why it was so difficult for me to become an embraced part of any group. In my family, anything less than A's or first place was viewed as failure. I was an average athlete, average in looks, horribly bashful, honest, trusting, genuine, and naive. I found myself trying to excel in everything but never being able to meet my parents' expectations and, therefore, not my own. I did not know how to recognize and enjoy how God had made me. In adulthood, my identity became incorrectly centered in striving for and achieving levels of excellence in business. I envisioned and required results that were not obvious to others, and once again, that put me on the outside of most cultures.

As you undoubtedly also experience, there was and is constant pressure to be the person that others wanted me to be. The message was and remains, "Be like us, and you will be accepted and liked." I did not (and do not) want to be accepted if that is the requirement. Since I did not comply, the rejection was pervasive. As I was excluded for my passions and my true self, defensiveness and anger became unhealthy coping mechanisms. I soon began to consider modifying myself as I thought, "All these people must be right, and I must be wrong." They were correct regarding some of my broken behaviors, but *they were injuriously incorrect in that they were always attempting to pressure me to live in a way that made them comfortable and denied my true identity.* As the tensions continued, I increasingly asked the Lord, "What is wrong with me? Why can't I just fit in and still be myself?" Life in both the workplace and church was often crushing, even though I was successful.

Beginning God's Journey of Embracing My Identity in Christ and Helping Others to Do the Same

My breakthrough came while I was attending a leadership-development week at The Center for Creative Leadership. One exercise involved assessing where participants operated on a continuum ranging from Adaptive to Innovative. I registered off the chart on the Innovative scale. As my instructor reviewed this with me, he said, "No wonder you have difficulty fitting in. Most organizations, including families, are structured to operate through individuals who conform to the central behaviors and processes that are valued by leadership. Compliance is valued more than innovation. You are not *wired* to fit into standard organizations. Most of your peers are not able to understand and value why you are not like them, and they cannot hear what you are saying. They are not there and may not be wired to ever function there." He also described troubling and recurring experiences that were common to highly innovative individuals. These perfectly mirrored my experiences. I was stunned, but more importantly, *I was also liberated.* Central cultures had taken my differences as failures and weaknesses and pressed me to change. He described them as strengths that needed to be understood, embraced, and utilized *by the individuals and cultures that God had prepared to value them.* Normal cultures stifled me, and I pressed all the buttons of individuals who were comfortable there.

I had spent decades confused by why I defined success and effectiveness much differently from almost every other culture, why I did not fit in, and why I could not communicate in the languages of most of them. Now I knew that, although I had plenty to learn and was pretty messed up in some areas, my core identity *was not broken.* I was to fully identify and pursue the unique identity that God has given me. What an amazing revelation and relief. I had never understood that God intentionally created me in this way, not better or worse than anyone else, but *specific to His unique calling on my life.* These years of conflict were necessary, as they helped shape me for the purposes and missions that He has for me.

Core Mission

This personal revelation became a kingdom passion, because I was made aware that, in differing ways, each of us is experiencing similar situations and potential brokenness. My core mission became helping individuals and organizations shake off the incorrect expectations and inappropriate criticisms of those around them and embrace their true masterpiece identities in Christ. My greatest passion is for God's Spirit to live in and through me to touch others so that they become all that He created them to be and experience all of the incredible life He designed. This book is one part of His plan to free His Church.

He has instilled the following belief within me. *One of the greatest tragedies in the Christian Church is that many believers leave this Earth with much of God's masterpiece life left caged within them. Why? Because we become actors on a stage who seek the approval of the worldly and religious influences that surround us. We are progressively blinded to God's incredible design for our lives and correspondingly choose potentially misdirected and frequently compromised and comfortable Christian lives. Much of our true identity and the abundant and powerful life that Christ has for us is lost unless we awaken to His unique call and embrace His journey of living under the authority and in the power of His Spirit. This Christian life is not to be taken lightly. God has entrusted people's lives and eternity, and portions of the role of His Church to each of us through our unique kingdom missions. He designed us to thrive in all that He created us to be and do.*

This Book

This book is about Christ and you and your journey of learning to live in the fullness of Christ's life. It helps you to *Choose the unique and incredible life that God designed for you,* as you decide "Whose Life Are You Living? Whose Life Are You Going to Live?" There is an enormous difference between *Being a comfortable Christian* and *Living the masterpiece life that God has for you.*

Your Life in Christ

God has designed you uniquely to walk in His specific missions. Whether you have been embraced by many cultures or do not fit in, you, too, have been playing on a stage for many influences other than Christ. (Each of us surrenders some of our true self.) Interestingly, if you *do* fit in with most cultures and are praised as a success, it may be extremely hard for you to understand whether you have or have not been living the life that Christ designed. This is especially true if your church or career honors and recognizes you because you say and do the right things and serve in areas where they need you. That may be appropriate, or it may be distracting you. Regardless of whether you have been embraced or rejected, God's question is, "Are you pursuing the unique life and missions that I have for you?" Neither rejection nor being embraced confirms you are in God's masterpiece life. Do you know the *Real* you, the unique person that Christ created you to be? Are you willing to set all else aside and live for Him alone? He will open each of our eyes to the incredible purpose that He has placed within us.

God's heart is for each of us to truly live the unique masterpiece life He designed. Through His daily walk with us, He invites us to be released from the detours and distractions of inappropriate expectations and thrive in His victorious kingdom life. He loves us unconditionally and desires an intimate and personal relationship and walk. Journey with His Spirit through this book, and embrace His victorious life of *Being and Becoming* the masterpiece God designed.

> *The abundant life, where Christ lives both in and through each of His children in the power of His Spirit, is to be the normal life for Christians. It results in each individual living as His masterpiece. We learn to know Him, to see ourselves and others through His eyes, and to honor others in the same way He honors us, as we surrender all of our self to Christ and learn to walk in His Spirit.*

PART TWO

ONLY CHRIST KNOWS THE REAL YOU

DO YOU KNOW WHO YOU ARE IN CHRIST?

CHAPTER 2

WHOSE LIFE ARE YOU LIVING? WHOSE LIFE DO YOU CHOOSE TO LIVE?

MATT 6:24
No one can serve two masters; for either he will hate the one and love the other, or else he will be loyal to the one and despise the other.

GAL 1:10
For do I persuade men or God? Or do I seek to please men? For if I still pleased men, I would not be a bondservant of Christ.

GAL 2:20
It is no longer I who live, but Christ lives in me.

Living each day for Christ and Him alone transforms us into being fully effective at every level of His design for our lives. Walking in His Spirit with His missions as our first priority allows us to no longer be torn apart by trying to meet the conflicting expectations of others who make claims on our lives. Permitting God to prioritize and fulfill all other expectations according to His purpose, love, and power allows us to thrive in Christ and glorify His Kingdom as He lives in and through us. As Galatians says, we will no longer seek to please men but will experience the incredible wonder of being the bondservant of Christ. Christ's love and power will flow through us.

If you are on God's path, this chapter will help you stay there. If you are not walking in His plan, this chapter will help you to choose between the fulfilling and powerful life God designed and the side-tracking expectations of all other sources. Only Christ knows who you really are! You can know and become your true self when you permit the Holy Spirit to reveal and develop His identity in you. Walking your journey with Him results in the fullness and joy of *truly living*.

This chapter is presented in three sections that ask: Whose Life Are You Living? Whose Life Do You Choose to Live? What Realities and Challenges Accompany God's Incredible Walk?

Whose Life Are You Living?
What Audiences Are You Performing For?

Are you living for Christ alone, or are you defining your life by seeking to please others who want you to meet their expectations? Is God's design for your life simply one more input you consider along with the rest? Do you recognize that many expectations placed on you by family, culture, friends, workplace, church—and significantly your own self-driven voice—will conflict with much of God's design for you? Many people's intentions are good, but they might not recognize the real you and God's purpose for you. Others' intentions are selfish and destructive to your purpose in Christ. *Whose life are you living?*

Consciously or not, each of us reacts to significant influences around us, people from our past and present, as though we're performing on a stage. Authority figures such as parents, school administration, coaches, pastors, Sunday School teachers, and police play impactful roles. Social structures such as families, neighborhoods, clubs, gangs, cliques, sports teams, and our ethnicity influence our identity choices. Portions of these influences are to be embraced under God's direction, but many are to be set aside. Envision yourself in the center of a large stage, surrounded by an audience. Each person is asking you to meet their needs or to be who they want you to be. These demands are impacting you, no matter how mature and independent you are.

Where is God in the crowd, and what is His current role in your life? Let the loving voice of God's Spirit replace all others. He will help you to determine which voices you are to respond to and how to let Him provide them what they truly need *through you*. It may not be what they are requesting. He will bring His discernment and healing into your life.

You may hear the echoes of destructive voices, but He will break their authority over you. As you choose to live solely for Him and walk in His Spirit, you will *Be and Become* all that He created you to be. Even so, life lived solely for Him is filled with challenges and victories. Only by staying in constant, obedient fellowship with the Holy Spirit will you know if you are staying on His path.

Are You Trapped or Free?

Consider the following analogies. How do they reflect your life or the lives of others you know? Are you freely living in the purposes and passions God has wired into your very being?

An Eagle or a Chicken?

An eagle egg dropped out of its nest onto the straw in a chicken yard. An industrious and loving Mother Hen got the egg into her nest and hatched it with her own. The family embraced and nurtured the eaglet, and it grew up emulating chickens. Regardless, it could not fit in. It was never healthy, and it had strivings and passions imprisoned within that it could neither understand nor fulfill. It was dying, emotionally and physically, though its family and the *wise* leaders of the flock tried to help it be *a good chicken.*

The farmer was saddened by the impact of this circumstance on both the eaglet and flock and began the process of introducing the eaglet to its true nature, including how to fly, hunt, and ride the winds. God had infused this nature into it.

Over time, the eagle became fully alive, physically and in its identity. Its inner being and passions began to be realized. When it was set free, it *soared* into the heavens with a cry of exhilaration. For the rest of its life, *it truly lived.*

Some well-meaning chickens were saddened. They felt the eagle was not acting as a chicken should. They believed it had been misled. His adoptive mother understood that her child was becoming what God created it to be, instead of what she and others had incorrectly thought it should be.

(God places unique and equal value on eagles and chickens, all parts of His Body, the Church. Neither is to attempt to be like the other, even though both are to learn from each other. Even as eagles (or chickens) learn from other eagles (or chickens,) they are to always recognize and honor each other's God-given uniqueness.)

The Apprentice Juggler

The story of *The Apprentice Juggler* is part of the outstanding work presented in David and Karen Mains' book *Tales of the Kingdom*.

It talks about an apprentice who desires with all his heart to be a juggler. He has the skills, but something always interferes with his success. The apprentice trains and trains, but he can maintain a juggler's rhythm for only so long. Suddenly, another and stronger rhythm takes over from deep within. He hides it and attempts to overcome it. He believes he is a failure and will ruin every performance of the juggler troupe.

When the time arrives for the troupe to perform for the King, the Christ figure, the apprentice is so afraid that he is willing to quit and seek another direction. Heartbroken and in desperation, he permits himself to privately follow his own rhythm. A beggar, the King in disguise, sees him practicing and encourages him to trust his rhythm. It is *who he is*. Recognizing the beggar is the King, the apprentice performs for everyone in his unique rhythm and finds incredible success. His rhythm is that of a clown, which is the most difficult and impactful juggler rhythm.

The Mainses finish this story with a Godly exhortation to us all. We are to live by the passions and gifts God has confirmed and wired into us. (Only He is to be the source of their validation.) When we follow God's calling, though we may lose some things that we enjoyed, we will find the incredible wonder of embracing the unique life and specific missions of our true Kingdom identities.

Each of us has Christ-given missions and passions that are fulfilled only by living in God's unique rhythms which reside within. Permit Him to reveal these and be your source of life. It will no longer be your efforts, but Christ's life, power, and results that live both in and through you for His glory. Nothing else will be fulfilling, regardless of how the world or the Church embraces it.

The Canary in the Cage

A group was discussing the concept of their identities in Christ when God presented the additional example of a canary in a cage. He asked, "Whose cage are you in?"

Canaries were created to live in the open world, free and part of a flock. Some were captured and sold, and most eventually adapted to life in a cage. They gradually forgot who they were. Bred and raised in cages, they never knew their life's potential. They thought their current situation was great. If the cage door opened, most would not know what to do, and many who left would die in the wild. They had learned to feel safe and happy in their cages. Yet, if *they were taught to be themselves*, their cages opened, and they escaped, they would then *truly live*!

God Has a Unique Design for You as His Masterpiece

God's question to each of us is, "Whose life are you living?" When living to please anyone but God, we are eagles attempting to be chickens, jugglers attempting to be clowns, or canaries agreeing to stay trapped in cages. Regardless of how comfortable or glamorous our situation (farmyard, vocation, or gilded cage) might look or feel, God offers real freedom and the most incredible life we could ever imagine.

Identity and validation are to be sought only from God. Unfortunately, we do not learn to intimately interact and fellowship with God until later in life. By then, others have filled us with their expectations of who and what they want us to be. God's revelation has been minimized. We are to listen to others and learn, but in the end, nothing must replace the revelation that grows out of our intimate relationship with Christ and the instruction He provides through His Bible and His Spirit. We find freedom, light, and life when we commit to follow Christ alone.

Real Life Example: The Gifted Leader

Joe was a man of vision and action who led his organization from start-up to excellence. It had significant global impact, and Joe was highly regarded. He was task oriented and, in many ways, a private man who preferred smaller-group interactions to general glad-handing. People embraced him and his leadership and were impacted by God's Spirit through him.

Desiring improvement, Joe contracted organization consultants. They sought to modify Joe's style to meet their desires for Him to be an administrator, less driven and more openly people focused. The change proved inappropriate for the organization, which then became comfortable with itself and pursued only slight improvements. Much new ground was lost. Christ placed Joe in his position to be the visionary leader He designed, not an administrator.

It was appropriate for Joe to improve and refine his skills, but it was not God's will for him to become someone he was not. By attempting to be what others wanted instead of living fully in Christ's wonderful design, God's mission through him was negatively impacted until he refocused.

My Mistakes

I have made mistakes helping others find their God-created purpose as well. The most difficult one was with my son. My wife and I love our son and two daughters completely and are proud of who they are and who they are becoming.

Although I mostly understood my daughters, for years I did not understand my son. I tried to parent him to be the extraordinary and impactful person I thought he was. I strived to see him with God's eyes but was blind, unable to recognize and embrace the real him, as he was becoming his own unique, extraordinary, and impactful person. I created destructive situations for us and our family. It was only after the Lord intervened that I could see how I was interacting, and it broke my heart. Subsequently, I have been able to see him as the phenomenal individual that God is developing. I have reveled in that person and am proud and excited about who he is and who he is becoming. My son and I are not to be like each other. If we tried, neither would be effective in God's unique missions.

My wife and I truly have these same feelings about our daughters, our children's spouses, and our grandchildren. All are incredibly God-designed individuals, who are blessings to our family. All have unique callings in God's kingdom, and we ask Him to help us to always see them through His eyes.

Whose Life Are You Living?

Through personal time with the Spirit, determine what He has for you to internalize. Please document your thoughts as you engage in continuing discussions with Him, not only for the next few minutes, but moment by moment throughout life as He reveals "Whose Life You Are Living." Consider the following, and go where He leads:

- As you read, were you willing to drop your guard and let the Spirit speak to you, or did you protect yourself from what He desired to introduce?

- What excites you about knowing more about yourself and your life's potential for *truly living*?

- Whether you know Christ personally or only know about Him, are you willing to move forward by honestly seeking Him and His plans for you, or are you going to insist on holding the reins of your life? Will you insist on being in control at the cost of missing His masterpiece life?

- Whose life have you been living? What have been the greatest sources of influence in determining the identity and purpose for your life to this point?

- What priority have you given Christ among all the forces that shape your life and daily walk?

- Are you a canary in someone's cage, an apprentice juggler denying your internal God-given rhythm, or an eagle who emulates chickens? Or are you on the journey of living God's unique purpose?

- Identify the next steps that the Spirit is revealing, and put them into action through His power, not yours.

Whose Life Do You Choose to Live?

As individuals, we have three basic choices:

1. Live the victorious life that Christ designed for us, as we choose Christ, hold nothing back, embrace the Bible as God's inspired word, and joyfully surrender *all* to His lordship.

2. Choose a *safe and comfortable* Christian life, in which we withhold much of ourself from Christ's authority, redefine the Bible's truths to conform to our personal desires, and seek to blend in by pleasing our church, our cultures, and their definitions of us and the Christian life.

3. Choose to reject Christ and the church and spend little or no time with the Bible and God as we do things our way.

If we have truly encountered the living Christ, both of the first two choices will result in eternal life with Christ. Only the first will result in the incredible journey of experiencing the masterpiece life God designed. The third results in an eternity without Christ.

When we choose to live for Christ, there is no guarantee of fame, wealth, health, and popularity, even though those things are appropriately part of many Christians' lives. Individuals who preach that these are guaranteed are preaching a distorted and false gospel. God promises we will experience trials and tribulations and be rejected as Christ was. The lives of His apostles were far from easy, and most ended in early death, yet they experienced incredible lives. His life does guarantee that those who intentionally walk fully in His Spirit will experience

His abundant life—life unlike any other. The world may never know us, but that will not matter. When we leave this Earth, we will have given our all to Christ. Nothing will have been caged within.

Our choice now and every day is about releasing incorrect expectations and control, and saying, "I belong totally to You, and I want only the life that You have designed. I want all of You! When I join You in Heaven, my desire is that not even a smidgen of the masterpiece life you created for me will remain unlived for your glory."

What Will Living the Life God Designed Be Like?

Only you and God can answer the specific details of this question as you experience life's journey together. However, you can answer broad questions that should excite and encourage you to give Him complete control. Consider the following with God. Explore additional thoughts with Him. What will life be like when you:

- Live each day in close fellowship with your loving Father, aware of His delight in you, even as He lovingly corrects you.

- Surrender your expectations to Him and permit Him to accomplish His purpose and missions through you each day.

- Learn to identify, enjoy, and obey the voice of the Holy Spirit.

- Live the biblical Christian life, where it is the Spirit's power, authority, and love that flow in and through you to transform you and achieve His will in and through you. It is never your efforts.

- Know the joy of being loved for who you are in Christ and not for what you do.

- Permit Him to have you see others as He sees them and you, with the same spiritual insight, love, and grace.

- Know you are *Being and Becoming* your true self, free to seek validation from only one source, your Heavenly Father

- Know He is in control, even when life makes no sense and may not be looking or feeling at all like you had envisioned it, and you fully trust Him.

- Know your heart is pure, your life pleases Him and therefore brings you the joy of *Being and Becoming* all that you are created to be.

Much Will Attempt to Get in Your Way

Living in Christ as his unique masterpiece is exciting and rewarding but requires vigilance, as much will challenge you.

- Your natural self, carnal nature, will always seek to wrestle control from God's Spirit.

- The daily activities of life will seek to displace your highest priority of developing and walking in your ever-deepening relationship with God. Reading the Bible, prayer, and worship may begin to feel like religious obligations, if you are not engaging them through your spirit.

- Your priorities will be continuously tested.

- Your family and peers may attempt to dissuade you from being a Christian *kook*. Even when you are on course, safe Christians and society will consider you as unusual, because you are! Walking in unity with Christ's Church does not mean conformity to human expectations within His church. (If you get off God's course, you won't be there long as you walk in God's Spirit.)

- Your church may not understand you. If tension is present, you need to get away and get clear about what God is teaching you, instead of becoming what others want.

- Strongholds, including substance addictions, pornography, fear, judgmentalism, impatience, anger, and non-biblical sexual activities will seek to destroy your walk with God.

- Lack of balance in your use of time will deceive you.

- False areas may become sources of your identity and validation instead of gifts to enjoy in Christ. These might include athletic prowess, academic prowess, good looks, financial accomplishments, or finding your personal identity in God's use of your spiritual gifts.

- You may be tempted by secular and human wisdom, which dominate society and many of today's churches, where they are held in higher esteem than the Bible. (Corinthians teaches that "the natural man does not receive the things of the Spirit of God, for they are foolishness to him; nor can he know them, because they are spiritually discerned.")

God Walks With You

PHIL 1:6

Being confident of this very thing, that He who has begun a good work in you will complete it until the day of Jesus Christ.

While much will seek to pull you aside, God walks the journey with you. He has already defeated the enemy and made His way straight for you as you Walk in His Spirit. (The enemy is relentless at identifying and probing our weak areas. Listen to God's Spirit and stand on God's scripture truths. These stop the enemy at every level.)

Your Path Forward

Summarize all God has revealed about the wonder of releasing incorrect expectations for your life and learning to live completely in Him. You will not have to give up anything that brings real value to your life on Earth or that is of eternal importance. You will have gained everything. In time, chains will be broken as you permit God to release all of Himself in and through your life. At the end of life, there cannot be any comparison between the futility of life expressed through one who closes the casket and says, "I did it my way" and the miracle of life experienced through one who says, "Thank You, God, for living in and through me so that I lived Your way! You poured out all of me for Your glory, and nothing was left caged within."

- What are you thinking and feeling right now? What do you accept? What do you reject? What do you have questions about?

- What did God desire to share with you from this chapter?
- Whose life have you been living? Why?
- Whose life do you want to live? Why?
- Whose life are you choosing to live?
- Does He want you to walk with Him through the rest of this book? Are you willing to let Him show how you and He are to move forward, instead of either quitting or forging ahead on your own?
- Do you believe that He has really created you as His masterpiece? Can you trust Him to achieve this in and through your life?
- Are you willing to Live for Him and Him only?
- What are your next steps with Him?

As Christians, we are designed to choose God's life, to be the unique individuals Christ created, and to fulfill the specific kingdom missions He designed. Only His validation is to govern our life. We are not to be distracted by playing on a stage designed to please other audiences.

PART THREE

SOLID FOUNDATIONS ARE ESSENTIAL FOR TRULY LIVING CHRIST'S LIFE

HOW STRONG ARE YOUR CORNERSTONES?

CHAPTER 3

Nothing Can Change the Depth of Christ's Love for You

Jer 31:3
The Lord has appeared of old to me, saying: "Yes, I have loved you with an everlasting love: Therefore with lovingkindness I have drawn you."

Eph 3: 17-19
... that Christ may dwell in your hearts by faith; that you, being rooted and grounded in love, may be able to comprehend with all the saints what is the width and length and depth and height to know the love of Christ which passes knowledge; that you may be filled with all the fullness of Christ.

What would it mean to comprehend the immeasurable dimensions of the love of Christ and to know His love which passes knowledge? How would our daily lives with Him and others change? Paul's prayer in Ephesians 3 tells us God's Spirit will enable us to comprehend the dimensions of His love and be filled with all the fullness of Christ. His indescribable love will pulse through our being. We will learn to live in His love and permit Christ to love others through us. We will shed the image of viewing ourselves as spiritual paupers and grow into the inconceivable life of "being filled with all the fullness of Christ." How many of us realize that all of Christ's fullness is to be part of our identity in Him?

> *God's Love Is Beyond Human Understanding but Comprehensible through God's Spirit*

This journey begins as the Spirit provides revelation of the Bible's truth that *nothing you have done or ever will do can change the depth of His love for you. You cannot earn or destroy it!* Mistakes do not deter Him as He accompanies you on your journey. He loved you before time began, and His love will not change. Our attempts at doing good do not increase His love. As Isaiah 64:6 shares, "All our righteousnesses are like filthy rags." He embraces the real you (righteous in Christ) and delights in you as you "be" who you are in Him today and "become" who you are to be tomorrow.

Religious or Spirit-Generated Love?

Many Christians struggle with accepting and living in Christ's unconditional love. We either try to earn it or prove we love Him by following the rules or doing good works. Both are works of our flesh.

I had always heard the term "unconditional love." The meaning was clear, but I did not know how to believe it. Perfection ruled in my family, which always felt like "conditional" love. I viewed the world and relationships through this screen and could not find freedom.

My Testimony:

The Freedom of His Love Received Through Faith.
What Binds You?

At seven years old, I sang in the children's choir during a special service. I loved it and was "so" proud. When we finished, we moved down the aisle to find our parents. I walked with a delighted swagger, which included hands in my pockets and a huge smile on my face. As I sat down beside my mother, she said, "A gentleman never walks with his hands in his pockets." I was crushed. That was the last time I enjoyed doing anything in front of others. Due to innumerable incidents like this, performance anxiety and the false need for perfection became unhealthy burdens in all of life. I blame no one. My parents were great. However, for a child, these situations were real, and still require God's healing.

Accordingly, all relationships, including mine with Christ, were constricted by this ingrained requirement for perfection. In many situations, I withdrew. Loss of sleep and anxiety prevailed. After high school, I turned to alcohol. I "thought" it relieved my tensions and allowed me to be myself. Instead, it began to imprison me. God later freed me, and I praise Him that I did not die or kill others.

Could God's Love Be Unconditional?

Given this background, I had a very mixed view of God and little understanding of His love. I was saved and went to church, but I did not have a relationship with Him. I was a social drunk. I swore most of the time and did not even know that it was obnoxious. Anger often drove me.

At twenty-two, I recognized the Lord calling me back. My cry to Him became, "There must be more to being a Christian than this!" I visited a number of churches in my attempt to find it. Pastors were very warm and welcoming, but they could not hear my heart, and they all gave me books. Church members were genuinely nice to me and invited me into their families. However, I remained broken, totally confused, and longing for something that I did not understand.

Christ Made His Love Real for Me

I desperately pleaded with the Lord to help me find His life. I tried radio and television preachers and continued seeking help in local churches. Nothing worked, and I got more books. I was in crisis.

On a Sunday in October of 1972, I was dressing for yet another church. I looked into my apartment's living room. Jesus was standing there. He was dressed in conventional clothes, khaki and white. He had the most amazing persona, including the sense of an unseen aura surrounding Him. His smile was embracing, and His personal warmth and love drew me to Him. He said, "Nothing that you have ever done or ever will do can change the depth of my love for you." In my mind I instantly understood that He had always totally loved me, and He always would. His love did not depend on my good *or* broken behaviors. It was unchangeable and unconditional. He desired a deeply personal relationship. As I received all of this, He quietly disappeared.

Even now, I remember His presence and love as though He were still before me. However, in that moment, I was so defeated that I merely continued to dress and drove to another church with no additional thought to His visit. Incredibly, I did not remember this experience for several weeks. I believe that I had given so much ground to the enemy and was so focused on myself and my failures, that he was able to temporarily draw a curtain over that life-changing event.

God continued His miraculous intervention. The church I visited had an evangelical pastor. After the message, which was good but did not help, the Pastor gave an altar call, because as He explained later, "The Holy Spirit directed him to." I sat there. My response to the Lord was, "I can do this only one more time. If I don't find my way to You this time, I don't have anything left to give!" This was not a challenge; it was my last hope. So, I went up to pray for true life in Christ.

Afterwards, I met with an Associate Pastor, who was not evangelical. He gave me a book. I was heartbroken, with nowhere to turn, and left in despair.

The following week, the Senior Pastor visited. He sat down and mostly listened. I remember defensively saying, "Don't ask me to stop drinking!" His loving answer was, "I'm not going to ask you to do anything like that—that is between you and Jesus." This man understood what I could not express. He talked with me about faith in the completed work of Christ instead of in my actions and attempts to earn Christ's love and fellowship. He led me to my initial understanding of God's gift of faith and Christ's love. I was then able to pray in the faith of all that Christ is and has done and know that "My life was His. He loved me just as I was." My prayer was not just a re-commitment but a prayer for receiving God's gift of faith and permitting Him to release it in my life. I had an extremely long way to go, but I knew inside that I was different. A man of God had been with me. Christ had touched me through him.

This pastor mentored me and connected me with others who accepted me and did the same. I soon remembered Christ's appearance in my apartment. Life in His gifts of love and faith had begun, and His Spirit's transformations followed, each in their appropriate season.

Life with Christ has not been easy, but it has been wonderful. Christ planted my life on His truth: "Nothing Can Change the Depth of My Love for You."

He wants you to know this about His love for you. Stand on it in unquestioning wonder, faith, and victory.

From My Design to Christ's

The enemy did not let go without significant resistance, as I had surrendered much ground to him. This struggle was fierce and difficult, but Christ always led me. A significant example occurred weeks after. I lay awake wrestling with life. Christ showed me an image of myself at the right side of my bed. It vividly displayed my broken condition and was crushing to view. Christ said, "This is the person that you have made of yourself. I am going to take out each of the bricks that you used to build your life and replace them with my own, so that you become the person I created you to be." He advised this was going to be painful and time-consuming. It was and at times still is, but He is marvelous and true to His word.

Transformations and Blessings

He began to change me, and my life started to reflect Him. Profanity quickly disappeared, except for instances when self-focus took over. He transformed me from the inside out, as He replaced my sinful ways with His identity. Strongholds of anger and impatience began the long journey of healing as He replaced (and continues to replace) them with His character.

God's Word became alive. I loved reading it and found it personal and life changing. Its truths and the beginning of a personal relationship with Christ took up residence within me.

God never asked me to stop drinking. Instead, He pointed out that I was being two people. I drank with my old friends, and I did not with Christian mentors. I was working with high-school students who saw me as a person coming alive in Christ. He asked why I avoided disclosing my drinking. He asked what behaviors, including drinking, would most help or confuse them in finding their walk with Him. I was free to make the decisions, but I was to be a person of integrity who presented myself consistently to all groups. He also taught me that His love never does things that injure the faith and life of others. The drinking was soon over and never missed.

Performance anxiety dissipated but remains, and I believe it is like Paul's affliction. It keeps me fully dependent on Christ.

He "Cares About Every Aspect of My Life"

Within fourteen months, He had changed me so much that He could now introduce me to the phenomenal Christian woman Joanne, who would become my wife. Had I met her a year before, she would have correctly not found anything attractive in me.

Friends connected us, and we scheduled a blind date. On my way to pick her up, the Lord said, "This is the woman that you are going to marry." I was not used to having conversations with the Holy Spirit, but I told Him, "That is not funny. I'm going to meet her, and she will not be my type at all. We will have a horrible night." I met her and was enchanted. As I drove home, I was filled with joy. I remember the full moon and how it lit the countryside. At one point, the Lord opened a portal from the left side of my head that extended deep into the universe. He did this for reasons that I do not fully understand, but it was incredible and revealed aspects of His wonderful and powerful presence. Then, He said, "You think that you are so full of joy because of Joanne, but your joy is because you are beginning to understand how much I care about every aspect of your life!" What an incredible message of relationship and truth.

As Joanne and I dated, I was careful and walked with God to confirm the relationship, but He had me when she opened the door. (I did not share any of this with Joanne until long after we were married. That would have been manipulation.)

Joanne and I were engaged in three months and married in eight. God has blessed us with forty-nine years, and counting, of an incredible marriage. He has always been the center and the driving force of our relationship. We do not recommend this eight-month pace, but neither do we challenge God-led relationships. Second to Christ, Joanne is the best portion of my life. I do not understand how He could love me enough to bless me with marriage to such an amazing, Christ-filled woman.

What Is Your Story?
God Meets Us Where We Are

Why did the Lord meet me so dynamically over these months? Why did He appear personally to me? Why did He communicate so powerfully on several occasions? Because I sought Him fervently, and He knew the types of personal encounters I needed to draw me deeper into His transformational journey toward life in Him.

We all have unique needs. Accordingly, Jesus designs unique personal encounters through which He builds personal relationships. No one's personal encounter is to be viewed as more or less dramatic. Many like to highlight the God-experiences of others because they seem to be spectacular. We may dismiss our own salvation and transformation experiences as less dynamic. Every encounter with God is miraculous and is to be shared with honor and thanksgiving. Little could be more inappropriate than diminishing God's touches on our lives by comparing them to another's.

Learning to Love God, Yourself, and Others

MARK 12:30, 31

And you shall love the Lord your God with all your heart, with all your soul, with all your mind, and with all your strength. This is the first commandment.

And the second, like it, is this; "You shall love your neighbor as yourself." There is no other commandment greater than these.

Christ speaks these truths not only as the greatest commandments but also as His very words of life and freedom. We are able to learn to truly love God, ourselves, and others only when we have received the incredible and unconditional love that Our Father has for us. We are set free from all fear regarding our relationship with our Father and from all doubts about our ability to trust Him. When times are toughest, and we hardly have the strength to stand, we are able to trust in His love and purpose. When it is hard to love ourselves or others, we are then able to surrender to His Spirit within, who provides His love.

What is God's Spirit revealing about your love relationship with God, yourself, and others? Ask Him to teach you to differentiate His words from your own or the enemy's.

> *The Spirit's voice is always edifying and uplifting even when He is correcting and exhorting us to grow and live more effectively in Him. Momentarily, it may not always "feel" good, but it always brings freedom. If you are hearing something that makes you feel rejected or unworthy, that is not the Spirit; it is either you or the enemy. Reject it. God loves you unconditionally. Nothing you have done or will do can add or detract from His incredible love. Nothing Can Change the Depth of Christ's Love for You!*

Each of us hears and experiences life through filters that affect how we respond or react to information. Permit the Spirit to transform you so that you experience life through the healthy perspective of His all-consuming love. When He is our filter, we will know who is speaking into our lives (the enemy, our self, or others) and how to process all inputs through Him.

Application
What Do You Think?

What is your response to the information in this chapter?

- Do you absolutely and undisputedly know that the Lord loves you totally and unconditionally?

- Do you agree that nothing you have ever done or ever will do can change the depth of His love for you? Are you holding onto shame and guilt over things which He forgave and forgot the moment that you asked for His forgiveness? Are you letting these "ghosts" break your heart? If so, what is God's truth, and what does He want you to do with these? *He is righteous & just to forgive us our sins, & to cleanse us from all unrighteousness.*

- What stirred in your soul as you read this? What excited you? What challenged you? *God loves me unconditionally right from before I was born.*

- What do you disagree with and why? What does the Bible say?

- What kind of a loving, personal relationship do you have or desire to have with Christ? *Something closer ---*

- What kind of relationship does the Lord want with you?

- What actions does He want you to take with Him, right now? *to ask Him to be the filter of all my thoughts, words, plans & actions.*

CHAPTER 4

YOUR SALVATION: REAL OR CLUB MEMBERSHIP?

EPH 2:8

For by grace you have been saved through faith, and that not of yourselves; it is a gift of God.

Our incredible Christian lives begin with salvation through faith in Christ, which must be rock solid for us to move forward in God's masterpiece lives. Is your salvation biblically real? Do you understand how to confirm and embrace it and to help others do the same? What could be worse than believing we are saved when we are not or doubting we are saved when we are? How can we tell the difference?

In this chapter we will first review the deceptions that blind sincere individuals to true salvation and then examine the Bible's truths regarding it. Please remember to permit God's Spirit to lead as you guard against blocking Him by holding onto tribal beliefs.

WHOSE LIFE ARE YOU LIVING?

Beliefs That Deceive and Block God's Salvation

MATT 7:21-23

Not everyone who says to Me, "Lord, Lord" shall enter the kingdom of heaven, but he who does the will of My Father in heaven.

Many will say to me in that day, "Lord, Lord, have we not prophesied in your name, cast out demons in your name, and done many wonders in your name?"

And then I will declare to them, I never knew you: depart from Me, you who practice lawlessness!

JOHN 3:3 (JESUS IS SPEAKING)

Most assuredly, I say to you, unless one is born again, he cannot see the kingdom of God.

JOHN 14:6

Jesus said to Him, "I am the way, the truth, and the life. No one comes to the Father except through Me."

Deceptions

Many deceptions about salvation ensnare individuals. Most of these people are genuine and sincere. Many are incredible people. However, if they have not had a personal encounter with Jesus, they are not saved. Three of the most prevalent deceptions apply to individuals who are in some ways associated with the Christian Church.

Deception: Salvation by Head Knowledge

JAMES 2:19
*You believe that there is one God. You do well.
Even the demons believe and tremble.*

1 COR 2:14
*But the natural man (the flesh) does not receive the things
of the Spirit of God, for they are foolishness to him, nor can
he know them, because they are spiritually discerned.*

This deception results in an almost impenetrable condition for those who embrace it. They have *head knowledge* without the Spirit's *revelation*. They know the basic truths about Christ, and they accept them just as they accept historical information about Abraham Lincoln. They think that knowing the truth *about* Jesus is the same as *knowing Him.* It is not, and without a personal encounter with Him, they are not saved. Some churches and families permit and encourage this belief because they do not recognize the difference.

Head knowledge without the Spirit's revelation is of the natural man. Even the demons have this knowledge and know that Jesus is the Son of God, but they have no part in Him. Most of the individuals in this condition cannot hear God call them to salvation, because they believe that they are already saved.

There is an incomparable difference between knowing *about* Christ and knowing Him personally. In like manner, although most of us can say we know person "A" is the President of the United States, we would agree that we, in no way, have a personal relationship or friendship with him or her. We only know *about* them. Knowing about Christ is not *knowing Him* and does not result in salvation. Being drawn by the Spirit to a personal encounter with Jesus and responding in the supernatural faith that He provides is God's narrow way (Eph 2:8). We may speak His name and do things in His name, but if we are not saved, He will state as He did in Mark 7, "I never knew you: depart from Me."

Deception: Salvation by Association

JOHN 6:44 (JESUS IS SPEAKING)
No one can come to Me unless the Father who sent Me draws Him; and I will raise him up in the last day.

Association with the church does not equate to salvation, yet many are deceived as they claim salvation through it. Perhaps their families were church members for generations and called themselves Christians, whether they were or were not. They have been baptized and erroneously believe that saves them. They are members in good standing and take comfort because *they serve in church positions. They are pastors, teachers, or deacons. They even tithe.* However, if they have no personal encounter with Jesus, they are not saved. Club membership does not count as salvation.

Believing in salvation by association is an easy deception to slide into. Many families and churches teach this error by stroking individuals who attend, serve, say most of the right things, and live their lives in a *good* way. Once again, this is like being in a club. All have gone through the rite of passage, have made a statement of commitment to the group, and do the things that are expected of good members. They then tell others that they are members/Christians and even believe it themselves. Have they encountered Christ personally?

If they have not, they will walk through life believing, "I am a Christian and will go to heaven," when they are not. Once again, it is extremely hard for them to hear God call them. They disregard His messages as being for someone else.

My wife, Joanne, and I were raised in a Protestant denomination that had a standard format of taking twelve-year-olds and placing them in a confirmation class. We learned doctrine and other excellent Bible truths. At the conclusion, all went forward and joined the church—club membership. Whether or not it was intended, most of us believed joining made us Christians, saved in Christ. God may call some to encounter Him in this way, but the rest are being deceived. Age and mental knowledge are not God's standard for salvation. John 6:44 states that the Father must draw us through His Spirit. John 14:6 speaks of a personal encounter and acceptance of Christ. God revealed this immediately to Joanne. I was deceived and therefore confused for years. Because I thought I was saved, I could not understand my failures and lack of connection with Christ. He revealed Himself to me according to His timing and began setting me free.

Deception: Righteousness and Salvation by Good Works

Rom 3:10-12

There is none righteous, no, not one
There is none who understands
There is none who does good, no, not one

Is 64:6
But we are all like an unclean thing,
And all our righteousnesses are like filthy rags

Gal 2:15-16
Knowing that a man is not justified by the works of the law but by faith in Jesus Christ, even we have believed in Christ Jesus, that we might be justified by faith in Christ and not by the works of the law; for by the works of the law no flesh shall be justified.

This deception results in individuals believing or hoping that their good works will outweigh their bad, and, thus, they will be saved and go to heaven. Many church members even tell them that they are surely saved because they are such "good and loving" people. They attempt to follow the Ten Commandments and the Golden Rule. Because they believe they are "good," they hope to be saved and often believe that they are. The Bible is clear that good works will never get anyone into heaven.

This deception is a burden and a destroyer of the abundant life of Christ. Those who believe they must earn salvation through their works have missed all that Christ is and has done, and His salvation is not attainable for them. Others who are truly saved may mistakenly think every sin breaks their salvation. These are chained to a deception instead of growing in the true victory of life in Christ.

The scriptures are clear. No person is righteous through their good works. God's righteousness is gained only through the work of Christ. God's revelation is required to break this stronghold of seeking salvation and relationship with Christ through good works.

I struggled with this *Good Works* deception before and after salvation. Afterward, I was entangled in the lie that, if

I were truly a Christian, my life would always be godly, and I would not experience repeat sin. My sins left me doubting that I was really saved, and I was impatient and often in bondage to my failures. Some impatience is good, and we are to be deeply grieved, in a godly manner, by our sins. The problem was that I was focusing on myself and my efforts, instead of on Christ and drawing closer to Him. God calls us to live godly lives, but they are to *result from His Spirit's life in and through us, not our efforts in the flesh.* I was stuck in the futility of attempting to live Christ's life through my own efforts. This is a destructive approach that Satan encourages and delights in.

We have all met incredible people who believe that they are right with God, because they try to be good and are better, in their eyes, than many Christians. Christians errantly teach this when they say and believe, "Surely God would never send 'Jane' to hell. She is so good!" When confused Christians teach this *Good Works* philosophy, they are making it extremely difficult for others to hear God's truth.

Biblical Salvation

MATT 16:15-17

He (Jesus) said to them (His disciples),
"But who do you say that I am?"

Simon Peter answered and said, "You are the
Christ, the Son of the Living God."

Jesus answered and said to him, "Blessed are you,
Simon Bar-Jonah, for flesh and blood has not revealed

this to you, but My Father who is in heaven" (God's revelation comes through His Holy Spirit.)

JOHN 6:44

No one can come to Me unless the Father who sent Me draws him: (The Spirit draws them.)

EPH 2:8

For by grace you have been saved, through faith, and that not of yourselves; it is the gift of God.

JOHN 3:3, 6, 16

Most assuredly, I say to you, unless one is born again, he cannot see the kingdom of God.

That which is born of the flesh is flesh, and that which is born of the Spirit is spirit.

For God so loved the world that He gave His only begotten Son, that whoever believes in Him should not perish but have everlasting life.

EPH 1:17

That the God of our Lord Jesus Christ, the Father of glory, may give to you the spirit of wisdom and revelation in the knowledge of Him.

Salvation Through Christ

Biblical salvation is dependent on the *revelation of the Spirit*. It includes a call from the Father, a personal encounter with Jesus, and the individual's acceptance of Christ through faith that is not conjured up by their human will but is the gift of God. There is no other way. Salvation is not based on head knowledge, family, church association and membership, or good works. It is not based on infant or adult baptism.

Christ's way to salvation is through a personal encounter with Him, where, through the revelation of God, we absolutely *know* that Jesus is who He says He is, the Son of the Living God. We recognize our brokenness and absolute need of Him. Through *God's gift of faith*, we appropriate Christ's redemptive work through the cross and His resurrection life. Acceptance of Christ is to usher in a lifelong journey of experiencing an ever-deepening personal relationship with Him as He transforms us into the masterpiece that He designed. (Many block this by choosing to remain immature Christians.) The transformations in our lives are accomplished by His Spirit within us, not by our fleshly efforts. Without true salvation, we are no more than club members, even though we take on the name of "Christian."

Revelation Knowledge

We discuss revelation knowledge thoroughly in Chapter 13. For now, consider Peter's experience in Matthew 16. After Peter shared, "You are the Christ, the son of the living God," Jesus told him how blessed he was to know this truth by revelation, *"for flesh and blood has not revealed this to you, but My Father who is in heaven."* Revelation truth was alive in the very core of Peter's being. It transformed him and governed how he lived. Peter did not decide to believe because he was impressed by Christ. That belief is of the flesh. He received and acted on the revelation of the Spirit, which is like the fuel that propels a rocket. It results in Christ's transformation of our lives. Receiving and believing the Spirit's revelations of Christ result in biblical salvation through our personal encounter with Him.

Head knowledge is the opposite of revelation knowledge. It results from human experience and does not necessarily represent God's truth. It may affect the way that we live, but it does not have the power to radically transform the core of our being. It does not lead to salvation.

Application

Have you had a personal encounter with Christ where, through God's revelation (like Peter's), you *know* Jesus is the Son of God, and you place all of yourself under His authority? Head knowledge does not count. Christ's encounters with each of us are as unique as we are. Do not compare or attempt to copy another's experience. You will know if you have encountered Him through the Spirit's revelation and have embraced Him. The Spirit is your confirmation within. Satan will tempt you to deny that your Christ-encounter was real. Tell him to depart as you stand on the truth of the scriptures and the miracle of Christ's Spirit living within you.

What did you experience through this chapter? Some thoughts were from you, and some were from the Holy Spirit. Shouts of denial and rejection may have come from the enemy. Process what the Spirit shared. Identify where you are in Christ and what His Spirit has for you. Always begin time with Him by asking for His revelation, and He will provide it.

- What specific emotions and revelations were experienced as you read? What concepts and scriptures impacted you the most?

- What do you agree with and why?

- What are you uncomfortable about and why?

- What do you reject and why?

- What scripture verses support each of your positions?

- If you are not saved, what are you going to do with your life? If you reject salvation in Christ, be sure you understand the consequences of casting God's Son aside.

- If you believe you are saved, why are you certain? Have you avoided the deceptions and embraced salvation through your personal encounter with the living Christ and God's gift of faith?

- Build your life on God's biblical truths.

- What have you and the Holy Spirit agreed are to be your next steps? *More deliberate prayer, Bible study + finish this book.*

CHAPTER 5

KNOW GOD THROUGH HIS REVELATION. HOW DO YOU SEE HIM?

Knowing Jehovah (God) as He reveals Himself is essential for enabling us to become the masterpieces He designed. Each of us views God through paradigms that contain both truth and falsehood, and He desires to replace falsehood with His truths. We cannot know everything about Him, but we can know what He has chosen to reveal. One of His central truths is that He loves us and desires a deeply personal relationship with each of us.

In this chapter, we consider many ways that culture and human relationships impact our views of God. Then, we examine how God reveals Himself through creation, the Bible, and the person of the Christ of the Gospels. You are asked to permit Him to replace mistaken beliefs so that you know Him as He is, your loving God and incredible Father. Only the Spirit can reveal God's truths.

Culture and Relationships Have Impacted Our Views of God

Cultural beliefs and healthy or hurtful relationships were forming our perspective of God long before we cognitively sought to know Him. These deeply held views impact and draw us either toward or away from His true identity.

Cultural Views of God

Below are common cultural views of God and their corresponding potential impacts. Add your own. Identify which have the greatest positive and negative impacts on your view of God, and document how they affect your life and walk with Him.

IDENTITY OF GOD	IMPACT ON INDIVIDUALS
UNTRUTHS	
Distant & Uninvolved	No reason for me to care about Him.
He's Either Not Real or Dead	Those who believe in God are weak, deceived.
Judgmental	I can't trust Him.
Critical Perfectionist	Same as above.
Watching My Every Move, to Catch Me in Sin	Same as above.
Harsh Disciplinarian	Rejection, hatred, rebellion.
Unforgiving	Why try? I'll do this on my own.
"Do Not Disturb"	I'm not important.
He's Some Mystic Force of Energy	All religions are equal. I'll define my own spiritual journey.
TRUTHS	
Nurturing and Patient	Wow, He loves helping me grow.
Joyous	Let's walk through life together.
He Loves Me Unconditionally	He loves me just as I am. Wow!

Know God through His Revelation. How Do You See Him?

IDENTITY OF GOD	IMPACT ON INDIVIDUALS
He has a plan for me.	
Always There to Help and Show the Way	I can trust Him.
Creative	He embraces uniqueness, including me.

Relationships Impact Our Views of God
Relationship Approaches Have Great Impact

Our ability to relate with God and others is significantly impacted by past and present relationships. Consider the following list of positive and hurtful relationship approaches, and add your own.

POSITIVE	HURTFUL
Unconditional Love	Conditional, Performance-Based Love
Accepting and Nurturing	Impatient and Perfectionistic
Happy and Relaxed	Angry and Distant
Optimistic and Full of Faith	Pessimistic and Fearful
Fun/Adventurous	Cautions and Withdrawn
Positive Gender Role Models	Negative Gender Role Models
Open Communications	Limited Communications
Listens and Truly Hears You, Including Emotions	Tells You. They are in charge, and you are to submit.
Admits Mistakes and Genuinely Asks Forgiveness	Is "Always Right." Might say "Sorry" but "Whatever"
Reconciles Quickly/Forgives/Releases the Situation	Carries Grudges. Forever Hits You with Past

POSITIVE	HURTFUL
Disciplines with Love for Development Versus Punishment	Disciplines for Control or Avoids Discipline and Enables Brokenness
Encourages, Exhorts to Support Your Identity	Demands Compliance to Their Desires *Somewhat relevant*

Impact of Different Categories of Relationships

Consider the following categories individually. What relationship approaches have you experienced, and how did your relationships within each group (including specific individuals) strengthen or injure your ability to: trust God; be the person He created you to be; and interact with others? How did they impact your self-image, ability to trust, willingness to be vulnerable, and ability to live in your true identity? (We are not assigning blame.) God desires understanding, healing, and, ultimately, freedom. Ask the Spirit to help you receive all that He has for you. Document all of this for your future work with Him.

- Family: Father, Mother, Siblings, Foster Parents, Grandparents, Uncles, Aunts.

- Authority Figures: School officials, law enforcement, gang membership, coaches, leaders in church and work.

- Social and Community: Your family's cultural identity, your community's identity, academics, athletics, cliques, ethnicity, and social/economic groups.

- Intimate Relationships: Dating experiences, marriage experiences, and close friends.

Your Current View of God

For some of you, even calling Him "Father" makes your stomach churn. For others, it is incredibly easy. Wherever you are in this, He understands and loves you. He has a unique plan for drawing you into the amazing relationship that He designed.

List the five to ten most important areas that govern how you view God and how much you trust Him. Be brutally real, and avoid religious answers. You and He will compare this to His revelation of Himself. The items listed are examples.

HOW I VIEW/KNOW GOD	WHERE DID THIS COME FROM?	HOW DOES THIS AFFECT MY RELATIONSHIP WITH HIM?
He's God, but He Doesn't Care	Distant, Abusive Parents	I Don't Want to Be Around Him.
I Know I Can Trust Him.	Family That Embraced Me	I Believe He Truly Loves Me

God's Revelation of Himself

God reveals Himself primarily through His creation, the Old and New Testaments, and the life of Jesus Christ on Earth. We provide an introduction to each category and encourage you to engage in an increasingly intentional journey to know your Heavenly Father. All learning is to be based on scripture, with God's Spirit as your source of revelation.

Through His Creation

> **ROM 1:19-24A**
>
> Because what may be known of God is manifest in them (humankind), for God has shown it to them.
>
> For, since the creation of the world, His invisible attributes are clearly seen, being understood by the things that are made, even His eternal power and Godhead, so that they are without excuse, because, although they knew God, they did not glorify Him as God, nor were thankful, but became futile in their thoughts, and their foolish hearts were darkened.
>
> Professing to be wise, they became fools, and changed the glory of the incorruptible God into an image made like corruptible man—and birds, and four-footed animals and creeping things,
>
> Therefore, God also gave them up to uncleanness.

Humankind has no excuse for claiming that they do not know about the one true God. "His invisible attributes are clearly seen, being understood by the things that are made, even His eternal power and Godhead, so that they are without excuse." There is no excuse for worshiping nature in place of Him. Work with the Holy Spirit to record what you know about God through creation. Here are a few thoughts.

CREATIVE	ENJOYS VARIETY AND DIVERSITY	ENJOYS BEAUTY
Provides Precise Order	Is Uncontained	Restores
Powerful	Eternal	Exists Everywhere
Loves His Creation	Is Good	Is Personal
Permits Choice	Loves Diversity	

Through His Bible

2 TIM 3:16

All Scripture is given by inspiration of God, and is profitable for doctrine, for reproof, for correction, for instruction in righteousness.

HEB 4:12

For the word of God is living and powerful, and sharper than any two-edged sword, piercing even to the division of soul and spirit, and of joints and marrow, and is a discerner of the thoughts and intents of the heart.

MATT 24:35

Heaven and earth will pass away, but My words will by no means pass away.

The Inerrant Word of God

To know God and become His masterpiece, we must know the Bible is the inerrant and Spirit-inspired word of God. This is the statement of the scriptures themselves, both Old and New Testaments. It is the truth that Christ presented throughout His ministry. Without this truth we have nothing but the vacillating, vain thoughts of ourselves and others.

Embracing this truth is critical and a fork in the road that separates carnal from spiritual Christians. Billy Graham shared how he faced this giant of a decision in His early preaching years. He read, prayed, and wrestled. He knew that either the Bible was/is God's truth, and He could build his life on it and share its truths unapologetically as the very word of God, or he had nothing of value to believe and share. He made his choice for the Spirit-inspired inerrancy of God's word, and God utilized him to bring Christ's life into the lives of millions. We must all choose to either embrace this truth and our empowered lives in Christ or set it aside and have nothing but our own religious and secular philosophies. Only the Holy Spirit can bring this truth alive for us.

The Bible's Revelation of God's Character and Identity

The Old and New Testaments are filled with God's revelation of His identity and character. Review the following scripture examples, and add your own. Cultivate a lifestyle of spending time with Him through Bible reading, praying, and fellowship, and you will begin to really know Him. No book study can replace the revelation gained through your personal relationship with God. The Spirit's revelation through scripture is our source of understanding. Therefore, we present examples. Search out additional hundreds in God's word.

ETERNAL	DEUT 33:27A The eternal God is your refuge.
THE CREATOR	GEN 1:1 TO 2:28 In the beginning, God Created the heavens and the earth . . .
ALL THINGS EXIST BY HIM	REV 4:11 You are worthy O Lord, to receive glory, honor and power; For You created all things, And by Your will they exist and were created.
HOLY	LEV 19:2B You shall be holy, for I the Lord your God am holy.

Know God through His Revelation. How Do You See Him?

SPIRIT	**JOHN 4:24** For God is Spirit, and those who worship Him must worship in Spirit and truth.
LOVE (UNCONDITIONAL)	**DEUT 7:9A** Therefore, know that the Lord your God, He is love, the faithful God who keeps covenant and mercy for a thousand generations ... **1 JOHN 4:9-11** In this the love of God was manifested toward us, that God has sent His only begotten Son into the world, that we might live through Him. **JER 31:3** The Lord appeared of old to me, saying, "Yes I have loved you with an everlasting love; Therefore with lovingkindness I have drawn you."
GOD CREATED US FOR RELATIONSHIP	**JOHN: 14:20** At that day you will know that I am in the Father, and you in me, and I in you.
ALL POWERFUL	**JER 32:17** Ah, Lord God Behold, You have made the heavens and the earth by Your great power and outstretched arm. There is nothing too hard for You.
EVER PRESENT	**PSALM 139:7-10A** Where can I go from Your Spirit? Or where can I flee from Your Presence? If I ascend into heaven, You are there; If I make my bed in hell, behold, You are there. If I take the wings of the morning, And dwell in the uttermost parts of the sea, Even there Your hand shall lead me
ALL KNOWING	**1 JOHN 3:20B** God is greater than our heart, and knows all things.
UNCHANGING	**HEB 13:8** Jesus Christ is the same yesterday, today and forever.
ALL FRUIT OF THE SPIRIT	**GAL 5:22-23** These verses list the fruit of the Spirit. Since the Father, Jesus Christ, and the Holy Spirit are one being with three roles, they embody these fruits.

JUSTICE	AMOS 5:24 But let justice run down like water, And righteousness like a mighty river.
MY STRENGTH, MY FORTRESS, MY STRONGHOLD	PSALM 18:1-2 I will love you O Lord my strength. The Lord is my rock and my fortress and my deliverer; My God, my strength, in whom I will trust; My shield and the horn of my salvation, my stronghold.
TRINITY	SEE CHAPTER 13
RIGHTEOUS JUDGE	PSALM 98:9 For He is coming to judge the earth. With righteousness He shall judge the world, And the peoples with equity.

Which of these do you either believe or question and reject? Ask the Holy Spirit to prioritize these with you and help you embrace God's true identity. When doubts arise, declare Bible truths by stating these scriptures.

God's Specific Revelation of His Identity Through Jesus Christ

JOHN 14:9

Jesus said to him, "Have I been with you so long, and yet you have not known Me, Philip? He who has seen Me has seen the Father, so how can you say, "Show us the Father?"

In the four Gospels, we see God's identity through the life of Jesus—how He walked, talked, prayed, and interacted with individuals and life. His actions convey not only His and His Father's identity *but also* the ways that He desires to express Himself through us. Do not permit secular, cultural, or church constraints on Christ's character to replace scripture. Jesus is the very essence and definition of love, peace, patience, gentleness, and grace. Everything He did reflects these characteristics, including His actions of overturning the tables of the moneychangers and His often-direct correction of His disciples.

Characteristics of Christ are noted below. Scripture verses are included in Chapter 20. At this point, we ask you to study the Gospels, confirm the following, and fill in your additional understanding from the Spirit's revelation. The scripture is your final authority. How do your beliefs about God and Christ align or conflict with these Bible truths? Document your findings. Permit the Holy Spirit to align your beliefs with God's truths.

HOLY	FORGIVING	NEVER LOSE ONE OF HIS
Loving	Connects Through Truth and Relating Personally	Healer
Righteous	Merciful	Defeated the Enemy
Just	Humble	Restorer
Without Guile	Strong	Joyous
Eternal	Forgiving	One with the Father
Full of Grace	Creator	Exhorter
Gentle	Lord of All	Confronter of Sin
Teacher	Brother	Confronter of Leadership Errors in Teaching and Action
Loving	Friend	Directed His Disciples to Live What He had Taught, Instead of Walking without Faith

> *God unconditionally loves you and desires an intimate, personal relationship with you. You are His masterpiece; He delights in you; and He will accomplish His missions in and through you, as you surrender your all and learn to walk in the Spirit.*

EVER DEEPENING PERSONAL RELATIONSHIP IS GOD'S ULTIMATE REVELATION OF HIS IDENTITY

Do You Desire to Know God Personally, with All Your Heart?

Do you want to get to truly know God? The only way is through a personal relationship that includes walking in His Spirit. Depth and intimacy are dependent on the time and commitment that are invested in the relationship. God is "all in." Are you? Decide how you will jump in and move forward in this life. Healing of hurts is necessary, and He will help. Never bury and ignore hurts; get the help you need.

Application

Creation, the Bible, and the life of Christ reveal God's true identity. Compare and contrast His revealed identity to your view of Him. Permit the Holy Spirit to guide you as you consider:

- ✦ Which of the Bible's characteristics of God do you totally embrace?

Know God through His Revelation. How Do You See Him?

- Which of His revealed characteristics conflict with your view of Him?
- Select three or four biblical characteristics that you can't believe.
- Identify the forces that have hurt you or let you down in these areas.
- Begin the process of differentiating your past and present hurts from the true identity of your Father God and His desired relationship.
- As you seek healing, surrender to the Holy Spirit, and ask Him to help you replace any broken view of God with the reality of who He is in your life and who you are in His.
- Declare His identity through scripture verses.

CHAPTER 6

SEEING YOURSELF WITH GOD'S EYES

EPH 4:22, 24
put off... the old man which grows corrupt... put on the new man which was created according to God, in true righteousness and holiness.

The way we view ourselves and others determines who we become and how we treat people. What would our lives be like if we viewed ourselves through God's eyes and followed His Spirit's leadership? We would *be* His unique masterpieces and experience the fullness of life in His Spirit. We would help others to do the same.

Utilize this chapter to determine whether you see yourself and others as God does. To what extent are you living His life or your own? Permit His truths to transform your walk with Him. We consider scripture revelations of how God views mankind's identity from three perspectives.

First: Prior to salvation
Second: Following salvation
Third: As unique masterpieces

Identity of Mankind: Before Accepting Christ

All individuals share certain God-given characteristics, whether they are saved or not. Consider the following and determine what you accept or reject. Which scriptures support your beliefs? How would you modify this list?

CHARACTERISTIC	SCRIPTURE
Made in the Image of God	Gen 1:27 So God created man in His own image;
Loved by God	John 3:16 For God so loved the world that He gave His only begotten Son,
Dominion over the Earth	Gen 1:28 And God ... God said to them, "... have dominion over the sea, over the birds of the air, and over every living thing that moves on the earth."
Unique	Psalm 139:15-16 My frame was not hidden from You, when I was made in secret, ... Your eyes saw my substance, ... And in Your book, they were all written, the days fashioned for me,
Free Will; Consequences	Gen 3. The man and woman made the choice to disobey and hide the truth from God. (Consequences resulted).
Eternal Beings	Matt 25:46 ESV And these will go away into everlasting punishment, but the righteous into eternal life.
Guilty before God, without Christ.	Is 64:6 But we are all like an unclean thing, And all our righteousnesses are like filthy rags;

IDENTITY OF ALL CHRISTIANS

2 COR 5:17

Therefore, if anyone is in Christ, he is a new creation; old things are passed away; behold, all things have become new.

In Christ, we are new creations. We have unique roles in His kingdom and are adopted into His family. His Holy Spirit has taken up residence in us, and we are to walk under His loving lordship.

Permit the Spirit to plant the following scripture truths in your heart. If you do not understand, study and work with Him. Stand on His truths about your identity in Christ. Living otherwise robs you of His gift of kingdom life.

CHARACTERISTIC "I AM/I HAVE..."	SCRIPTURE
CHARACTERISTICS WHETHER I AM SAVED OR NOT.	LISTED ON PAGE 78
THE RIGHTEOUSNESS OF GOD THROUGH CHRIST.	2 COR 5:21 For He made Him who knew no sin to be sin for us, that we might become the righteousness of God PSALM 37:23 The steps of a good man are ordered by the Lord, And He delights in his way.
UNCONDITIONALLY LOVED	PSALM 36:5, 7 (NLT) Your unfailing love, O Lord, is as vast as the heavens ... How precious is your unfailing love, O God!
FORGIVEN OF ALL SINS	EPH 1:7 In Him we have redemption through His blood, the forgiveness of sins,
NO CONDEMNATION	ROM 8:1 There is therefore now no condemnation to those who are in Christ Jesus,
GOD'S CHILD	1 JOHN 3:2A Beloved, now we are children of God
A NEW CREATION	2 COR 5:17 Therefore, if anyone is in Christ, he is a new creation; old things are passed away; behold, all things are become new.

THE TEMPLE OF THE HOLY SPIRIT WHO LIVES WITHIN	**1 Cor 6:19-20** Or do you not know that your body is the temple of the Holy Spirit who is within you, . . . you are not your own?
HAVE A HOLY CALLING	**2 Tim 1:9** (God) who has saved us and called us with a holy calling,
GOD'S MASTERPIECE	**Eph 2:10** For we are His workmanship (masterpiece), created in Christ Jesus for good works, which God prepared beforehand that we should walk in them.
UNIQUE GIFTS AND PURPOSE	**1 Cor 12:4-31**
ABLE TO DO ALL THINGS THROUGH CHRIST	**Phil 4:13** I can do all things through Christ who strengthens me.
APPROACH GOD BOLDLY	**Heb 4:16** Let us therefore come boldly to the throne of grace,
DELIVERED FROM THE POWER OF DARKNESS	**Col 1:13** He has delivered us from the power of darkness and conveyed us into the kingdom of the Son of His love.
SATAN CANNOT TOUCH	**1 John 5:18** We know that whoever is born of God does not sin (live a lifestyle of sin); . . . the wicked one does not touch him. (Without the loving permission of God)
A SAINT	**Rom 1:7** To all who are in Rome, beloved of God, called to be saints:
AN HEIR OF GOD	**Rom 8:16,17** The Spirit Himself bears witness with our spirit that we are children of God, And if children, then heirs—heirs of God and joint heirs with Christ.
COMPLETE IN CHRIST	**Col 2:10** and you are complete in Him

AN AMBASSADOR	**2 COR 5:20** We are ambassadors for Christ,
SALT	**MATT 5:13** You are the salt of the earth;
LIGHT	**MATT 5:14** You are the light of the world
DEAD TO SIN	**ROM 6:2** How can he who died to sin live any longer in it?
EVERLASTINGLY LOVED	**JER 31:3** The Lord appeared of old to me saying: "Yes, I have loved you with an everlasting love; therefore, with lovingkindness I have drawn you."
HEALED	**1 PETER 2:24** Who Himself bore our sins in His own body on the tree, that we, having died to sins, might live for righteousness—by whose stripes you were healed.
EVERLASTING LIFE WITH CHRIST	**JOHN 10:26-28 (JESUS IS SPEAKING)** And I give then eternal life, and they shall never perish; neither shall anyone snatch them out of My hand.
CHRIST LIVES IN ME	**GAL 2:20** I have been crucified with Christ; It is no longer I who live; but Christ lives in me
BLESSED	**EPH 1:3** Blessed be the God and Father of our Lord Jesus Christ, who has blessed us with every spiritual blessing in the heavenly places in Christ,
SHALL DO GREATER THINGS	**JOHN 14:12** Most assuredly, I say to you, he who believes in Me, the works that I do he will do also; and greater works than these he will do,
FREE OF THE PAST	**PHIL 3:13** Brethren, . . . this one thing I do, forgetting those things which are behind and reaching forward to those things which are ahead, I press toward the goal for the prize of the upward calling of God in Christ Jesus.

HOLY AND WITHOUT BLAME	**EPH 1:4** He chose us in Him before the foundation of the world, that we should be holy and without blame before Him in love.
CHRIST'S FRIEND	**JOHN 15:15** But I have called you friends,
CONFIDENT	**JOSHUA 1:9 (GOD SPEAKING TO JOSHUA)** Be strong and of good courage; do not be afraid, nor be dismayed, for the Lord your God is with you wherever you go.
A CITIZEN OF HEAVEN	**PHIL 3:20** For our citizenship is in heaven,
SEATED IN HEAVENLY PLACES	**EPH 2:4-6** But God, who is rich in mercy, because of His great love... raised us up together and made us sit together in heavenly places in Christ Jesus,
FULLY KNOWN BY GOD	**PSALMS 139:1-3** O Lord, You have searched me and known me. You know my sitting down and my rising up; You understand my thought afar off; You comprehend my path and my lying down; And are acquainted with all my ways.
A SON/DAUGHTER OF GOD	**GAL 3:26** For you are all sons of God through faith in Christ Jesus.
LED BY THE SPIRIT OF GOD	**ROM 8:14-15** For as many as are led by the Spirit of God, these are the sons of God.
CREATED TO: BE FILLED WITH AND WALK IN THE SPIRIT	**EPH 5:18B** ... but be filled with the Spirit. **GALATIANS 5:25B** If we live in the spirit let us also walk in the Spirit
SEEN BY GOD AS WHO I AM IN CHRIST	**1 SAM 16:7** ... for man looks at the outward appearance, but the Lord looks at the heart.

GOD'S FUTURE	**JER 29:11** For I know the thoughts that I think toward you . . . to give you a future and a hope.
HIS CHOSEN	**1 PETER 2:9** But you are a chosen generation, a royal priesthood, a holy nation. His own special people,
ALIVE WITH CHRIST—SINS ARE WIPED CLEAN	**COL 2:13-14** He has made (you) alive together with Him (in Christ,) having forgiven all trespasses, Having wiped out the handwriting of requirements that was against us . . . And He has taken it out of the way, having nailed it to the cross.
NOTHING CAN SEPARATE YOU	**ROM 8:38-39** . . . neither death nor life, nor angels nor principalities nor powers, nor things present nor things to come, nor height nor depth, nor any created thing, shall be able to separate us from the love of God which is in Christ Jesus our Lord.
SEALED	**2 COR 1:22** who also has sealed us and given us the Spirit in our hearts as a guarantee
MORE THAN CONQUERORS	**ROM 8:37** Yet in all these things we are more than conquerors through Him who loved us.
HE WILL COMPLETE	**PHIL 1:6** He who has begun a good work in you will complete it until the day of Jesus Christ.
ONE IN CHRIST	**EPH 4:3-6** There is one body and one Spirit, just as you were called in one hope of your calling; One Lord, one faith, one baptism; one God and Father of all, who is above all and through all, and in you all.
RENEWED MIND/ NEW CREATION	**EPH 4:23-24** And be renewed in the spirit of your mind, And that you put on the new man which was created according to God, in true righteousness and holiness.

CHOSEN TO BEAR HIS FRUIT	JOHN 15:16 You did not choose Me, but I choose you and appointed you that you should go and bear fruit.
SPIRITUAL GIFTS	1 COR 12:7 But one and the same Spirit works all of these things (manifestations of the Spirit/gifts of the Spirit); distributing to each one individually as He wills.
A THREE-PART BEING —SPIRIT —SOUL —BODY	SEE CHAPTER 12

EACH CHRISTIAN IS ALSO UNIQUE IN THEIR PURPOSE AND RELATIONSHIP WITH GOD

EPH 2:10

For we are His workmanship (masterpiece), created in Christ Jesus for good works, which God prepared beforehand that we should walk in them.

1 COR 12:4, 11

There are diversities of gifts but the same Spirit

But one and the same Spirit works all these things, distributing to each one individually as He will.

1 COR 12:18-19

But God has set members, each one of them, in the body, just as He pleased,

And if all were one member, where would the body be?

Learn to See Yourself and Others with God's Eyes and to Daily Live Your Unique Walk, Purpose, and Missions in His Spirit. Only Christ's Spirit Can Reveal Your Unique Identity and Accomplish It in and through You. This is Not About Human Perfection.

Application

Do you accept yourself as the unique masterpiece God created and delights in, or do you live a broken image? Are you willing to embrace God's incredible and unique design and missions as you permit His Spirit to transform you?

- How do you view your identity differently than God does? Why do you think this is so?

- Where is the Spirit directing you to begin as He replaces broken images with your true identity?

- The mature Christian life is experienced by those who commit to the lifelong journey of "walking in God's Spirit" (Ch 15). Will you ask the Spirit to provide His revelation regarding this truth and lead you into this life? If not, what is blocking you?

- Walking in God's Spirit is a lifelong adventure of *Being and Becoming*. It begins in each moment (each now) and is lived one moment at a time, as you listen to His voice. Ask Him to set you free to begin right now. The Christian life is not about trying to act like Jesus in the flesh but about walking in the Spirit and *being the masterpiece He designed.*

- Do not attempt to copy someone else's journey with Christ. Yours is unique.

- Freedom from deep scars and hurts does not occur overnight. Some may take a lifetime. Even so, He will accomplish His purposes in and through you, often utilizing them.

- Christ's transformation happens from the inside out. It is the work of the Holy Spirit, not your efforts. Your role is to walk in Him.

- Do you focus on perfection and yourself? This is deception. Focus on Christ and following Him. Mistakes are part of moving forward in faith. God understands that they are part of learning when they result from the efforts of a pure heart.

- The greatest failure is to let fear, religion, and unbelief shackle you into being frozen where you are. Do not block God's Spirit.

- Are you willing to let the Spirit teach you to view others from this same perspective?

CHAPTER 7

TRUE CHRISTIAN FAITH IS THE GIFT OF GOD

EPH 2:8
For by grace you have been saved through faith, and that not of yourselves; it is the gift of God.

HEB 11:6A
But without faith it is impossible to please Him,

2 COR 5:7
For we walk by faith and not by sight

HEB 11:13
These all died in faith, not having received the promises, but having seen them afar off were assured of them, embraced them, and confessed that they were strangers and pilgrims on the earth.

God's gift of faith connects every aspect of our lives with Him, His purpose, and His power. It is impossible to live for Christ or please God without it. Yet many sincere Christians replace His gift with the powerless imitation of faith that results from their own efforts. Do you know the difference, and have you learned to live in His faith, which Ephesians states is *not of ourselves but is the gift of God?* God's faith has its source in the revelation of His Spirit, and it transforms our lives. Embracing this gift permits us to live, serve, and pray in His confidence and power. Flesh-generated faith is powerless and results in burden and frustration. It teaches, "If we just believe hard enough and have 'enough faith' through our own efforts, God will honor our desires." It focuses on us, our understanding of biblical truths, and our flesh-generated efforts to believe. Permit God to free you of this counterfeit and fill you with His gift of faith.

What Is Christian Faith?
The Gift of God, Not Human Efforts

Faith is God's gift for all of life. We now evaluate this truth as it applies to salvation and then expand our application to all aspects of Christian life. Do you believe that your faith for salvation resulted from your efforts, or was and is it the gift of God? You may never have thought about it, but Eph 2:8 presents one of the most important and empowering truths of scripture. Our faith to receive God's salvation is *the gift of God. It is not something that we are able to create through our self-will.* We cannot take any credit. God provides not only the sacrifice and grace for salvation through Christ but also the faith to receive it. We are responsible for receiving and acting on God's gift of faith. If you believe the Bible (Eph 2), then *you know your faith for salvation is God's gift.* It is His gift for not only salvation but for living all of His life.

Faith: God's Gift for All of Life
Human Efforts at Faith Are Futile

GAL 3:3

Are you so foolish? Having begun in the Spirit are you now being made perfect by the flesh?

ROM 8:8

So then, those who are in the flesh cannot please God.

GAL 5:17A

For the flesh lusts after the Spirit and the Spirit against the flesh; and these are contrary to one another . . .

GAL 6:7-8

Do not be deceived—God is not mocked; for whatever a man sows, that he will also reap. For he who sows to his flesh will of the flesh reap corruption, but he who sows to the Spirit will of the Spirit reap everlasting life.

Our lives in Christ begin through the Spirit's gift of faith. Are we now to continue our walk with God through His gift of faith or through our imitation of His faith, generated through efforts of our flesh (minds, wills, emotions)? Galatians 3:3, above, asks a similar question and makes it clear that attempting to accomplish anything of kingdom value through efforts of our flesh is foolishness! The subsequent three verses state reasons for this truth. The Spirit and flesh have no part in each other. A Christian's works of the flesh, beginning with fleshly efforts at generating faith, cannot please God. Faith for all aspects of life in Christ is a gift of God.

WHOSE LIFE ARE YOU LIVING?

> *The Spirit is to be the source of all that occurs both in and through each Christian's life. This includes faith, actions, and transformation. What is achieved/sown in the flesh is of no kingdom value. The ability to have biblical faith cannot be found within humankind.*

Having embraced the Spirit's revelation that God's gift of faith is for all aspects of life, we are ready to engage life as He designed it. We learn to trust Him in every situation. As His Spirit brings revelation to specific areas of the Bible, they become alive within. His truths and promises transform us. (Ultimately, we learn to "walk in His Spirit," Chapter 15. Without this, we are merely trying to act like His masterpieces instead of being them.)

Many in the Christian Church have been misled into believing that they are responsible for creating faith by the efforts of their flesh. They are trapped by this false teaching which pleases Satan and is an anchor that constrains their spiritual lives. Works of our flesh never please God. Are you free of this deception? Do you walk in God's "gift" of faith?

The Believer's Role in Appropriating God's Gift of Faith

Believers have an active role in walking in God's gift of faith. With intentionality, we are to receive it, accept it, and stand on it, based on God's biblical truths. Even this is accomplished in the power of His Spirit. Often this involves great struggles when outcomes seem to deny our understanding of His promises and conflict with our desires. We err in many ways. Some attempt to control God, by thinking they have the right to define what His promises mean. Others focus prayers on asking God to make things work out according to their desires without leaving room for His wisdom. Many believe their perspectives of earthly life must define how God interprets His Bible truths. Each of these errors place our beliefs above God's sovereignty. He views our lives and purpose from His eternal perspective. It always results in our best. His sovereign will determines both when and how He fulfills His promises.

Victorious lives require faith without sight as we will often not understand or even feel like embracing His plans. We require His gift of faith. When we rely on flesh-generated faith and we are disappointed, we most often turn to self-will, disappointment, distrust, and even bitterness. However, we mature every time we choose to stand in His gift of faith. He has given us free will, and when we insist on our way and our flesh-based faith, our lives experience detours, confusion, and even loss. When we stand in His faith, we grow in Him, and our masterpiece lives blossom.

recipe for a fulfilling life!!

God's Incredible Life of Faith

HEB 11: 33-34

who through faith subdued kingdoms, worked righteousness, obtained promises, stopped the mouths of lions,

quenched the violence of fire, escaped the edge of the sword, out of weakness were made strong, became valiant in battle, turned to fight the armies of aliens.

Look again at the above verses and then at the entire eleventh chapter of Hebrews. This is the life of faith God has for you. He designed you to be listed among this group of heroes of the faith, not by your efforts but through His Spirit's life in and through you. God does not measure heroes based on their worldly accomplishments but on their lives in His faith.

> True Christian faith is the gift of God and never results from mental and emotional efforts of humankind. It is the very life of those who believe in and walk in Christ, for without faith you cannot please your Father. Flesh-generated faith has no power, because the works of the flesh conflict with the works of the Spirit.

What Christian Faith Is Not

Although we know Christian faith does not result from mankind's efforts, there are other misconceptions we are to confront and eliminate.

Faith Is Not Presuming of God to Bless Human Plans

Many well-intended Christians chase after beautiful rainbows, in God's name, when He is not their source. Spiritual-sounding ideas hit them. Because the ideas feel so wonderful, are so exciting, or so logical, the individual decides, "It must be from God!" They forge ahead. They may pray with much fervor, claim to seek God, and use scripture, but they never really engage and listen to Him. In truth, their prayer is, "Bless my idea, God. It is so wonderful that it must be Yours!" They then testify that they have "faith" that God will provide and bring miracles. Unless they have received it from His Spirit, this is not Godly faith at all; it is presumption. Their flesh is in charge, through their minds and emotions. Do not include this kind of flesh-faith in your understanding of Godly faith.

Worldly Success Measures Do Not Necessarily Equate to the Presence of Godly Faith or His Blessing

Neither success nor lack of success in human terms reflects the presence of His faith or His blessing. Consider two actual ministries:

One ministry enjoys financial success, recognition, and impressive connections, even though it is not executing God's mission effectively. They have dreams for expansion. They push until doors open. Donors of substance line up to contribute as they flock to images of worldly success and declarations based on flesh-faith. Ministry leaders declare all financial progress is confirmation of God's blessing. The new endeavor proceeds and is celebrated, but it is again run with the same lack of excellence. Everyone glorifies God, while they pat themselves on the back. Was this an example of God's initiative? There is strong reason to wonder.

Another ministry is effectively led by the Spirit, and it operates in His power. The Lord touches and transforms lives. This ministry remains small. Finances are a challenge, but God is always faithful. God's power is present and operating. Many might say that this ministry is not as successful as it should be because of size and money. They would be using the wrong metrics.

Graciously, God often works despite our mistakes and waits for His purposes to prosper and blossom. He stands by all who have good hearts and are growing in Him, even when we miss His Spirit's leadership. The flesh loves to declare that logical, exciting, and spiritual-sounding ideas are all of God and that flesh-generated faith will move the hands of God. Both are deceptions of the enemy that drain God's kingdom.

God's Faith Brings His Truths Alive

Mature walks with God are founded on key biblical truths. We stumble and falter if we *try* to believe them in our own faith. We thrive in Christ only as our faith is His gift from His Spirit, and it results in transformed life within us. Where do you stand on the following?

In Whom Do You Believe?

One definition of faith is that it is a complete trust or confidence in someone or something. We may say our faith is in God, and that may be true, but it must be explored further. Mankind has created its own definitions of "god." Christian faith is in the One true God, Jehovah, who reveals Himself through the Trinity. Is your faith in Him? Only through the Spirit's revelation and God's gift of faith can we absolutely know Jehovah is the one true God. Anything less resides in our flesh. Do the biblical truths of God's identity (Chapter 5) reside in your very being through God's gift of faith?

God Is Sovereign

Most Christians say this is true. Only those who walk in His gift of faith grow to truly trust and rest in His sovereign will.

They embrace His loving and sovereign decisions governing "how and when" He responds to every prayer (Hebrews 11:13, above.) The truth that many promises of God are not achieved in the time and manner His people desire is exciting for them. It does not weaken their faith; it, in fact, strengthens it. Such faith cannot originate in our flesh.

The Bible Is God's Inerrant Word

As we discussed previously, one of the early decisions each Christian faces is, "Will I believe the Bible's statement that it is the inerrant word of God?" (Remember Billy Graham's story.) Only God's gift of faith can result in confidence in, and life based on, this foundational truth of Christianity. Life without it drifts with every tide of human thought. We have three choices.

First: Reject this truth because many religious people, including some defined as Christian, and basically all secular individuals and groups work hard to convince us it is foolishness. Accordingly, we set God's word aside and make ourselves (and others) the ultimate judge of truth. Life is built on a foundation of sand, and our definitions of truth vacillate in rhythm with every whim—ours and many others.

Second: You choose to try "obediently and religiously" to believe everything in the Bible because religious authorities say "good" Christians must. This is a fruitless journey. It depends on your will instead of the revelation of the Spirit.

Third: Choose to explore this "question" under the guidance of God's Spirit. As He brings His revelation of this truth, embrace it through the supernatural faith that He provides. Life enters an incredible series of Spirit-driven transformations that occur only in those who receive biblical inerrancy through God's gift of faith. This truth now encompasses the *entire* Bible, and you do not have to test each word and promise separately. You will test much specifically as you mature through your journey, because you want the Spirit to make it fully "your" understanding, resulting from His revelation and faith. He brings revelation for each specific truth at times appropriate for you. God is not interested in blind robots, and He enjoys working with you so that each truth becomes your own through His Spirit.

Faith: Exercised Differently for Two Categories of Biblical Truths

2 COR 5:7
For we walk by faith and not by sight.

God's faith is expressed differently as we approach life in two categories of Bible truths. The first involves truths that are directly covered in the Bible. The second involves areas that are not.

Faith: Applied to Bible Truths, Promises, and Situations Specifically Addressed in the Bible

There are specific truths and promises throughout the Bible. These involve God's identity and character, our identity in Christ, His promises, the role of His Church, how we are to walk in His Spirit, and our kingdom roles. As we evaluate choices in these areas, we know His exact statements of truth. His gift of faith in these areas is specific. We know, "His truth is 'this' and He will do it." We will not know the "when and how," but we know that His truths and promises shall be met. This walk is not easy, as it depends on walking by faith and not by sight. Also, since He has given us free will, we may choose to either walk in His truth by His faith or follow our own desires into detours.

My life involves decisions concerning how to deal with physical situations (heart and muscle issues) that may impact longevity. Accordingly, I am often tempted to rush into His missions. When I do, I am wrong. I am walking in my flesh instead of His Spirit. He draws me back with gentle reminders to trust Him. He reminds me to receive His faith and stand on the following scriptures:

Is 54:17A
No weapon formed against you shall prosper,

Psalm 31:15A
My times are in your hand:

Phil 1:6
Being confident of this one thing, that He who has begun a good work in you will complete it until the day of Jesus Christ.

I do not merely "hope' that these are true—God has given me His gift of faith to "know" they are true. The Spirit establishes my life in them and removes anxieties and confusion. I trust my Father God to accomplish His masterpiece life in and through me, even when it conflicts with my desires. Whether His plan for me includes many more years or fewer, I know He will accomplish His will as I obediently follow His Spirit.

Faith: Applied to Situations Not Specifically Addressed in the Bible

In these situations, our faith is based on His revelation of the biblical truths about the righteousness, goodness, and trustworthiness of God's character. He cares about every aspect of our lives and will work all things for our good, according to His will. We approach Him with all our needs and trust Him *as we ask Him to reveal His direction*. We tell Him the desires of our hearts, *but place these under His sovereign will and eternal purpose*.

God's gift of faith in these instances is different. We present our needs and seek God's *revelation of His will*. We develop a full knowledge of His word regarding our situation and seek godly counsel. His revelation takes many forms. It is sometimes a complete vision of an endpoint and sometimes just the next tiny step. Sometimes, we hear nothing, because He wants us to mature by acting on what He has already taught us. In each case, we engage with the Holy Spirit until we believe He has released us to move forward. We then proceed in God's faith, trusting Him for redirection if necessary. We understand that no one always hears the Spirit accurately. Our faith is not based on how excited we are, how godly the decision seems, or how much sense it makes. It is based on His proven character. *We trust God for His will and results! Faith is strong and vibrant, but it is in Him, not what we believe is the exact outcome and approach that we pursue.*

Example: Faith for Obeying God's Role for You in Spiritual Gifts

God has given the gift of prophecy. The Spirit directs a person to speak edification, exhortation, and comfort into lives and situations. The Spirit has provided them with a process to confirm His instructions. After receiving confirmation, they proceed with great humility and a tremendous sense of responsibility. God provides His gift of faith, and He executes His gift of prophecy through them.

His gift of faith in the character of God is incredibly important in the lives of His people. It is lived with a different humility than faith in the specific promises of God, as it results from a deep personal relationship and obedience that is open to human error. *Without the willingness to step out in this type of God-given faith, no Christian would be able to walk **through their missions, including use of spiritual gifts,** in the power of the Spirit. They could step out in their own flesh, and some try this, but this never produces God's fruit.* Since we are human, mistakes will be made. When our hearts are right, He views these as honest learning events and works through them.

Example: Faith for Optional Decisions

A ministry thinks they need to expand. The leaders bring the entire opportunity before God as they pray, discern the facts, and evaluate alternatives. They believe their decisions are directed by God's Spirit. They correctly and humbly say that they stand in "faith." They have every reason to stand on and proceed in "faith." (Some report "they see this work done with their spiritual eyes," which is authentic when God has actually provided this vision. Sadly, some mimic this experience and claim it as a testimony to "their" faith, even though God has not shown them. This is false testimony.)

However, if they have misunderstood God, their vision and faith do not obligate Him. He did not promise this specific expansion in His word. Since they recognize this possibility of human error, their faith includes an awareness that plans may change as He brings clarity. No amount of human-generated "faith or eyes of faith" will require God to deliver on expectations that are outside His will. As we have noted, God honors pure hearts and may make provision for plans that missed His design. He loves to develop His children and uses all things to bring forth His ultimate purposes.

Faith for Miracles

When Jesus states that an individual's faith has made them whole, what is the faith He honors? Is it the faith that individuals generated through acts of their flesh, or is it God's gift of faith? What does the Bible promise? The subject of healing provides a superb study of faith. What we learn here is applicable to all works of faith in the Christian life.

Prayerfully consider the following examples, and ask the Holy Spirit to reveal, "Is there any significant difference between what you believe about Christ's abilities to heal and what Bible characters believed?" If you truly know Jesus, the answer is, "No, there is not." If there is no difference between what you and they believe about Jesus' abilities to heal, why does healing not always result from your faith-filled prayers? What is the faith that Jesus honored?

The Holy Spirit Is the Source of Biblical Faith for Miracles

The Spirit, not our flesh, provides God's gift of faith for claiming His promises and experiencing His miracles. He is the source of God-Honoring and miracle-appropriating faith. We are accountable for receiving and standing in His faith. In the following examples, Bible characters not only knew that Jesus *could* heal but also knew that He *would* heal. They stood and acted on that knowledge, the gift of faith. Where did that knowledge come from?

LUKE 8:43-48 YOUR FAITH HAS MADE YOU WHOLE

(Our first healing example testifies to the woman who touched Jesus' garment and her blood issue of twelve years was immediately healed.) Jesus said to her, "Daughter, be of good cheer; your faith has made you well. Go in peace."

MATT 8:5-13

As You have believed, so let it be done to you.

This next testimony to faith presents the centurion who came to Jesus, pleading for his paralyzed servant. When Jesus stated that He would come to his house, the centurion answered that he was not worthy for Jesus to be under his roof. He asked Jesus to "But only speak a word and my servant will be healed." Jesus marveled and said, "Assuredly, I say to you, I have not found such great faith, not even in Israel. . . . Go your way; and as you have believed, so let it be done for you."

Compare the faith of these individuals to your faith and that of every true believer in Christ. Both individuals believed that Christ "could heal" with either a word or a touch. You undoubtedly have this same belief and faith. Yet, the individuals in our examples went beyond that faith. They "knew" healing would occur if they acted. The woman knew that she was to touch His garment, and the centurion knew that he must ask, and Jesus must speak a word.

Why aren't our healing prayers always answered with immediate healing since we have absolute faith that Jesus *can* heal? Where does the biblical faith that healing *will occur* come from? Sadly, some Christians answer this question by chastising those who are not healed and stating that their faith is the issue. They declare it must not have been strong enough. Those who teach such judgment must believe that the individuals in our Bible examples had stronger personal faith. If so, it is not obvious, and those who declare that it is must create a picture that explains how people who did not even know Jesus personally could have a deeper faith than those like you, who have the Spirit resident within. They must place blame on the flesh-created faith of those who do not experience healing and give credit to the what they have designated self-generated faith of the Bible examples. We have demonstrated that, biblically, there is only one true faith. Only God's gift of faith results in the works of God, as it aligns our prayers with His will.

There are two realistic possibilities regarding how these two biblical individuals, and others in similar examples, received healing as Jesus honored their faith. First, Jesus may have honored fleshly faith for His own purposes of blessing them, bringing glory to God, and teaching all His followers across time that all things are possible. This does not fit the Bible's presentation of faith. Second, it is most probable that the Holy Spirit provided them with His gift of faith that Jesus not only could but would heal, and Jesus responded to that gift. The Spirit could have easily done this and conformed to His biblical definition of faith. Whatever motivated Jesus, scripture teaches that the individuals did not "earn" healing through flesh-faith. Jesus honored the gift of faith. Believers are to have faith *in God through His gift of faith*. We are not to have faith in our faith.

True Christian Faith Is the Gift of God

> There is a significant difference between God's gift of faith as it applies to every word and promise in the Bible and as it applies to situations that are not specifically covered. However, presumptive "human faith" that asks God to support our flesh's initiatives is not biblical faith. Permit the Spirit to lead you in understanding and living in His gift of faith.

Summary: Elements of God's Gift of Faith

God's gift of faith to believers is firmly planted in understanding and embracing the following:

- Biblical faith is the gift of God that is transmitted from His Spirit to your spirit. It cannot be found within the efforts of an individual's flesh (mind, will, or emotions). Trying to create God's faith through your flesh is following a major deception of the enemy. It results in futility and robs your life of God's purpose and power.

- Everything that God reveals in the Bible is true, and we are to stand unwaveringly on His truths and promises.

- God can do anything, with the exceptions that He will not lie or change. (Num 23:19; 1 Sam 15:29; Psalms 89:35; Mal 6:18; Heb 6:18)

- We are fully able to trust in the biblically revealed character of God and, therefore, are exhibiting mature faith when we surrender our desires to His loving and sovereign will.

+ God will keep all His promises. How and when He does this is always for our best. His eternal perspective is to be trusted, even when it hurts incredibly from our limited earthly view.

+ God desires that we always share our hearts, our hopes, our needs, our heartbreaks, and our frustrations (even anger), as we seek His will. He loves forthright interactions, emanating from pure hearts that long to be fully His.

+ Godly prayer and faith result in aligning our desires with His will and not insisting on our own.

+ God's gift of faith results in actions that the Bible and His Spirit direct.

Application: Faith through the Holy Spirit

+ From this chapter, what are you embracing, and what are you uncomfortable with?

+ What is the Spirit asking you to rethink?

+ What are you not willing to accept? What is He revealing to you concerning your beliefs about faith that are different from the scripture conclusions above? How do you validate the differences within the context of the entire Bible, instead of isolating on one or a few verses? Which carries the greater weight of God's truths, the context of the entire Bible and the character of God or the isolated statements of a limited number of verses?

+ Will you embrace God's teachings about His gift of faith and live in His power? Begin now, and you will live every aspect of His masterpiece life for you!

+ What are the next steps that you and the Spirit will take?

CHAPTER 8

Prayer: Intimacy and Kingdom Impact

Matt 14:23

He went up by Himself on the mountain to pray.
Now when evening came, He was there alone.

Luke 11:9-10, 13

So I say to you, ask, and it shall be given to you; seek, and
you shall find; knock, and it will be opened to you.

For everyone who asks receives, and he who seeks
finds, and to him who knocks it will be opened.

James 5:16b

The effective fervent prayer of a righteous man avails much.

Biblical Prayer

For Jesus, prayer was intimate relationship with His Father and the very foundation of His life. It is to be the same for us. God has designed His kingdom work to be greatly affected by the prayers of His people.

What does it really mean to pray as Jesus prayed, and how might our lives in Christ be different? Prayer will become ever-present in our lives. Our relationships with Him will grow in intimacy, trust, and love. We will ask God to align our desires and prayers with His will. Accordingly, we will experience the incredible faith and power of His Spirit flowing in and through us. Peace and purpose will fill us even in the most difficult situations. We will learn that just as His Church is His hands and feet on Earth, He has made the mature prayers of His people, our prayers, *essential for releasing His power and accomplishing His will in both the spiritual and earthly realms.*

In other words, the Spirit transforms us to embrace the irreplaceable position that prayer held in Christ's life. We learn to walk in faith regarding James 5:16: "The effective and fervent prayer of a righteous man avails much."

Achieving your unique purpose in Christ and experiencing His abundant life is possible only through a lifestyle built on Spirit-led prayers of faith and loving fellowship with God. As you read further, sincerely request, and expect the revelation of the Spirit regarding the truth of scripture and His plan for developing the role of prayer in your life.

Prayer Is God's Incredible Dynamic for Life

The great preacher Charles Spurgeon said, "Prayer has become as essential to me as the heaving of my lungs and the beating of my pulse." Clearly, he knew that he could not truly live without connecting personally and continuously with God through prayer. May it be the same for us!

> *Prayer is our Father's gift for receiving and giving love and life between Himself and His children. It is communication of His Spirit with our spirits! It is about being wonderfully freed to abide in life with the Father, the life we were born to live. The more we know our Heavenly Father, the more we thirst for and develop our prayer relationship with Him.*

Prayer: Personal Relationship with God

MATT 6:6

But you, when you pray, go into your room and when you have shut the door, pray to your Father who is in the secret place;

Prayer is relationship, communion, and intimacy with God. It is not limited to knees bowed, eyes closed, and hands folded. It is a two-way intimacy that is to happen every conscious moment, even as we interact with others. Prayer includes respectfully coming to God with questions, a broken heart, and even healthy anger and confusion. *God loves you and wants you to approach Him openly and honestly about everything.* He knows what you are feeling better than you do. Worshipful prayer/relationship is His fountain of life. It draws you to Him and solidifies the inconceivably intimate relationship that He desires. You join with Him in all seasons of life, including celebration and grief, and become more closely united than you are in any other relationship.

Some of us have trouble with relationships. We may have parents who wouldn't tolerate challenging their decisions or beliefs, even if we did so respectfully. As a result, it may be hard to trust God and approach Him with love and freedom. Others had an easier start because our parents instilled relationship confidence. They encouraged us to engage in every type of issue, contentious or not. Relationships are easier for us. Either way, we have much to learn about living in the trusting and fully accepting relationship of His unconditional love. Growth through Spirit-led prayer and faith is essential.

God is not looking for religious words, phrases, or canned prayers. Effective prayer is meaningful, mature conversation. We are speaking with God and are not to pray to please those around us. Prayer includes talking, listening, and understanding, as well as crying, challenging, laughing, requesting, trusting, and praising. Above all, it involves being fully present.

We are to be as forthright and comfortable as we would be with our most trusted friend—actually *more* so. Do we listen as much as we talk? We are blessed to interact with the righteous God of all creation, our loving Father. Nothing is more incredible. Intimacy in prayer is based on committing time together where nothing is hidden or held back. God is all about truth, grace, love, and growth. He has given His all and is "all in." Are you?

God-Honoring Prayer Aligns Us with God's Will

1 JOHN 5:14-15

Now this is the confidence that we have in Him, that if we ask anything according to His will, He hears us and

> *if we know He hears us, whatever we ask, we know that*
> *we have the petitions that we have asked of Him.*

JOHN 15:16B
> *... I chose you and appointed you that you should go and*
> *bear fruit, and that your fruit should remain, that whatever*
> *you ask the Father in My name He may give you.*

LUKE 22:40-42
> *He (Jesus) knelt down and prayed, saying,*
>
> *"Father, if it is Your will, take this cup away from Me,*
> *nevertheless not My will, but Yours be done."*

It is normal for believers to view prayer as their way of asking God for what they need or want. There is nothing wrong with this, but we are to grow so our prayers include much more. In Luke 22:42, Jesus is asking for His desires. However, *the central purpose of His prayer is to align Himself with the will of His Father*, as He says, "Nevertheless, not my will but Yours be done." In 1 John 5, the Spirit instructs that we are to "ask anything according to His will," and we will have our petitions. Through John 15:16, Jesus instructs us to ask "in My name" which conveys asking for what is in the will of Jesus (also the will of the Father). Our prayers are to be seeking and praying for Jesus'/God's will, not our own. Like Jesus, we share our desires, *but we end by praying solely for His will.*

Many have been taught that ending prayers with "In Jesus' name" is like a magic phrase that commits God to do whatever they have wrapped in that phrase. They mistakenly believe they have met Jesus' statement in John 15, "whatever you ask in My name." They have been misled. Asking in His name is *praying for His will, specifically or generally, and yes, doing so in the power of His name.* As Jesus did, we are to express our desires, but we truthfully seek and trustingly surrender to His will. Jesus' name is holy, and we are to use it with the utmost respect, always believing that we are asking for His will and not our own.

As we learn to trust our Father, we become comfortable with the position that it is His will that we truly desire, even if it conflicts with our heart's desires. Thus, prayer extends beyond building a wonderful relationship *to aligning our entire being with Him and His will.* We may begin with what is on our hearts. As we interact with Him and surrender, we enjoy how He draws us to His loving will, even as it sometimes hurts incredibly. We always have the choice of embracing or rejecting His will. God-Honoring prayer brings us into *alignment with what He is doing instead of insisting He bless our desires. When we embrace and pray for His will, we receive His gift of faith.*

Our loving Father wants us to engage with Him about all things during each moment of life. By doing so, we learn that He is always there for us. He hears our every word and respects our every need and desire. He loves walking hand in hand with us. *If we permit Him, He will align the desires of our hearts with His.*

God's Power Results from Praying His Prayers

JOHN 15:13 (JESUS IS SPEAKING)
However, when the Spirit of truth has come, He will guide you into all truth; for He will not speak on His own authority, but whatever He hears He will speak; and He will tell you of things to come.

Ultimately, we are to pray God's prayers by asking Him to reveal them. This is a natural and powerful progression that results from always seeking His will. We then pray His prayers/His will with the incredible faith He pours into us. His Spirit's power is present. When His prayer is for immediate resolution or healing, we speak it with absolute faith and great joy. It is just as incredible when He reveals His prayer is for something else, such as end of life. We then join in His prayer, which brings His blessings and grace into all who are present. *His Spirit-led prayers are just what is needed to bring His blessings in every circumstance. Our self-guided prayers are often off-target and often run counter to His will,* even though they sound appropriate or are warmly received.

If I am in a group that is praying, and I do not hear Him, I do not pray. When I am asked to pray in public, He has always provided His words.

Desires of the Heart: Are These Always Met?

PSALMS 37:3-7

Trust in the Lord and do good. Dwell in the
land, and feed on His faithfulness.

Delight yourself also in the Lord, And He shall
give you the desires of your heart.

Commit your way to the Lord, Trust also in
Him, And He shall bring it to pass.

He shall bring forth your righteousness as the
light, And your justice as the noonday.

Rest in the Lord and wait patiently for Him:

Most of us have taken truths and promises of the Lord out of context and then wondered why "the Lord isn't keeping His word." A prevalent example is the misuse of the verses above, which in part state, "He shall give you the desires of your heart."

Many approach God with the desires of their hearts and claim this verse. If their prayers are not granted, they cry out, "He promised to give me the desires of my heart. I am praying and praying, and He is doing nothing. He has not kept His word, and it feels like He does not love me. I know better, but that's how it feels." This is a difficult and hurtful position, and most of us have been there. Is the Lord breaking a promise? Never! We are claiming His promise out of context. The entire passage conveys the following:

- Trust in Him and do good.
- Dwell in the land (where He has placed you.)
- Feed on His faithfulness.
- Delight yourself in the Lord.
- And He shall give you the desires of your heart.
- Commit your way to the Lord.
- Trust also in Him and He shall bring it to pass.
- He shall bring forth your righteousness as the light.
- Justice as the noonday.
- Rest in the Lord.
- Wait patiently for Him.

God promises that He will bring the desires of our hearts to pass *as we seek His will and walk with Him according to scripture.* He never promises to do anything, regardless of how good it may sound to us, that will injure us or others in His eternal wisdom and plan.

We all have heart desires that are not "wrong" in any way but are not part of His plan for our eternal good. Surrendering these and trusting Him involves great pain and sacrifice. It also *results in great spiritual growth.* Note that we are to surrender these, not give up, as we approach God as Jesus did.

If we ignore God's loving plan and insist on pressuring Him for our desires and our timing, there is a good chance that our hearts will harden as we interpret His "No" as rejection. Resentment, rebellion, even bitterness may follow. We, like Abraham, may take matters into our own hands and make big mistakes that carry significant consequences. God wishes to spare us. Ultimately, if we do not surrender our desires to Him, He may permit us to receive them and the accompanying brokenness. He will do this in love, desiring that we learn and are drawn back into close relationship. Israel's biblical history demonstrates this reality.

Maturing into vibrant Christians results from God's Spirit transforming us from the inside. This always includes transforming the "desires of our hearts." The difficulties associated with unfulfilled desires of the heart are replaced with faith and trust. As we *abide in Him, we find our true desires being met as we permit God to lovingly mold and align them with His.*

Prayer: Living in the Flow of Christ's Power

Have you tried to swim against or across a strong current or tide? It is exhausting. It is so much easier to swim with the current.

When our prayers and our obedient walk align with God's will, timing, and methods, we thrive in the flow of His plan and power, not in the futility of our own efforts. Even so, life will not be easy. He states we will face trials and tribulations.

When we bullheadedly pray for and insist on our own desires, we are probably swimming against His plan. Life feels broken and devoid of His wonder and fruit. The masterpiece life in Christ is founded on His Spirit connecting with our spirit. Those who attempt to live it through their flesh (mind, will, and emotion) will miss much of His blessing.

Living in the flow of God's will and power requires ever-maturing surrender to the authority of God's Spirit. Compare this victorious life in Christ to riding through fast-flowing and often turbulent whitewater rapids. Sometimes the stream is smooth, and the rest of the time the turbulence ranges from Class I to Class VI. You may think that you can navigate the smooth water and the lower-class rapids on your own, but the full journey requires a trained guide to handle all that is upcoming. In the less turbulent waters, you learn to trust your guide and work under their development, both as individuals and as teams. When the rough water comes, you are then able to succeed together and experience exhilaration, often in the midst of fear. When you fall in, your guide has taught not only how to survive but to be victorious. Even in the smoother, fast-flowing water, the dangers are there, hidden but capable of trapping and drowning you. Your guide has prepared you for life and victory instead of injury or death. The victorious and abundant Christian life is similar. *It depends on God transforming you from insisting on being in control to living under the authority and counsel of the Holy Spirit. Maturing prayer is essential.*

Answers to Prayer Are Uniquely Designed
James and Peter

In Acts 12, we are told of two different outcomes for similar situations. First, Herod has killed James by the sword (verse 2.) He saw that it pleased the Jews, so he proceeded to seize Peter. Peter is in prison, under close guard and chains, and Herod plans to put him to death. Verse 5 points out that "constant prayer was offered to God for (Peter) by the church." As a result, an angel appears in the prison and miraculously frees him.

We wonder why Peter was spared, and James executed. Both were apostles with important roles in the Church. Was the Church praying differently, or were they praying the same for each apostle? Was God teaching them about praying His will instead of their own? We have no insight into their prayers for James. God may have guided them to pray for different victorious outcomes and witness through both the freedom of Peter and the death of James. At the least, He had them surrender to His will. Hopefully, the Church was asking God to reveal His prayers and joining Him there.

Examples: Seeking God's Prayers

Many of us instinctively pray that individuals will find relief from trials and blessings. *When we do this, we may indeed be praying against God's plan and design.*

An individual approaches you and asks for prayer. They seek God's relief from great personal stress. Believing, innocently, that God wants to free all from unhealthy circumstances, you pray accordingly with great boldness. Be careful! This individual may have been ignoring the Lord and His will. It may have taken

God years to patiently move them into this position where they are desperate and ready to turn to Him. Praying against the immediate situation may easily be praying against God. *Learn to ask God for His prayers.*

Many Christians believe that peace and healing are defined in human terms. They ignore God's wisdom that defines these from His perspective, where His peace is founded in Christ, not in circumstances. We are to pray according to His revelation, not human desires.

> *Do not find yourself unintentionally praying against God's will. Instead, always ask Him what His prayer is, and pray in His faith, power, and love.*

We Are Not to Pray What Others Want to Hear

Some Christians learn to pray to please those around them, instead of talking to God. They pray what they think the individual(s) wants or needs to hear. *Our prayers are to be conversations with God, not speeches to impress or please those around us.*

Do Our Prayers Change the Mind of God?

The biblical answer to this question is, "No, they do not."

Parables and examples of interactions with God have been mistakenly used to present the position that our prayers can change His mind. Interpreting these within the context of the entire Bible results in a different answer.

God is all-knowing and unchanging.

> *For I am the Alpha and the Omega, the Beginning and the End, the First and the Last (Rev 22:13)*
>
> *For I am the Lord, I do not change; (Mal 3:6)*
>
> *God is not man that He should lie, or a son of man that He should change His mind (Num 23:10 ESV, 1 Sam 15:29.)*

God Does Not Change His Mind

"God is not a son of man that He should change His mind." He is all-knowing, all-powerful, ever-present, and does not make mistakes. He knows the beginning from the end. It is not possible for Him to improve His plans. In order for God to change His mind, He would have to learn something new, improve who He is, or gain insight into the way He "previously" viewed and understood situations. He would in essence have "made a mistake." His plans are perfect, and He does not change His mind. He knows what others will do and what He will do before situations unfold, before we have even thought to pray, and before time began. However our prayers are instrumental in His kingdom plans.

Why do examples and parables teach us to keep inquiring of Him? *His heart's desire is for us to draw closely to Him and communicate in all things.* Therefore, He has provided us with real-life Bible interactions and parables that tell us to do just that! These interactions draw us into deep and trusting relationships with Him. *He teaches that we are not only welcomed, but encouraged, to discuss all things with Him at all times.* We are to interact like Abraham did for Sodom and Gomorrah, as *He is bringing us into deep personal fellowship and aligning our will and understanding with His.*

When God Relents, He Is Not Changing His Mind

God's desire is always for mankind to repent so that He may withhold destruction. Throughout scripture, God shows us that He will prophesy and deliver destruction for His righteousness' sake, but He takes no pleasure in the death of the wicked. His desire is always for mankind to turn and be saved (Ezekiel 32:10-16.) In verse 11, He says, "Turn, turn from your wicked ways. For why should you die, O house of Israel." In Jer 26, God tells Jeremiah to speak His words to all of Israel so that "Perhaps everyone will listen and turn from his evil way, *that I may relent* concerning the calamity which I purpose to bring on them because of the evil of their doings." He knew that they would not, but He gave (and still gives) everyone many opportunities to repent and escape His wrath. When His people did (and do) repent, He did not change His mind about punishment. He got what He desired and knew would occur.

What is God teaching through parables/examples where it seems like prayer or persistent prayer causes God to change his mind? *He is drawing us into close and trusting relationship.* He is teaching us to bravely approach Him in every situation. *He then aligns our desires and understanding of His character with His truths. He reinforces the reality that righteous prayers, in the end, always lead us to praying the will of God with the gift of God's faith.*

Examples

First: In Exodus 32:7-14, Moses is on the mountain with God. God reveals that the people have sinned greatly and instructs Moses to leave Him alone so that His wrath may consume them. Moses pleads with God to spare them for His own reputation and the sake of His promises. God "relented." Did Moses change God's mind? God long ago knew what Moses would say and what He would do. He was teaching Moses (and through him each of us) to engage with Him and trust Him. He was also developing Moses as His leader, molding Him into a powerful instrument in His plans.

Second: Some parables of Jesus teach this same relational truth. They do not indicate our persistent prayers can do the impossible—change His mind. God is not "a son of man that He should change His mind." Persistence is encouraged to draw us to Him and His will. *These teachings assure us that we are invited to continuously engage with Him about our every desire and question, as we learn to trust Him. He always loves, hears, and honors us.*

In Gen 22, God taught Abraham that He could be trusted, even if it meant slaying Isaac. In Gen 18:23-32, the Lord was about to destroy Sodom and Gomorrah, and taught Abraham to approach Him in all things. Abraham persistently asked God if He would spare them if He found righteous people. Abraham began by asking if there were 100 righteous, would God spare them and worked his way from 100 to 50 to 45 to 30 to 20 to 10. At each level, God patiently said that He would. Through Abraham, God was/is teaching all to come to Him. He listens to our every plea. Abraham must have found it incredible to face the God of creation and survive as He asked Him six times to consider sparing the righteous. *It is equally incredible that we are to engage Him with such trust.* Did the Lord God break His scriptural truths and change His mind in these cases, or did He know how these interactions would proceed and utilize the situation to build fellowship and trust with Abraham and through him, with us? *God always knows what will transpire. We are being taught to interact and walk victoriously with Him.*

Third: These types of interactions, including Christ's parables about the friend and the bread, and the judge and the administration of justice, are about building our relationship and trust. They are about His righteous and loving nature, not about changing God's mind.

Our Prayers Do Change Things!

JAMES 5:16B
The effective, fervent prayer of a righteous man avails much.

DANIEL 10:12-13
Then he (the angel) said to me, "Do not fear, Daniel, for from the first day that you set your heart to understand, and to humble yourself before your God, your words were heard; and I have come because of your words.

But the prince of the kingdom of Persia withstood me twenty-one days; and behold, Michael, one of the chief princes, came to help me, for I had been left alone with the kings of Persia."

EPH 6:11-13, 18A
Put on the whole armor of God, that you may be able to stand against the wiles of the devil.

> *For we do not wrestle against flesh and blood, but against principalities, against powers, against rulers of the darkness of this age, against spiritual forces of wickedness in heavenly places.*
>
> *Therefore, take up the whole armor of God, that you may be able to withstand in the evil day and having done all, to stand.*
>
> *Praying always with all prayer and supplication in the Spirit, being watchful to this end with all perseverance and supplication for all the saints*

Although our prayers do not change the mind of God, *they do change things*. The prayers of a righteous man avail much. *Clearly, they carry the power of God*, but why and how?

Just as God chose to use saved individuals as His voice, hands, and feet for impacting this world, He has chosen to make the prayers of His saints crucial for the release of His power and the accomplishment of His will. Because He has designed life this way, our obedient, Spirit-led prayers are instrumental elements in God's plan for bringing His will into being and for releasing His power. Righteous prayers absolutely change things. God utilizes them to impact both the spirit and the natural realms. He instructs us to "pray always" because our prayers are instrumental in His plans for bringing about His will. Prayer that is guided by the Spirit avails much.

His power resides in the prayers of His people. They are part of His conditions for impacting the spiritual and natural kingdoms. If we refuse His prayer opportunity, He will offer it to others until His people obey. His Church is one of His instruments for activating His will. We have meaningful roles in His plans, and these include prayer. *If He chose to always provide miracles without the fervent prayers and faith of His Church, we would be like immature children who were handed everything. He develops spiritual warriors with specific kingdom missions.*

We Have Choices

We do have choices. We can choose to pray for our will, instead of seeking God's. We can refuse to pray. If our prayers are for us, we can choose to ignore God's guidance and seek a fate that is not His preferred will. The Book of Jonah provides practical examples. God directed Jonah to go to Nineveh to cry out against their wickedness. Jonah refused and fled. He was swallowed by a great fish. When He returned to the Lord, he was spewed out onto dry land. The Lord again commanded Jonah to preach a message of repentance. He did. The people repented, and God "relented." This was His desire from the beginning, and Jonah suspected what would transpire. Jonah became depressed. His pride was hurt as He felt foolish when his prophecy of destruction did not take place. Twice, he asked God to take his life. Our Father asked Jonah if it is right for Him to be angry. He restores Jonah's relationship with Him. Jonah had choices, and the people

Our obedient, Spirit-led prayers are instrumental elements in God's plan for bringing His will into being. He blesses us by giving us active roles in His kingdom. Spirit-led prayers carry His power; selfish prayers of our flesh do not.

of Nineveh had choices. God knew what choices each would make. However, He did not dictate their actions and choices. *He does not manipulate us. They had free will, just as you do.*

Two Elements of Every God-Honoring Prayer

Matt 8:2-3 and Mark 9:21-24 teach us to honor both Jesus' *ability* and His *willingness/sovereignty* in every prayer of faith. He is able in all things. His sovereign will is not to be taken for granted, especially as it determines "how" and "when" prayers are answered.

In Matthew, a leper worships Jesus, saying, "Lord, if You are *willing*, You *can* make me clean." Jesus put out His hand and touched him, saying, "*I am willing*; be cleansed." Immediately his leprosy was healed. This leper knew Jesus could heal him, but he also knew Jesus had the choice to heal or not. He honored Jesus' sovereignty by surrendering his request to the will of Jesus.

In Mark, a father asked for removal of a mute spirit from his son. He says, "But *if You can* do anything, have compassion on us and *help us*." Jesus said to him, "If you can believe, all things are possible to him who believes." Immediately the father cried out, "Lord, I believe. Help my unbelief!" Jesus cast out the demon. The father began by not having faith that Jesus either could or would heal his son but asked anyway. When he heard about faith and knew that his was weak, he asked Jesus to provide his faith.

The Bible's teaching through these examples takes us to a higher level of living in God's faith and prayer. *Jesus teaches there are two components to faith and prayers of faith. These are faith in God's ability, and surrender to God's willingness/sovereignty, including His decisions regarding how and when He answers. It takes true faith to focus our prayers on His will instead of our own.* This is the "if you will" portion of mature prayer. It takes the focus off God's ability (we know He can) and puts it on His sovereignty. Godly faith leaves the results and timing to the Lord, even though we share our desires. It takes no true faith to ask the Lord to do what we *know* He can do, *without being willing to surrender to His will.* Jesus is our example, as in the garden He prayed, "Father, if it is your will, take this cup from Me; nevertheless, not my will, but Yours, be done (Luke 22:42)." Our lives become incredibly richer as we learn to do the same.

God Fulfills His Promises According to His Sovereignty, Not Man's Interpretation

Many brothers and sisters in Christ live under the belief that God will fulfill His promises, in the way that humans interpret them and want them to mean. They may not say that, but their negative reactions to God when His answers do not conform to their desires clearly indicate their attitudes and expectations.

Some "faith" churches apply this concept to healing, as they interpret Is 53:5 and 1 Peter 2:24. They take the truths that "by His stripes we are healed" and "He bore our sicknesses and diseases" and combine them with James 5:14-15, "Is anyone among you sick? Let him call for the elders of the church, and let them pray over him, anointing him with oil in the name of the Lord. And the prayer of faith will save the sick, and the Lord will raise him up." From these truths, some create a "doctrine" that physical healing on Earth is the will of God for every person in the present. We discussed this in Chapter 7. The burden of healing and the resultant guilt if healing doesn't occur is placed on the "faith" of those praying or on the "faith" of the suffering individual. *This "credit or guilt" view of "self-generated faith" conflicts with the biblical truth that faith is the gift of God.* These churches constantly face the question of, "What was wrong? We believed with all our might." Their answer is, "We don't understand God's ways, but we will continue to stand in our belief that healing is for all, at all times!"

We agree—we do not understand God's ways. However, we interpret His ways under God's sovereignty. *He is sovereign, and He keeps every promise in His word. He does so in the integrity of His eternal perspective, not mankind's restricted view. It is mankind's interpretation that requires adjustment when they do not believe that God's promises were fulfilled. Healthy questions draw us to reconnect with Him.*

No individual or collective work of the human mind has the ability to grasp the eternal meaning of God's word to the point they can insist their understanding encompasses the entire perspective and will of God!

Prayer: We Do Not Wrestle Against Flesh and Blood
"Stand against the wiles of the devil."

This empowering instruction of God is often unknown or ignored by many believers. Instead of following His word, they wrestle against the people and situations that can be seen. This is not where the real battle is engaged. It is in the spirit realm. Our prayers are to be directed there, under the guidance of God's Spirit. As we stand in the armor of God, our prayers are vital to releasing His actions in that realm. Read Daniel 10:12-13 again, and grasp the insight these verses provide regarding the spirit realm and our prayers.

We are to stand against the wiles of the devil and pray. As we open our lives to God's Spirit, He leads us to ask for His discernment regarding what He is doing in the spirit realm and to guide us to pray from this perspective. This is quite a learning journey. Yes, we are to pray for people and situations in the natural realm, but we have better insight and effect after seeking God's prayers first for the spirit realm.

Read and meditate on Eph 6:11-18. How is the Spirit guiding you to embrace and incorporate these scriptures in your life and prayers?

Power in the Lives and Prayers of Believers

Consider Bible truths about the power that resides in those who live kingdom lives by walking in the Spirit. Christ's power resides in the prayers and actions of those who permit His Spirit to live both in and through them.

The Kingdom of God Is Not in Word but in Power

1 COR 4:20
For the kingdom of God is not in word but in power.

2 TIM 3:2-5
For men will be lovers of themselves ... despisers of good ... lovers of pleasure rather than lovers of God, having a form of godliness but denying its power.

(God's power resides in those who walk obediently in His Spirit.)

Mustard Seed

MATT 17:20

... for assuredly, I say to you, if you have faith as a mustard seed, you will say to this mountain, move from here to there, and it will move; and nothing will be impossible for you.

(When we pray for His will, with His faith, all things are possible.)

Prayer and Fasting

MATT 17:21

However, this kind (of demon) does not go out except by prayer and fasting.

(Truly effective Christian prayer warriors are building their lives in Christ. They know Him. They know His voice, and they walk in obedience to His Spirit.)

Greater Works Than These

JOHN 14:12-13

Most assuredly, I say to you, he who believes in Me, the works that I do he will do also; and greater works than these he will do, because I go to the Father.

And whatever you ask in My name, that I will do, that the Father may be glorified in the Son.

(This promise is beyond the comprehension of most of us. Yet it is Christ's promise, and it is there for all Christians who will but surrender their wills and live His life, by walking in His Spirit. We believe it applies to each Christian.)

God's Power: His Gift of Faith—Evidence of Things Unseen

HEB 11:1
Now faith is the substance of things hoped
for, the evidence of things not seen.

HEB 11:13
These all died in faith, not having received the promises,
but having seen them afar off were assured of them, embraced
them, and confessed that they were strangers in a strange land

(The how and when God chooses to provide His answers and power lie in His hands. Maturing Christians rejoice in and walk in this truth.)

Pray as He Taught You

Recently, God has desired to bring greater maturity to my prayer life. I did not fully understand what He meant and continued to ask Him to teach me. Not much growth was occurring.

Patiently, He revealed that I have been waiting for Him to bring some "magic revelation." Then He kindly said, "I want you to pray as I have taught you!" His point is that I (we) am responsible for diligently walking in all that He has taught me, including prayer. I had been avoiding maturity by asking, "Teach me how to do this, Daddy," when He has taught all I need to know for this stage of life. True learning takes place through walking out what we know, in the power of His Spirit.

The Spirit was not impatient or critical. He was speaking as Christ did to His disciples when they did not live out what they knew. He was firm and lovingly direct.

Do You Ask for What God Has Already Promised?

The Bible contains many wonderful promises of God. He is faithful and righteous, and His promises are to be embraced by faith. Many Christians spend lots of time and energy, pleading with their Father to provide what He has promised and already given. Their focus is on the wrong place. We are to know God's promises and approach Him to help us embrace and appropriate them instead of asking for what is ours already. Consider two different prayers for peace.

JOHN 14:27

*Peace I leave with you. My peace I give to you;
not as the world gives do I give to you. Let not your
heart be troubled, neither let it be afraid.*

PHIL 4:6, 7

*Be anxious for nothing, but in everything by
prayer and supplication with thanksgiving,
let your requests be made unto God:*

*And the peace of God, which surpasses all understanding,
will guard your hearts and minds through Christ Jesus.*

We all experience times when peace evades us, and grief or despair descends. In 1 Cor 1:8b, Paul shares, "we were burdened beyond measure, above strength, so that we despaired even of life." This is not a lack of faith but learning to trust in God instead of ourselves.

One approach to prayer for peace is, "Father, please give me your peace." A second is, "Father, I bring these promises for peace from John and Philippians to You. You have given peace. I trust in Your word, and I ask you to help me receive Your peace as I stand on these scriptures."

Neither prayer is wrong. One embraces God and His promises through appropriation. The other asks for what is already theirs. Our Father God is constantly encouraging us to live in His promises instead of begging for what He has already provided.

> *Prayer is to be an incredibly personal communication and relationship-builder between God and you. He draws us into deepening love and understanding of His will and our roles in it. Relax, enjoy, and learn to listen to His Spirit at all times. Pray His prayers with the faith that is His gift to you.*

Application

Consider the following as you think about this chapter.

- What has prayer meant to you, and what do you agree with or disagree with from this chapter? What scripture verses confirm your positions?

- Did you read this chapter under the leadership and revelation of the Spirit or under the constraints of your mind and emotions? Did you meditate on God's truths or rush through? What we receive from God's Spirit is in direct relationship to our willingness to surrender to His revelation and authority.

- What does the Spirit wish you to learn and apply regarding prayer?

- What are your next steps for growth in your prayer and faith relationship with your Father God?

- Consider getting a book on the promises of God and making His promises foundations of your life in Him.

CHAPTER 9

AN INITIAL LOOK AT HOW GOD WIRED YOU

PSALMS 139:14
I will praise You, for I am fearfully and wonderfully made,
Marvelous are Your works,
And that my soul knows very well.

God has wired you to be uniquely suited for your specific kingdom roles and missions. The more you understand and embrace your identity in Christ, the more effective you become. Have fun as we begin by looking at your *personality type*, your *life passions*, and your *Love Languages*. Whether this is new or a review, enjoy as you permit the Spirit to provide His revelations. Our scope does not include the detailed instruction appropriate for those who wish to engage focused resources on these topics.

Remember, we must walk in God's Spirit in order to operate where and how He wants us and not where we or others want us. Don't let anyone convince you that you "have to be" more like they are or want you to be. Learn from everyone and every situation, but stand in God's unique identity and purpose, confirmed by the Bible and His Spirit. He designed and loves your uniqueness.

Strengths and weaknesses are to be lived under the control of the Holy Spirit. When we utilize our strengths in our own power, our actions bring no glory to God.

Even when He is in charge, others, including your church, will often not understand or value who we are in Christ. As we walk in Christ, we are walking in His love.

Remember that no individual is self-sufficient. Those who think they are, are deceived and are going to achieve less than God's unified Body will achieve.

Your Personality Type

There are a number of personality assessments, and all have specific purposes. Myers & Briggs is comprehensive but complex. Two easier, yet effective ones, are the "Four Animal Type Personality Test," found on focusonthefamily.com and the "DISC Assessment" located on multiple websites. The OSPP Four Temperaments Scale is slightly less intuitive. Try all four if you enjoy exploring, but select one that you will use consistently. We discuss DISC below. These assessments help us better understand ourselves and others, so that we increase effectiveness. They are indicators. Each of us is a fluid and dynamic individual. We are being transformed by God's Spirit, and we are not to put ourselves or others into boxes.

DISC Personality Test

Please search the web for "DISC Personality Test." Review two or three free options; select the one that best fits your style. Take the assessment, and study this approach to understand DISC, your personality type, and the strengths and development areas of each personality type. Consider how to utilize this method most effectively so you become more effective individually and in strengthening your relationships with others.

The DISC Model focuses on the following four personality types:

Dominant/Driver:
Usually focus on results, problem-solving, and the bottom line

Influencing/Inspiring:
Usually focus on interacting with people, having fun, and/or creating excitement

Steady/Stable/Supportive:
Usually focus on preserving relationships and on creating or maintaining peace and harmony

Conscientious/Correct/Cautious:
Usually focus on facts, rules, and correctness

There Is No Best Profile

Each brings strengths and challenges. We need to be operating in unison for His will to be accomplished. He wired you with your personality type for optimum effectiveness in your kingdom purposes.

Working with Others

Most of us are more comfortable with certain personality types. Some seem to be polar opposites, and they tend to drive each other "up the wall." We may think, *Just get them into another group, and let us get this done.* This tension is not bad, if we learn to identify its source and choose to value the unique God-given skills of each person. Leaders need to ensure that individuals have responsibilities which align with God's wiring. Accepting a mismatch of individuals to responsibilities is not loving and godly; it is failure on the part of leaders and administrators.

Application

- Now that you have studied this one element of God's wiring, let Him guide you in its utilization.

- We are not only to gain personal freedom and effectiveness in Christ but also to extend these opportunities to others. What if we understood:
  - Our spouses better
  - Our children better
  - All those around us better?

- What if we helped them become all that Christ created them to be instead of trying to make them become what we'd like them to be?

Your Life's Passions

Your Heavenly Father created you with a love for doing certain things and being in certain situations. These areas of life reflect the "passions" God has built into you. Recognize these as another revelation of how God has wired you and where He may utilize you most effectively. Pursuing these passions will often help you in choosing to say "Yes" or "No" to opportunities in life. Work through the following exercises to help you identify your life's passions.

How Do You Want to Be Remembered?
Funeral and Epitaph Thoughts

Give the following your full energy. Close your eyes and place yourself in each situation. Document your answers to the questions. Brief statements are best, but they must express your heart.

1. Visualize yourself walking unseen among the individuals attending your funeral. What would you most like to hear them saying about you and your impact on their lives?

   [handwritten: She was kind, thoughtful & helped people find the Lord.]

2. Envision yourself standing at your gravesite. What brief epitaph would you most like to see inscribed there?

   [handwritten: Loved by all who knew her...]

3. Combine your thoughts into one sentence that really states your heart's desire. You will have it "right" when you experience yourself saying a resounding, "Yes" to the statement. Here is an example: "He saw who I really was and helped me become it."

WHAT ROLE AND AREAS OF AUTHORITY HAS GOD ASSIGNED?

JER 1:5

Before you were born I sanctified you;
I ordained you a prophet to the nations.

Ask the Spirit to guide you to fill in the last four words in this scripture with your God-decreed calling and areas of influence for your life. These grow with seasons and maturity. Often the calling stays similar as it matures and broadens, while the areas of influence expand.

Prayerfully fill in the following.

God ordained "you" a ". _healer_ . . . ." to the ". . . _suffering_ . ."

Where Do You Thrive?

Read the following with the Spirit. Utilize a table similar to the one below, and write down one answer for each row. It is to give you the most energy and passion.

1. Identify natural time frames in your life. These may be by age, school experiences, employment, or others.
2. For each time frame, ask for the Holy Spirit's revelation of your responses to the following question: "In what situations did I . . . ?"
   - Find that I become so deeply involved that I lose all track of time? I look up and am shocked to see that so much time has passed.
   - Experience great pleasure and energy whenever I do these types of things?
   - Have a natural skill that others are drawn to or respect?
   - Feel fulfilled?
   - Feel I am effective and really touch others?
   - Simply love doing these activities and/or being there?

An Initial Look at How God Wired You

Considering all situations and answers, ask yourself, "In what ways do my answers resemble each other?" Look for very clear and very subtle similarities that include: the type of activity, the settings, the needs of individuals involved, the type of results, and the specific energy and joy you experienced. Condense your answers into one concise statement.

Identifying Similarities in Fulfilling Situations

PERIOD	ACTIVITIES, EXPERIENCES WHERE YOU THRIVED	WHY THEY BROUGHT YOU LIFE AND FILLED YOU WITH PASSION
Before Jr. High		
Jr. High		
High School	Lessons; music	
Subsequent Education	Maths	
Ages twenty and older in ten-year increments	Nursing — hospital n homes	
The last five years	Church; Sunday School	
Employment or volunteer time frames	Bookclub	meeting people + helping the enjoy books

Validate and Finalize

Identify what God has taught you through these three exercises regarding your passions (the funeral exercises, God's assignments to you from Jeremiah 1:5, and situations where you thrive.)

Over the next few days, take time with the Spirit to process and validate your work. Have you received all that He has for you?

These passions are part of God's wiring, His gifts to you, and the purposes that He has for you. Stand with Him in this part of your identity, and He will continue to develop your understanding. Deny them, and you will probably not find fulfillment. You are identifying areas where you experience the great passion of Christ moving both in and through you, as His masterpiece tool.

Your Love Languages

Everyone is wired to give and receive love in ways that really work for them. Dr. Gary Chapman developed an effective tool for improving relationships and presented it in his book *The Five Love Languages*. It is not the purpose of this book to present his work. Therefore, we suggest that you purchase his book, take the test, and apply this tool in important relationships. The five love languages are:

- Quality Time
- Receiving Gifts
- Words of Affirmation
- Acts of Service
- Physical Touch

One website for Dr. Chapman's work is listed https://www.5lovelanguages.com/5-love-languages/. Be sure that the site you choose is free for at least taking the test and understanding the concepts. Have fun and enjoy experiencing improved relationships.

Application

Ask the Spirit to confirm these elements of your "wiring" and guide you in utilizing them for God's purposes in yourself and others.

Live with God's Spirit as your source, not your flesh.

PART FOUR

Mature in Christ and Experience the Life He Designed for You

CHAPTER 10

You Are God's Unique Masterpiece

Eph 2:10
For we are His workmanship (masterpiece), created in Christ Jesus for good works, which God prepared beforehand that we should walk in them.

Do you know what it means to live as God's unique masterpiece in this very moment? He sees you as His fully loved creation and delights in you just as you are, even as He develops you for future good works. He draws you into His masterpiece life with all the love that is in Him and will not easily surrender you to a lesser existence.

However, we must each choose to embrace or reject His life. He will not force us. It comes only to those who surrender their flesh's desired position on the "throne" of their life (seeking to control it) and permanently invite Christ's Spirit to occupy that position. All control is voluntarily and joyfully yielded to Him, as we submit to His sovereign authority. Our lives are then His to be lived according to His design. As knights of earthly kings served at the will of their sovereign, so we then serve Christ as He lives in and through us. Our natural man/flesh is continuously placed on the cross. We do not lose our identity. We embrace our true identity through our free will. This life does not come to nominal or carnal Christians, because they retain control of their lives and miss all or most of God's incredible design. They live in the shadows of His calling. What life are you going to live?

Masterpiece Life or Shadow of His Design?

Consider these additional scripture cornerstones of our identity in Christ:

PSALM 37:23-24

The steps of a good man are ordered by the Lord
And He delights in his way.
Though he fall, he shall not be utterly cast down;
For the Lord upholds him with His hand.

PSALM 139:14

I will praise You, for I am fearfully and wonderfully made.
Marvelous are your works.
And that my soul knows very well.

JER 1:5

Before I formed you in the womb, I knew you;
Before you were born, I sanctified you;
I ordained you a prophet to the nations.

JER 1:10

See, I have this day set you over the
nations and over the kingdoms.
To root out and to pull down,

You Are God's Unique Masterpiece

To destroy and to throw down,
To build and to plant

Do you view yourself and others as God's masterpiece? Has brokenness, false teaching, or even false humility caused you to deny this calling of God? Opposingly, have your earthly "successes" led you to walk in self-confidence and make little room for God's Spirit to control and direct your life? Many of the hardest Christians for God's Spirit to reach are those whom the church and the world embrace as successful.

God's masterpiece life is not about focusing on ourselves. It is about Christ and His life in us. It is not about what we do, but about who we are in Christ and what He does in and through us. It is about honoring others and supporting them in their walks in Christ. It is also about Christ's Church being His masterpiece full of *His love and power, unafraid to stand firmly for Him*. It is not quoting scripture, attempting to act like Christ, or being satisfied with salvation and living as safe, comfortable Christians. We are to live His unique masterpiece lives, radiating His love and power, regardless of circumstances. We are not to settle for less but to break loose and become all He created us to be, as we permit His Spirit to transform us as He lives in and through us.

His Masterpiece Identity

Are we willing to embrace God's scripture and view ourselves through His eyes, beginning with Eph 2:10? Will we seek and embrace the Spirit's revelations regarding the truths of these verses? We are children of the King, His masterpieces, unconditionally loved. He has given us unique kingdom roles and His authority to accomplish them through His Spirit. We cannot live for His glory when we deny His truths and act like impoverished victims. Neither will we be able to see, honor, and support others who are on their kingdom journeys with Him.

Ask His Spirit to reveal your identity as His masterpiece, and view God's relationship with you and His kingdom purposes from this perspective. Regardless of mistakes and brokenness, He is not going to walk away or reject you. He sees you as His finished product, through all stages of your journey together.

God Delights in You:

Consider Psalm 37:23-24. Do you understand that a "good man" is one whose heart is right with God and is righteous through Christ and Him only, not one who is good through their deeds? Is it clear that our Lord is always with His people, regardless of mistakes? He orders their steps and upholds them as they journey together through their masterpiece life. The God of all creation walks with you and "delights in your way." Will you permit His Spirit to implant this image into your very being? You are fearfully and wonderfully made (Psalms 139.)

God Created You with a Specific Kingdom Mission

Review Jeremiah 1:5 and 10 above. The Lord has "ordained"/commissioned Jeremiah in his position of *"prophet" over nations and kingdoms* (his areas of influence.) Jeremiah is to obey the Lord by fulfilling specific missions through the three steps of *spiritual warfare* that are set out in verse 10: "To root out and to pull down, To destroy and to throw down, To build and to plant."

As we discussed in Chapter 8, these verses apply to every Christian. God has "ordained you" in a calling and mission and has "set you over" areas of influence. His authority through you begins in the spirit realm and then extends into the natural. His spiritual authority and power for achieving His missions reside and operate in and through you. We are not to limit His authority to what feels safe and obvious, but permit Him to extend us. Living in His purpose and power is not a game. *You have a unique calling from God that is as important as Jeremiah's. Pray, listen, trust, wait, and act in His Spirit.* God's kingdom role for you exists every day of your life, and He is calling you forth to stand in your missions, as His power works in and through you.

Spiritual Warfare and Authority

As noted above, the last three lines of verse 10 are spoken not only to Jeremiah but also to each of us. These are about spiritual warfare, which is developed in Chapter 17. In our areas of influence and under the Spirit's direction, we are "to root out and pull down, destroy and throw down" all that is not of God. Then, "build and plant" all that is. Walking in Christ involves His application of scripture in His power. He exercises it both in and through us to impact both the spiritual and the natural realms for kingdom purposes.

> *Humbly grasp and embrace your commissioning by God, and your life will be revolutionized. Frequently review and embrace it with Him. Living as less is saying "No" to God and forfeiting much of the wonder and joy of living His masterpiece life. God directs and accomplishes His purposes through His Spirit operating in and through you. You are responsible for intentionally listening, hearing, and walking obediently in His Spirit.*

Called into His Light

1 Peter 2:9

But you are a chosen generation, a royal priesthood, a holy nation, His own special people, that you may proclaim the praises of Him who called you out of darkness into His marvelous light;

As His masterpiece, you are called out of the darkness and into His marvelous light. He is the light. Through His Spirit, His light shines in and through you as you permit Him to transform you. Before this, you lived in another kingdom and served another master. You are free to leave behind the old life and replace it with Christ's life, but you must choose. Many choose to hang onto old ways. That is not God's design, and it is a tragic waste. The real you is to walk in God's Spirit in the love, joy, authority, and victory of all scripture.

God's gift of "free will" embodies unconditional love. Every moment, we can choose Him and His ways or walk away into the shadows and darkness. Initially, we can refuse salvation. Once we've received Christ, we can refuse His sovereign authority, our identity, and His missions. He will not give up on us. However, when we refuse opportunities, He will offer them to others as His kingdom plans move forward. We will have lost some of the blessings He designed for us as His masterpieces.

Some Christians do not grasp the importance of placing laser focus on God's unique commission and missions for their lives. They are satisfied with an average Christian life that is blind to His unique purposes and is therefore lived without intentionality and His power. It is a tragic waste of all God placed within them. We are to be Holy Spirit and mission focused.

Three examples:

First: Doctor Martin Luther King was a pastor. He could have limited himself to that role and ignored God's call to bring his influence into the civil rights movement. Had he ignored God's commissioning and the influence that God exercised through him, Dr. King would have squandered part of God's kingdom purpose. He would have remained "safe and comfortable," but he would have forfeited much.

Second: Jesus could have ignored His mission and purpose and sacrificed all for temporary comfort and worldly gain. Satan would have won.

Third: A spiritually gifted woman serves in many areas of ministry. She is a clarion voice to the Church, regarding setting aside safe and comfortable cultures and replacing them with specific, Spirit-empowered lives. She has followed God into this life that swims against the current of American churches. She could choose a life of comfort.

Summary

God designed you to be focused on His unique missions. Living moment by moment, without aligning under God's Spirit and His missions results in a misspent life. Knowing the truths of God is to be followed by intentionally living them through the unique masterpiece lives God designed. This is truly living!

Just as Jeremiah, Ezekiel, John, David, Paul, and others were created and called for specific, unique, and Spirit-empowered purposes in Christ, *so are you*. Live God's life, not an alternate life in the shadows of God's call.

Masterpiece Life: An Incredible Journey with Your Loving Heavenly Father

Christ prepares us for our identity and purpose and accomplishes His missions through the unique circumstances that define our journeys with Him. The sooner we learn to walk with Him, instead of on our own, the sooner we discover and experience the true life of Christ flowing both in and through us.

A Transformation Testimony

For years, I could not understand and surrender to God's loving relationship. This was partially due to my distrust of human relationships. It was also due to my destructive belief that excellence and winning were to define my identity. I truly sought Him in everything and desired to live with Him leading every aspect of my life. I trusted Him, but a personal, loving, and joyous relationship wasn't there much of the time.

The Image and Transformation

The Spirit conveyed a stick-figure drawing (displayed early in this book) and the following concepts. The taller image represents the most incredible father imaginable, God. He is walking hand in hand through life with his child, me (or you.) Rays of light, representing God's light and life, surround them. The child lives in the wonder of exploring life with his father while living confidently in his total love. The father's love for his child is reflected and absorbed so it forms much of the child's identity. It includes:

1. Absolute, unconditional love. The father enjoys every step, every inquiry, and every detour of his child's explorations. Falls and bruises are a part of the child's learning.

2. Patience and understanding meet each of the child's needs and learning processes.

3. The father always sees who his child really is. He believes in and delights in him.

4. The child walks in absolute trust and confidence in his father's love and acceptance.

5. The child is not afraid to engage him about anything through questions and exploration.

6. He delights in the father's presence. Each step provides a new and marvelous revelation.

7. The child obeys even in fearful situations. He knows the thrill of truly "living" every minute.

8. The child grows through trips and falls; he is not defeated by them.

As they explore, the father introduces him to all His wonders. Everything is included, from soil to insects, animals, and the rain that feeds crystal streams. He shares them with such delight that the child catches his enthusiasm and grows more deeply in love with his father and his creation. They bond in an incredible relationship, and the son grows comfortably in his own identity. He embraces who he is instead of trying to be someone else.

Next, the Spirit stated, "This is who your Heavenly Father is. This is the relationship that He desires with you. He will pursue this through all of your life." I accepted this. I don't always remember to walk in it, but my Father always draws me back. His stick-figure picture conveys everything to me.

Do you have an image of your journey with your Heavenly Father? Is it an accurate image, or is it hurtful and distorted by life? Permit Him to provide you with His image of your daily walk. Use this one, if it works.

Learning to Walk in Christ

Learning to walk in our spiritual life often reflects the experiences of children learning to walk and run, and I believe God enjoys this as much as loving parents do. As we learn to walk in His Spirit, we make many mistakes and experience sins and failures. We trip and fall. Many of us who love God and desire to truly please Him deal with inappropriate distress over our failures. We find ourselves thinking, *Father, You taught me this ten years ago, and I am still messing up. What is wrong with me?* We may feel, *How can I approach Him again with the same sins and failures? I am ashamed, and He must be getting so impatient.* We may know what the scriptures say about His love and forgiveness, but our emotions and minds often shout that we may have driven Him away. These lies carry great power if we let them.

God views each step of our journey with a love that surpasses anything that we can comprehend. Our growth stages probably resemble infants as they learn to crawl, stand up, take the first step, walk, and run. Finally, they compete in their lives' races. At each stage, a healthy parent is loving, encouraging, supportive and full of joy. They also realize that each child progresses differently and in different time frames.

Envision how a healthy parent reacts when their child falls. The child lets go of support to take that first step. They take one and then tumble forward into the parent's loving arms. There is laughter, joy, and celebration. This process is repeated with each progression in the child's development. No healthy parent responds to falls or missteps with, "What is wrong with you? Why can't you get this? You are way behind others your age. I'm done working with you!" None.

Our Father God, the healthiest of all parents, embraces us at every step of our sincere journey of spiritual growth. When we fall and sin, He is there. He walks with us, knowing who we are and what we need. His patient and all-embracing love catches us when it's right and lets us tumble when we need to accept responsibility and gain confidence by learning through the fall. He is all about personal encounters and our journeys together as we *Be and Become* His masterpieces.

Application

Ask the Lord to show you how you view Him, yourself, and your walk with Him.

- Do you believe that you are His masterpiece?
- Do you believe that He has called you to walk through a unique and powerful life journey with Him? If not, why not? Do you want to accept this truth?
- What is your image of how He walks with you?
- What changes does He want to make in your image of who He is, who you are, and how He is ever-present with you?
- *Yes!* Are you willing to envision and experience the extraordinary relationship that He has for you, or are you going to be stuck with some lesser view?
- Do you understand that the Holy Spirit is to be your source of transformation? You cannot do it yourself.
- *Yes* Are you willing to place His Spirit on your life's throne and set laser focus on His life and missions?
- What are your next steps in your journey of "Being" the masterpiece He created?

CHAPTER 11

UNIQUE LIFE JOURNEYS SIGNIFICANTLY IMPACT KINGDOM MISSIONS

2 COR 1:5-6
For as the sufferings of Christ abound in us, so our consolation also abounds through Christ. Now if we are afflicted, it is for your consolation and salvation. . . . Or if we are comforted, it is for your consolation and salvation.

Through Our Individualized Life Journeys, God Hones Our Uniqueness, Missions, and Relationship with Him

How would our Christian lives be different if we embraced the truths of the above scripture and sentence? We would permit God to build on all that is part of our lives to refine us into His empowered masterpieces, instead of defining ourselves as either victims or self-defined victors based on destructive and positive events. Because God creates each of us with unique kingdom identities and missions, He also designs unique life journeys. They have incredible impact on the ways we interact with Him and engage in Christian life. *We are to recognize, value and embrace all He accomplishes through them.* We are not mistakes. (God did not cause our broken situations, and He is not responsible for our destructive decisions, but He does utilize them for good.)

The difficulty in this truth is that most of us, at least to some degree, think everything He has taught us should be known by others, the way we view life in Christ is the only correct way, and the way God accomplishes His missions in and through us is the singularly correct approach. Realistically, other than biblical truths, what God designed to help others may be of little help to you. What He designed to help you may be of limited value to them. Even when individuals have similar gifts, roles, and missions, their individualized journeys are designed to result in different approaches and forms of effectiveness. Unless God confirms it, we are not to let even respected and mature mentors attempt to reject our wiring and mold us into mirroring *their* God-wired characteristics and approaches.

This chapter helps us gain a keen awareness and respect for the journeys our lives have followed and to recognize how God is using them as one of the significant elements to empower us for kingdom impact. Learn to understand and honor others in the same way. If we ignore these truths and walk naively through our journeys, we will be distracted and taken down many unnecessary detours.

Analogy: Life Journeys Are Powerful Influencers

Compare the impact of your life's journey to alternative paths for approaching, observing, and describing a majestic oak. There are going to be innumerable accurate perceptions of both the tree and the journey.

Picture the ancient oak standing at the edge of an extended old-growth forest. On the northwest side is a thousand-foot precipice that descends into the sea. The southern side falls off gently into lush valleys, and the western cliff declines along this slope into distant sandy beaches. The north and northeast sides rise into a rugged mountain range, as the forest disappears into rocky pinnacles.

Individuals approach this tree from all directions and varying distances. One has been raised on the cliffs, where they engaged in steep and challenging climbs and descents as they approach the oak and serve by rescuing other climbers and helping them complete their ascent. Another tends flocks in the lush valleys and moves toward the oak along the gentle and embracing paths that intertwine through flowered fields. Others approach and serve from countless variations of geography and purpose, including some who continuously navigate the foreboding expanses of the mountain range.

Perceptions of the tree and the experiences that mold their skills and harden their muscles are different. Those approaching from the cliff gaze upon a tree with flat and stunted branches, resulting from constant wind and storms. Their muscles are hardened, and their character embraces danger as normal. Travelers approaching from the south view a tree whose branches extend uniformly and healthily into the welcoming sun-warmed spaces. They have different strengths, and they face different challenges. Every traveler's description of the tree is accurate but varies. Each also describes their journey accurately but in dramatically different ways. Some arrive scarred and breathless but invigorated, while others arrive at peace and rested.

Travelers who are not observant may never have seen the tree, just as some of us never actually meet God. Some travelers see the tree, are aware of its presence, but engage it only when they need its shelter. Both live stunted lives. Others have chosen to encounter this tree many times. As they go about their missions, they always stay in connection, often climbing ever higher to gain understanding of the tree and broadening perspectives of the world that surrounds them. These are called into broader journeys and approach the tree from many directions and in many seasons. If they are intentional, they gain an ever-deepening, personal understanding of both the tree and their broadening responsibilities. Even so, they will never have the one perfect knowledge and description of the tree and life.

Knowing God and Living His Masterpiece Life

There is one perfect description of God, His characteristics, and truths. Only God comprehends it. We gradually learn about Him and the Christian life through our intimate lifetime journeys with Him. Christians who visit Him infrequently will have little intimate knowledge and relationship. Those who visit, observe, and interact daily will grow continuously and intimately. Even frequent visitors know Him very differently because relationships are unique, though God remains unchanged. However, if anyone's "experience" of God and the Christian life differs from His biblical revelation, they have been deceived. Interpretation of His identity and character is never to conflict with the Bible's truth.

The analogy of God as a tree breaks down as God is ever present and is always interacting to draw us to Him. He is not waiting for us to approach Him. However, just as in our analogy of travelers above, we are responsible for choosing Him as the center of our lives and approaching and serving Him in ever-deepening personal relationships.

Your Journey Is a Gift

Each Christian's unique life journey with Christ is a gift. It influences how we know Him and how He utilizes us for His glory and His kingdom plans. We are to be His warriors in both the spiritual and natural realms. Some stand on dynamic battlefields. Some serve in the equivalent of logistics, training, medical support, and maintenance. All are equally important in God's eyes. Our unique journeys are to be embraced, as we revel in the intimate access and relationship God desires and pursues with us. Some of us choose this relationship, but many do not. Our kingdom effectiveness is proportionate to the intimacy of our walk with Him. Even so, some will know Him as a doctor, some as combat specialist, others as a master mechanic. We know and serve Him differently, but correctly if we are biblically focused and Spirit led.

Example

God taught me the above concepts through the following experience. I had been seeking mentoring from a gifted and mature Christian. Although I learned, I kept running into areas where his guidance did not align with what God was teaching me. Ultimately, God helped me see that this incredible man had consistently sought to draw me away from walking as God designed me, into walking as "he" did. He saw my walk as "defective" because, although God utilized us in similar situations, He worked through us in radically distinctive approaches. Neither was without error. He did not recognize this. (I have done the same to others.)

Different Journeys, Different Wiring: Different Godly Methods

God revealed how even individuals with similar gifts and missions are crafted to operate differently in His kingdom. Their journeys play significant roles in shaping them for His service.

My mentor was raised in a very conservative county in Pennsylvania. His family, his church, and his dominant culture valued obedience to religious rules, avoidance of conflict at all costs, and reconciliation even at the cost of resolving issues. God led him into a life where He learned to live and walk in the Spirit, and he grew rapidly and effectively. Conflict avoidance and reconciliation remained integral parts of his journey and God's purpose. Two of his major spiritual gifts are teaching and prophecy, although he has many. He is respected and serves God tremendously. The Lord utilized him to bring success and reconciliation. Thus, his environments reinforced minimization of conflict, which coincided with God's plans for him. One of his major focuses is "truth with mercy" as it *was taught Him* through the environments of his life journey.

I was raised in a cosmopolitan area of Ohio. I grew up in a mainline denomination which, at that time, provided a strong scriptural background but limited exposure to the dynamic life in the Holy Spirit. I did not know Christ personally until I was sixteen. I was raised to believe that I either excelled or I failed. Conflict was not desired, but it was not to be avoided. Results drove actions. My profession was in the competitive world of business, where success was defined by results. I learned about the Holy Spirit and the spirit realm later in life. God has humbled and blessed me by utilizing me in extremely difficult spiritual-warfare situations. Therefore, I am most comfortable with handling crisis situations and working where excellence is the standard. My passion is helping individuals and organizations recognize and achieve their God-given potential. Through my journey, Christ has taught me that His "truth with mercy" is to be demonstrated through the many forms He displayed on Earth, including those of the Lion of Judah.

Although this mentor and I have similarities in gifts and roles, we are generally utilized in very different situations. We are wired very differently, and our journeys were diverse. The mentor walked in environments of domestic culture, universities, and churches. I was brought up to break down walls in order to achieve what is right and what the Lord directed. God utilizes each of our backgrounds and journeys in Christ to develop us for *very different situations.*

If God had left our "wirings" just as they are (very different) but had reversed our journeys, each of us would be much different than we are today but still *not like the other*. God's designs of life journeys have significant impacts on how we are to serve uniquely in His Body. They are one of many factors.

Honor Your Uniqueness, Including Your Life Journey
Honor God's Uniqueness in Others

We are to honor the unique calling and journey (perspective) that Christ has for us and to extend that honor to every Christian we encounter. This does not mean we discard discernment—quite the contrary. We are to view others with the eyes and love of God. Recognize differences, and learn from others, but hear and conform only to the Bible and the leadership of the Spirit of God. Just as the heart in the human body is not to attempt to function as the brain, we are to be true to the Spirit's leadership as we live in His unique roles within His Body. This is accomplished by walking in the Spirit. Those of us with destructive and painful backgrounds often feel that these have disqualified us or reduced our effectiveness in some way. Reject this lie of the enemy. God uses all to His glory. You bring perspectives, strength, and healing that others cannot.

Live in unity with Christ's body, under His authority, and not as a maverick. However, understand that, as each Christian follows the Spirit instead of conforming to "groupthink," they will at times look like a maverick to many. That is not an issue for God, *if we are walking under the authority of the Spirit.*

The root of many destructive situations in the Church is that many pastors, mentors, teachers, and parents make the mistake of attempting to turn others into mirror images of themselves instead of helping them truly live their unique masterpiece walk with Christ. Thus, Christians are taught to be what influential individuals and cultures, including churches and families, want them to be, instead of being supported in their God-designed uniqueness. Many of us spend more time asking humans for guidance than we spend interacting with God and the scriptures, in order to know Him and accordingly trust His guidance to *Be and Become* his masterpieces. This is a serious mistake.

Application

God has great plans for you, and He is skillfully molding you as He walks with you through your unique journey in life. Your journey includes both His design and the detours that you have chosen or that others have forced upon you. He utilizes both for His good.

- What has your journey prepared you to be, and how are you to reflect Christ's love, truth, and mercy?
- The nuances of your journey and missions bring wonderful levels of individuality and kingdom effectiveness. No one is to be an exact replica of influential mentors, pastors, church and secular cultures, or other major influencers. We are to walk in the Spirit as God created us.
- What is the Spirit revealing to you?
- What transformations does He have for you?

CHAPTER 12

THE SPIRITUAL MAN AND THE NATURAL MAN

1 COR 2:14
But the natural man does not receive the things of the Spirit of God, for they are foolishness to him; nor can he know them, because they are spiritually discerned.

1 COR 3:1
And I, brethren, could not speak to you as spiritual people but as to carnal, as babes in Christ

Choosing to live as God's Spiritual Person is a requirement for living as His masterpiece. Are you actively and continuously choosing and living this life? It is essential. Only those who are saved in Christ can enter this life, but many do not choose to. How does this Spiritual life differ from the life of the Natural Man and the Carnal Christian? The Spiritual Person goes beyond salvation to intentionally submitting to and following the leading of the Holy Spirit. They permit Him to live in and through them. The unsaved, Natural Man/Person does not know the Spirit, does not receive His wisdom and blessings, and insists on personally controlling their destiny. Carnal Christians live immature lives as "babes in Christ." Although they are saved, they do not consistently submit to the leadership of the Holy Spirit, and, in most cases, insist on controlling their lives. Many Christians live in this state nearly all the time, even those who claim differently. God designed us to *Be and Become* His Spiritual Persons. Which life are you choosing?

Compare what you believe and what God has for you as we approach the transformational truths about the Spiritual Man/Person in three stages. First, we are *Made in God's Image*. Second, God created mankind as *Three-Part Beings*. Finally, explore the distinctions between individuals who live as God's Spiritual Men/Persons, as Natural Men/People, and as Carnal Christians. Determine which life you are living and which you are going to commit to live.

Made in God's Image

GEN 1:27
So God created man in His own image:

GENESIS 1:1-2
*In the beginning, God created the heavens and the earth.
... And the Spirit of God was hovering over the face of the waters.*

JOHN 4:24
*God is Spirit, and those who worship Him
must worship in spirit and in truth.
(Yahweh—Hebrew YHWH conveys "The Eternal.")*

God created us in His image. He is spirit and eternal, and we are therefore spiritual beings with eternal spirits. (Where our spirits spend eternity is dependent on our relationships with Christ.) Jesus stated that we "must worship Him in spirit and in truth." He placed our spirit's connection with God above all other forms of contact with Him. He could have said, "Worship with mind, will, emotions and body." Your eternal spirit is the real you.

God Is One Being with Three Identities

DEUT 6:4
Hear, O Israel: The Lord our God, the Lord is One!

2 COR 13:14
The grace of the Lord Jesus Christ, and the love of God, and the communion of the Holy Spirit be with you all.

GALATIANS 4:6
And because you are sons, God has sent forth the Spirit of His Son into your hearts crying out, "Abba, Father!"

God is One (Deut 6:4), and there are no other true gods. Scripture describes the One God as a three-part being (commonly referred to as the Trinity), reflecting His identities/roles of Father, Son, and Holy Spirit (Cor 13:14, Gal 4:6.) This is a difficult concept to understand. We may accept it as doctrine, but only the Spirit's *revelation truth* carries His power to bring this alive within us.

Analogies of the Trinity

Consider the President of the United States. Individuals may know him/her in three distinct identities/roles. These might be President, father, and husband. His wife would have no issue with viewing him in these three roles; neither would his mature children. There is no confusion that he/she is one person, who is correctly described as operating uniquely in each role.

Next, view your mother or father in this way. You will have no difficulty in recognizing their distinct roles as parent, spouse, and profession.

Third, consider your relationships with your children. My wife and I strongly value viewing our children in at least three identities. They are always going to be our children. As they mature, they become our trusted peers. Following mutual adoptions in Christ, we are brothers and sisters in God's family. We honor them through these perspectives, and our relationships transform naturally as our interactions mature.

Finally, consider the Trinity through the analogy of a triangle. The entire triangle is "God." Individual corners reflect the Father, the Son, and the Holy Spirit, and each of them is God. Each of them has a unique role or mission and is to be known personally and distinctly, but they are One Being.

These simple analogies help us understand God is a three-part being, and He is "ONE." He chose to reveal Himself to this world in the flesh, through Jesus Christ, but Jesus has always existed. He was not created; He was there with the Father at the beginning of creation. God's Spirit was also there. Today, God interacts with us primarily through the Holy Spirit and His Word, but He is free to engage as He chooses.

The Spiritual Man and the Natural Man

Mankind: Three-Part Beings
Spirit, Soul, Body

> **1 THES 5:23**
> *Now may the God of Peace Himself sanctify you completely; and may your whole spirit, soul and body be preserved blameless at the coming of our Lord Jesus Christ*
>
> **HEB 4:12**
> *For the word of God is living and powerful, and sharper than any two-edged sword, piercing even to the division of soul and spirit, and of joints and marrow, and is the discerner of the thoughts and intents of the heart.*
>
> **JER 1:5**
> *Before I formed you in the womb, I knew you.*
>
> *Before you were born, I sanctified you: I ordained you a prophet to the nations.*

We are spiritual beings made in God's image. Just as He is a three-part being, so are we, but in a different sense. In 1 Thessalonians and Hebrews, God describes us as being composed of spirits, souls, and bodies. These are distinct parts of one individual. Our spirits are eternal and come into being the moment the Lord creates us in our mother's womb (see Jeremiah). Before He formed us in the womb, He knew us. We are not accidents, left to the whims of fate.

The biblical view of our spirits is in direct conflict with the New Age hypothesis that our spirits come from some mystical force when we are born and return to it when we die. They may call this force "god," but it is not the God of Christians and Jews. Many New Age beliefs speak of spiritual journeys in a general sense that has limited similarity to the reality of the human spirit and the spiritual journeys of Christians. Unfortunately, growing numbers of individuals and churches who identify themselves as Christian are embracing similar views. Do not be deceived.

Some believe mankind is a physical being, who may or may not have a spirit. They are attempting to live from this broken perspective. This is similar to an eagle that views itself as a chicken, or a human who views himself or herself as an animal. Struggle as they will, neither will ever learn to truly live, until they embrace their God-given identity as His spiritual beings. The eagle may recognize its identity by instinct, but the human will find it only through the revelation of the Holy Spirit.

Spirit, Soul, and Body
Consider the Identities of Mankind's Three-Part Being

- Our spirit—This unique element of our being is eternal and receives revelation and instruction from the Holy Spirit. Our spirit then takes this revelation knowledge and makes it usable in the natural realm by processing it in our minds and taking action through our wills, emotions, and bodies. At the fall of humanity, our spirits became, in essence, dead to God. They come functionally alive only upon salvation through Christ.

- Our soul is the seat of passions, emotions, determination, and desires. The soul is either under the lordship of the Holy Spirit, communicating through our spirit, or it is under the control of self and, ultimately, Satan. It is unique for each individual and carries distinct attributes and personality

traits. Some natural gifts reside here. Many believe that its healthy characteristics remain with us into eternity. The soul consists of the:
- Mind
- Will
- Emotions

+ Our body engages the material realm through the five senses. This earthly body is ultimately replaced by our spiritual body. Many of our natural gifts reside in our bodies.

Some pastors, teachers, and friends misuse the terms "spirit" and "soul" by considering them equivalent. Spirit and soul are distinctly different, or our Father would not have differentiated them in scripture. It is a tragedy that many Christians have not been guided to differentiate between the Holy Spirit, their spirit, and their soul. Ask God to make this truth a vibrant part of your walk with Him. Only He can provide this revelation.

Fall of Humanity: "Death" of Mankind's Spirit

Our Father designed mankind to be in continuous, intimate fellowship with Him. This emanated through His direct interactions with our spirits. The fall of mankind, through Adam, broke that relationship. The entire race fell from God's designed relationship of His-Spirit-to-our-spirit fellowship to the state of the natural man (prior to salvation), where without Christ, our spirits are functionally dead to God, and mankind cannot experience relationship and life as God designed.

The Natural Man, the Spiritual Man, the Carnal Christian

Spiritually, humans live and operate under these three states of existence.

The Natural Man, the Flesh

> **1 Cor 2:14**
> *But the natural man does not receive the things of the Spirit of God, for they are foolishness to him; nor can he know them because they are spiritually discerned.*
>
> **Is 29:14**
> *I will destroy the wisdom of the wise and will bring to nothing the understanding of the prudent.*

The Natural Man, or the Flesh, is the state where one's life and actions are directed by their soul (mind, will, and emotions) and body. Due to the fall of man through Adam, all unsaved individuals operate in the flesh. Their spirits are not in connection with the Holy Spirit, as they are basically "dead" to God. They cannot understand the things of God because these are spiritually discerned. They may be wonderful, loving people, but their source is themselves. Some call themselves Christians but are not. They have no personal encounter and relationship with Christ. Their perceptions of truth and life are driven by soul and body, which are areas where Satan dominates.

Even after salvation, many are driven by soul and body instead of God's Spirit. I was driven by logic; I thought if something made sense, it must be of God, and I pursued it. For others, their iron wills define the direction of their lives. Many are also controlled by emotions. They think, *If it feels so right, and I am "so excited," it must be right to do and be God's will.* Others are driven by their bodies. All of the passions and lusts of the five senses have been embraced for so long they "must" be satisfied. In their minds, it is right to do so.

Mankind is created to be in intimate fellowship with God. The unsaved do not have this and experience a huge void, regardless of how "good" their lives seem. They seek to fill this void through efforts at self-aggrandizement, worldly identity, non-biblical spirituality and recognition. Wholeness will not be found through anyone or anything other than Christ. God constantly works in every person's life to offer salvation and the spiritual life through Christ.

A Reminder: Salvation Is Only Through Christ

JOHN 14:6
Jesus said to them, "I am the way, the truth, and the life. No one comes to the Father except by me."

GAL 2:20A
I have been crucified with Christ; it is no longer I who live, but Christ lives in me;

Immediately, as an individual responds to the Holy Spirit and personally accepts the salvation work of Christ, miracles happen.

- They are forgiven of all sin. 1 John 1:9
- The Old Nature/the Flesh, driven by the leadership of soul and body, has died with Christ on the cross. Gal 2:20a

(The individual continuously chooses whether or not to keep their flesh on the cross.)

- They become a new creation and are born again in the Spirit. 2 Cor 5:17
- Their spirit becomes alive within them. Rom 8:9-10
- The Holy Spirit takes up permanent residence inside them, and they are a temple of the Holy Spirit. 1 Cor 6:19
- They may choose or reject walking in their ever-deepening personal journey with God.
- If they live under the control of the Holy Spirit, it is Christ who lives in and through them. Gal 2:20

The Spiritual Man

JOHN 6:63

*It is the Spirit that gives life: the flesh profits nothing.
The words that I speak to you are spirit, and they are life.*

JOHN 4:24

*God is Spirit, and those who worship Him
must worship in spirit and truth.*

GAL 5:17, 24

*For the flesh lusts against the Spirit, and the Spirit
against the flesh; and these are contrary to one another,
so that you do not do the things that you wish.
And those who are Christ's have crucified the
flesh with its passions and desires.*

The Spiritual Man and the Natural Man

Gal 6:7, 8

Do not be deceived, God is not mocked; for whatsoever a man sows, that he will also reap. For he who sows to his flesh will of his flesh reap corruption, but he who sows in the spirit will of the Spirit reap everlasting life.

The Spiritual Man/Person is saved and chooses to live and operate under the leadership of the Holy Spirit. This person receives God's communications and instructions by *revelation* from the Holy Spirit to their own spirit. They joyously learn to surrender control of their lives to the Holy Spirit. Under His leadership, their spirit has authority over their soul and body. Thus, everything is aligned under the authority of God, and this person lives as designed by the Father. When the Spirit is in control, the person is living as Paul stated in Gal 2:20, "it is no longer I who live, but Christ lives in me." His Spirit is their source of both transformation and life as He lives in and through them. They are *Being and Becoming* God's masterpiece. No Christian reaches perfection in this life while on Earth.

Battle Between Flesh and Spirit

Although our flesh is crucified and died with Christ, it does not release control easily to the Spirit. The soul and body are real, and they have enjoyed the power of being in charge. They battle to stay there. Our flesh occasionally or frequently succeeds in grabbing control. As this is occurring, God's Spirit is revealing the danger to the Spiritual Person. They then choose to return control to the Spirit or take control and walk in their flesh. The second choice is a sin and must be dealt with through confession, repentance, forgiveness, and filling of the Spirit. Early in Christian life, taking control and living in the flesh occurs frequently, with many "learning" failures. The temptation is there all through life, but as we learn to hear God's Spirit and obey, we increasingly live in His victory.

Tragically, many Christians are not taught to live under the authority of the Spirit, and they live most of their lives in the broken state of Carnal Christian.

Carnal Christians

The Carnal Christian is saved. They received Christ. His Spirit is in them, and their spirit is alive to God, capable of communicating through the Holy Spirit. They may at times walk in the Spirit, but these times are limited. In the fully Carnal Christian, their spirit is totally dominated by their flesh (soul and body.) The flesh holds the reins and will not yield, because the individual chooses it over their spirit and the Holy Spirit. Even if this person is able to quote every scripture, speak marvelous-sounding religious philosophies and serve and bless many, their works are of the flesh and not of God. They do not bear spiritual fruit. When they are in the flesh, their actions are destructive to the work of God's kingdom, regardless of how "good" they appear. Many churches do not teach the difference. They leave their members trapped in tragic loss, and this delights the enemy.

Satan knows that he dominates the lives of both the unsaved person and the Carnal Christian. They operate in the "flesh," which is Satan's domain. Therefore, he does not care if that individual goes to church or lives a superficial "Christian" lifestyle where their spirit does not remain in continuous fellowship with the Holy Spirit. They may cry and wail and worship with great emotion, and, errantly, think they are spiritual. They may seek God with mind and will but only infrequently or never connect spiritually. They may diligently "serve" Him in their own power. He is not in these works. They are in the flesh, and our Lord receives no glory. Only actions accomplished by the Spirit of God through His people carry the power of our Lord and bear fruit that glorifies our Father. (John 6:63, Is 64:6)

Carnal Christians live most of their lives under the control of their souls. They try to "act like Christ" and keep God's laws, all in their own power. They normally believe that they are thriving Christians. Although they are saved and their spirits are alive to God, they generally give first priority to the world and its deceptions and distractions. Their lives and efforts bring little if any glory to God.

Holy-Spirit-to-Human-Spirit Communication and Action

Because we are, first and foremost, God's Spiritual Beings, intimate communication depends on the Holy Spirit connecting to and communicating with our spirit. As we listen and live under His authority, our spirit says, "*Wow!* I get that! That is direct 'revelation truth' from God!" It may come as we read the Bible, pray, meditate on scripture, worship, exercise, etc. Because Satan is the great imitator, our spirits must be discerning. Everything is to be confirmed through the scriptures. The Holy Spirit will never contradict or stretch the truths of God's word. He will not give "brand new truths" of God. (Rev 22:18-19)

After receiving revelation or direction from the Holy Spirit, our spirit then processes His truths into our minds, wills, and emotions. These truths are then utilized and lived out through our bodies. Soul and body are to function under the authority of our spirit, which is always to be under the authority of the Holy Spirit. When we live this way, *we are walking in the Spirit.* (Chapter 15)

The Enemy's Role

We have discussed the battle for supremacy that occurs between our spirit and our flesh. Be aware that Satan and his forces join this battle on the side of the soul and body. Satan cannot know the thoughts and mind of a believer—only the Holy Spirit has this relationship. But he and his forces are very familiar with each individual. They know what tempts them and how to introduce doubts and fears that mess with their faith and their obedient walk in the Spirit.

Thus begins a lifetime of growth for those who follow the Spirit or a lifetime of defeat for those who live in their flesh, often bound by the enemy. It is a journey of embracing our inconceivably wonderful lives when the Holy Spirit is obeyed. This is not an easy or problem-free life. When we follow the Spirit, we are in direct conflict with culture and often with human definitions within churches. We are never to be in conflict with *Christ's Church,* which may not always be reflected in individual denominations and local churches. Our journeys toward spiritual growth play out daily in every individual who is a born-again follower of Christ. Those who freeze their identity in spiritual infancy or teenage self-infatuation do not notice the battle. Satan works to keep them there, but their lives are no threat to his destructive plans. Their flesh remains in charge, and the Holy Spirit will not force Himself on them (Matt 23:37-39). Those who are growing in the Spirit are aware of the ever-present choice to accept or reject the leadership of the Spirit. The enemy pressures them continuously because God is accomplishing His will through them. No one is immune, from pastor to spiritual newcomer.

The Spiritual Christian's Victorious Life

Spiritual Christians continue their amazing and lifelong journey of walking with God in the Spirit. They consistently hear, learn from, and obey the Spirit of God. Their relationship with God deepens. They gladly yield control. Yes, they fail or trip and fall, sometimes frequently and repetitively, but they stand up, confess, repent, ask forgiveness, and move forward in Christ, They become stronger, more humble, more empathetic and more Spirit-controlled. Christ bears much spiritual fruit both in and through them for the glory of the Father.

Application

Are You a Spiritual Christian or a Carnal Christian?

At the moment of salvation, individuals are spiritual infants. They either begin a lifetime of choosing the empowered journey toward spiritual maturity or choose spiritual immaturity, immediately or at another point along life's path. Many choose immaturity because they have not been introduced to the truth and mentored. Some default to immaturity because they do not give priority to their relationship with God. The ultimate result of choosing immaturity is that, although saved, they never experience their God-designed purpose, and they miss intimate fellowship and masterpiece lives in Christ. This is like a Giant Sequoia seed deciding that it likes being a seed and determining to stay in that state until it decomposes and dies. Seeds are not able to make that decision, but we are.

What choices have you made? Do you know when the Spirit of God is in control and when your flesh is dominating? Do you listen for the Spirit to reveal this? Did you begin the spiritual journey but slow down or stop at a level you "feel good about," usually in comparison with church and secular cultures that embrace you? Are you intentional about the high calling (your kingdom mission) of God on your life? Although you have grown, are you blocking the leadership of the Holy Spirit and forfeiting your true calling and walk with Christ? Are you continuously learning to hear and obey the Holy Spirit as He draws you to Him and to living God's life under the Spirit's authority, instead of following your fleshly desires? Do you know *when you are in the Spirit and when you are in the Flesh?*

How is the Spirit directing you to walk differently with Him as you engage in your next steps as God's Spiritual person? Any lifestyle other than *Walking in the Spirit* will imprison His masterpiece plan within, and you will go to your grave with some or all of His kingdom purpose unlived and caged within.

CHAPTER 13

GOD'S REVELATION VS MANKIND'S HEAD KNOWLEDGE

Only the Holy Spirit Can Reveal the Truths of God to the Spirit of Mankind, and Only His Spiritual Revelation Transforms Us into Christlikeness.

1 COR 2:10-13

But God has revealed them to us through His Spirit. For the Spirit searches all things, yes, the deep things of God.

For what man knows the things of a man except the spirit of the man which is inside him? Even so no one knows the things of God except the Spirit of God.

Now we have received, not the spirit of the world, which man's wisdom teaches but which the Holy Spirit teaches, comparing spiritual things with spiritual.

But the natural man does not receive the things of the Spirit of God, for they are foolishness to him; nor can he know them, because they are spiritually discerned.

WHOSE LIFE ARE YOU LIVING?

> **EPH 1:17-19**
> *That the God of our Lord Jesus Christ, the Father of glory, may give to you the spirit of wisdom and revelation in the knowledge of Him...*
> *The eyes of your understanding being enlightened, that you may know what is the hope of His calling, what are the riches of the glory of His inheritance in the saints and what is the exceeding greatness of His power toward us who believe, according to the workings of His mighty power.*

Revelation Knowledge vs. Head Knowledge

Christians are created to walk in the revelation knowledge of God's Spirit instead of the head-knowledge of mankind. God teaches us the difference and shows us how incredibly our lives will be transformed when we choose to seek and follow only the Spirit's biblical revelation. This knowledge is the Spirit's communication of God's truths directly to mankind's born-again spirit. These truths take up "living" residence within us and through the power of God result in *His* lasting transformations. Head knowledge is a poor substitute. It results from personal observations and assessment of thoughts of others. It resides in the flesh and generally finds its identity in pride and self-reliance. Changes resulting from head-knowledge, true or not, do not touch the God-revived spirit of individuals and have no ability to result in God's transformations. As we seek the Spirit's revelation in all things, true spiritual growth results because we are discerning the difference and choosing the Spirit's wisdom, knowledge, and guidance. Then as Ephesians 1 reveals, "the eyes of our understanding will be enlightened" to the extraordinary things of God that no human mind can comprehend without the Spirit's revelation. When we do not recognize and honor this difference, we will err in many unnecessary ways.

Revelation Knowledge

For Christians, the Spirit's revelation is:

- The divine disclosure to humans of the knowledge that God desires to make known.

- First received in the individual's spirit and then processed through the mind, will, and emotions.

- Is always consistent with God's nature and His truths as revealed in the Holy Scriptures. If it does not align with scripture, it is not from God. It is a deception and a lie.

The Spirit's *revelation* is dynamic and instantaneously brings life. It immediately goes beyond information and becomes living truth within as it fills our being and becomes an integral part of who and what we are. The passion of God's revelation results in immense transformation, energy, and action. This is much deeper than mere joy or excitement. It is His truth and life. God has touched us with His unchanging knowledge. One of the first revelations for Christians is, "Christ is all that He said He is, and I know I need Him and cannot truly live without Him." Spiritual Christians also follow God-revealed plans for their lives.

Head Knowledge

> **1 COR 3:19**
> *For the wisdom of the world is foolishness with God. For it is written, "He catches the wise in their own craftiness."*

Head knowledge is potentially fact and truth, but it is accepted and applied because others or personal experience say(s) it is true. As sciences expand mankind's perceptions or actual understanding of truth, scientific "facts" are subject to alteration. Culturally established norms or "self-declared truths" that are not based on God's word are as fleeting as the patterns created by wind moving sand across a beach. Even so, secular society teaches its "truths" as correct for all. Each succeeding generation washes these "truths" away to be once again temporarily replaced by their next-favorite premises. Whether human-designated truths are correct or not, they are not alive spiritually. They are head knowledge. The Lord does use head knowledge. In fact, He provides His social and scientific truths to mankind. He designed us to explore and learn, but He is to be our source of spiritual knowledge through revelation.

Head knowledge impacts an individual through the mind. Mind and emotions become the final discerners of truth for those who do not depend on God. Their version of truth then drives their life, valid or not. The individual's development of themselves and their life is self-governed, and they seek to become what their preferred culture dictates. Unless they turn to God, they have a negligible chance of becoming all God created them to be. Many Christians are also driven by secular head knowledge and forfeit much of God's masterpiece life. The Christian's source is to be God's revelation through His Spirit.

Living the Difference

Once we know the difference between head knowledge and the Spirit's revelation knowledge, we are no longer willing to build life on anything other than His revelation. We test every significant teaching against the Bible. This particularly applies to spiritual learning and growth, as we no longer embrace any teaching just because some credible source (pastor, teacher, mentor, or author) says it is true. We similarly test what we believe the Spirit is revealing in order to block deception from the enemy and our minds. The Spirit of God, in full alignment with the scriptures, is our final authority. Mature pastors and teachers instruct their congregations and students to confirm their teaching through personal interaction with the Bible and the Holy Spirit.

How Revelation Knowledge Works

Revelation knowledge enters us straight from the Holy Spirit. He communicates it to our born-again spirits. It may come as a flash of light and a sudden understanding of the incredible truth of a Bible verse, regardless of how many times we have considered it. Our spirit receives this knowledge. It then communicates and processes it through the mind, will, and emotions, and it is integrated into our lives. This truth then transforms us and becomes a passion by which we live and follow Christ. It is not some religious or philosophical truth *that we try to apply or live up to. It instead is a life-changing reality that lives in and through us.* It includes deepening spiritual understanding of the Bible, the identity of God, our identity and purpose in Him, His identity for others, our kingdom roles and missions, and the way that He desires to live in and through us.

We are to be careful of individuals who claim revelations of "new" spiritual knowledge. God's word is not to be added to or removed. Rev 22 reads, "For I testify to everyone who hears the words of the prophecy of this book: If anyone adds to these things, God will add to him the plagues that are written in this book." We believe this applies to all scripture, not just Revelations.

Living by Revelation Knowledge: My Experience Revelation Life in Scripture

Before recommitting my life, I read the Old and New Testaments. I knew that they were true, and I worked in my mind to seek understanding and then application to my life. I was the focus.

Immediately after my recommitment, I experienced a new love and passion for the scriptures. They were alive. They were real. Daily, truths were *revealed by Him*, and they took up residence in my very being. Transformations spawned through His use of these revelation truths. I no longer read the scripture as some valued textbook. It was His living word. My mind played an important role, but it was no longer the initiator and discerner of knowledge. The Spirit conveyed His *living truth*. Emotional excitement and mental agreement followed.

The Spirit's revelation of the depths and meanings of scripture continues today and will never be over. He reveals His truth at the times and in the manners that are relevant for each person in each stage of our journeys. *Actively "listening" for His voice is required.* We are to always have our spiritual earbuds on.

The Spirit's Transformations

For several years after recommitting my life, I was still stuck in the religious mode of "trying" to be who He "wanted" me to be instead of living in His Spirit as He created and designed me. I read the Bible, listened to preaching, and prayed, but I was attempting to understand with my mind and then apply through my personal efforts. I had lots of religious knowledge but was stuck. My heart was right, but I did not know how to live as a Christian other than through my mind and my natural senses. I was confused, disillusioned, and broken. I was eventually able to permit God's Spirit to teach me to begin living through revelation knowledge. He then led me into the continuing journey of learning to walk in the Spirit, instead of the flesh. I have an immense amount to learn every day, but I enjoy walking with Him as He lives in and through me.

Revelation for Becoming His Masterpiece

In the middle of my Christian life, I accepted the truth that I am Christ's workmanship, created in Christ Jesus for good works that He prepared beforehand for me to walk in. It was/is great news, but I didn't know how to live in that truth. I tried to make things happen that I thought would please my Father God.

One day, the Spirit's revelation caused the truth of those words to take life. I then *knew that I was/am* His workmanship, His masterpiece. I have His purpose resident inside me, and I am truly alive in Him. I am not to "try" to live His life in my own power and skill, or to try to become something by my efforts. I surrender to Him and *Be and Become* His masterpiece by *permitting His Spirit to live my life in and through me* and teach me to live as He commands. "It is no longer I who live, but Christ lives in me." This truth moved from head knowledge to revelation knowledge that is transforming my life. Accordingly, I am totally dependent on Him. God is drawing every Christian to join Him in this life.

COMPARING SECULAR, CARNAL, AND SPIRITUAL CHRISTIAN TEACHERS AND PASTORS

General Comparisons

Only individuals who have the revelation knowledge of God's word and are walking in the Spirit can truly teach and live in God's power. As they live this way, they are Spiritual Christians.

Non-Christians and Carnal Christians may memorize the Bible and teach its truths, through head knowledge, but that is an imitation. They are merely teaching facts. Non-Christians cannot have the power of God flowing through them, *because His Spirit does not reside in them.* Carnal Christians will sometimes walk in the Spirit, but frequently they do not, because their flesh is normally their source. Either of these may influence others through human charisma, but their teaching will not carry the transforming influence of God. (Bible verses are the very words of God, and they always carry His power in and of themselves, regardless of who utters them. They are much more effectively delivered by God's Spirit through Spiritual Christians.) The individual who lives in the flesh (the Natural Man, the Carnal Christian) generally views the scriptures as religious truths that carry no more power than the principles of any other world religion, philosophy, or science.

Specific Comparisons:
Non-Christian Teachers/Pastors

Unsaved pastors or teachers, though they may call themselves "Christians," teach the Bible as head knowledge, equivalent to many other secular or religious sources. They may mentally know the Bible's content and may even embrace and teach portions as enlightened ways for society to live. But, for them, it is just human philosophy. They select what they like and reject the rest. Their knowledge is seriously limited compared to what God has to reveal, and it is always subject to the instructor's personal definition of truth. Their teaching presents a mere shadow of the light, life, and power of God's Bible. This is knowledge without revelation and application without the Holy Spirit. All who live in Christ's Spirit will recognize these are not alive in Christ.

Carnal Christian Teachers and Pastors

Carnal Christian pastors and teachers live most/much of their lives in the Flesh/Natural Man instead of in the Spirit. Their eyes are primarily focused on themselves and on head knowledge. They are infants or teenagers in the Christian life.

These teach the Bible or their idea of the Christian's walk with God from a position of pride in their minds, their superior academic knowledge, or their positional authority. They rely on head knowledge, assumed superiority, and charisma. They cannot effectively teach or mentor Christ-followers in the powerful life of walking in Christ because they do not experience it. An ever-deepening personal relationship with God is not a reality in their lives. Paul noted that he had to feed these Christians milk, instead of meat. They forfeit most of God's masterpiece life, even as they consider themselves superior.

Spirit-Filled Teachers and Pastors

These instructors have personal encounters and intimate relationships with Christ. They are not perfect. They mess up, occasionally misunderstand the Holy Spirit, and at times ignore the Spirit and walk in their flesh. However, their sincere commitment is to have the Holy Spirit in absolute control of their every action. The Spirit provides revelation knowledge for all that He desires to accomplish in and through their lives, including teaching, preaching, missions, mentoring, and utilization of gifts of the Spirit. They continuously listen for Him to reveal what He wants to say and do through them in each situation. They ask Him to reveal each student/individual through God's eyes. They choose to live under the authority of the Spirit and teach with the Spirit's transformational and contagious faith and power. God's work through them eclipses the impact of even the most charismatic unsaved or carnal presenter. Their preaching or teaching flows from the Holy Spirit to the individuals' spirits. The Holy Spirit is their source, as they recognize, "It is no longer I but Christ who dwells within me." The spirit of Christians experiencing their teaching recognizes this and responds to the Holy Spirit, even if the presenter is an obedient servant who is not a gifted speaker. Even the dormant spirit of the non-Christian may be stirred.

Summary: Intentionality and Obedience

Life in revelation truth and knowledge is dependent on the Holy Spirit, but it requires intentionality and obedience, as we are always to be listening for, confirming, receiving, and obeying the voice and revelations of the Spirit. After confirming He is the source, we are to obey. Our intentionality includes total surrender to the authority of the Holy Spirit, as our transformational life journey is accomplished by Him, not self. We recognize ourselves as humble but honored tools in the Master's hands. There is no place for pride. When we depend on our knowledge, our skills, and our desires, we are operating in the flesh, and the power of the Lord is not in our actions or results.

Living by God's revelation is a lifestyle that must be carefully taught and mentored. It can be lived only through the guidance of the Holy Spirit. Each person's natural man is easily deceived and may incorrectly believe their thoughts, desires, and passions of the flesh are from the Holy Spirit, when they may actually originate in either self or the enemy. The plans of God frequently do not align with what is exciting or logical from earthly perspectives, and we are to rely on the discernment provided by the Spirit.

God is the Only True Source of Knowledge, Truth, and His Transformation.
He Provides This Through His Revelation and His Power

Learning to identify the revelation of the Holy Spirit depends on many things, but especially on a deepening personal and intimate relationship with Christ. This relationship is founded on life that is constantly listening to the voice of the Holy Spirit, regardless of what we are doing. *We are to always have our spiritual earbuds on, and listen attentively to the Holy Spirit, regardless of what else is happening.* The living truths of God and the Bible are passed from generation to generation through the work of the Spirit and through Him only. Accepting the truths of God as head knowledge because someone with position or maturity has taught it is of the flesh.

Applications

- Think through examples in your life where Bible truths about Christ and walking in the Spirit have jumped off the page and become revelations that transformed your life.

- What do you agree and disagree with in the presentation of this chapter? What Bible verses are the foundations for your position?

- Do you live and grow by the Spirit's revelation or by religious and secular head knowledge?

- Based on what He reveals to you, what are you going to do?

- Are you willing to ask the Spirit for His revelation in every personal encounter, every scripture verse, every Bible study, sermon, or discussion? This is His desire.

CHAPTER 14

Always Ask, "What Is God's Truth?" and Stand on It Alone

John 8:31, 32
And you shall know the truth and the truth shall make you free.

Psalm 91:4b
His truth shall be your shield and buckler.

Eph 6:13, 14a
Therefore, take up the whole armor of God, that you may be able to withstand in the evil day, and having done all, to stand.

*Stand therefore, having girded your waist
with (the belt of) truth ...*

Victorious Christian lives are built on the foundation of God's truth. Everything that conflicts with biblical truth is to be identified and replaced with His word. The healthy Christian life is not passive but dynamic in its moment-by-moment application of His truths. We are to learn to live in His truths and avoid being "carried about by various and strange doctrines" (Hebrews 13:9), our emotions, or cultural pushback.

How Do We Respond to Confusion?

Everyone experiences times of confusion resulting from conflicting views presented by both religious and secular voices. Also, emotions, relationships, and our failures may cause us to question who we really are in Christ and what we believe. We must learn to ask God, "What is the Truth, Your Truth?" As He reveals it, we set aside deceptions, fears, and self-doubt, and mature in our relationship with Him. We stand with Him and say, "Yes, I embrace Your truths, and no feelings or lies can dissuade me." Tidal waves of doubt are then turned away as they crash against the cross.

One Night's Instruction

Confusion and turmoil often appear in the middle of the night. Eyes open, minds snap on, and larger-than-life issues pour over us.

During a particularly troubled time, I was awake and struggling with many actual and envisioned failures. These seemed to have destroyed my relationship with Christ, as my emotions shouted, "Your failures have separated you from Him." I could neither sleep nor find peace.

Christ then presented the following process for gaining His victory during times of great confusion and personal doubt. It was to be embraced by me. He later directed me to share it with you through this book. First, He showed me His empty cross next to me on a hill. He then communicated:

- "How you 'feel' about your relationship with Me does not impact either My love for you or the truth about our relationship!" Without words, He confirmed that His love is steadfast, and my feelings do not change either it or how He has bound us together through Christ. I am always to trust in His unbreakable bond of love and fellowship.

- Feelings matter, but I am not to be guided or distracted by them.

- During challenging and overwhelming situations, I am to stop operating in the emotional drama and face the situation by asking, "What is the truth? What is God's truth?" I do not proceed until I know His answer, accompanied by confirming scripture. This question elicits a redirection of my life. Regardless of what I "feel," I receive and stand on the truths of Christ.

- Next, I visually pick up each lie, audibly declare it for the lie that it is, and nail it to the cross.

- Immediately, I replace it with the truth of Christ in my life. In His gift of faith, I declare this truth as the foundation of my life and relationship with Him. Haunting lies disappear under the light of His truth.

God teaches us to always declare His truths as we stand against all that is not true in our lives. We are not to walk in the poverty of our emotions and mental responses. Every suggestion of the enemy and every lie that arises from our carnal thinking are to be immediately identified and met resolutely with God's truth. Many of these lies and deceptions reveal whose lives we have been living and the audiences we have been seeking to please by attempting to perform to their expectations.

Hearing God's Truth Through the Spirit

Once we know God's truths and are determined to stand on them, our lives take on new meaning. We become intentional about living this way. We recognize it is possible only as we walk in the Spirit (Chapter 15), instead of relying on our own efforts.

"You Believe, but Do You Trust Me?"

Do we understand the incredible difference between believing and trusting in God? Do we truly trust Him?

Once, as I was walking our dog, I was thinking about stressful physical conditions (atrial fibrillation, severe muscle degeneration) that were disrupting my life. I was practicing "standing on His truths." Even so, I was not able to find His peace and was struggling to understand what He was doing. The Spirit guided me to consider the following scriptures.

Is 54:17
No weapon formed against me shall prosper

Phil 1:6
Being confident of this very thing, that He who has begun a good work in you will complete it until the day of Jesus Christ

Psalms 31:15
My times are in Your hand;

He pointed out that though I had long believed these were true, I was struggling with the "What if's." What if God's will does not include healing and release from persistent difficulties? What if His purpose for my life did not include me living longer? What if God's missions and His passions in my heart were not to be fulfilled within my time on Earth? What if some of the struggles of my children were never relieved on Earth?

The Spirit clearly and lovingly asked, *"You believe, but do you **trust** me?"* He then taught me the important differences among belief, faith, and trust. I fully *believed* that His Word, including the above scriptures, was true. He had given me His *faith* to permit me to stand in His truths. However, the "What if's" often resulted in me fearing that His answers might not meet my heart's desires. Though I believed the scriptures, I was "hanging on" to concerns and seeking to *control* life. I believed that God uses all things for good in the lives of those who trust Him, but I struggled with the knowledge that some of His plans included outcomes that saddened me or might not materialize on this side of heaven. I often never really let go and *trusted* Him when His answers did not seem to match my desires.

He asked me to trust Him completely by leaving all outcomes to His sovereignty. Since His identity, character, and unfailing love are absolutely pure and faithful, I am able to rest in His goodness and the knowledge that He will never let me down, regardless of what is occurring in my life or the lives of those I love. He wants me to share my heart's desires, but I am not to *attempt to insist on my hopes* for results that *seem* so right to me. He knows what is right and good from His eternal perspective instead of my limited understanding of life as I viewed it through my limited earthly perspective. His sovereign will is the best possible answer in all situations.

Thus, He asked me to live by remembering His encouragement, "You believe, but do you trust Me?" I have been learning to walk with Him while asking this question, and answering it with an absolute, "Yes," even though I am often very uncomfortable with what I see in the natural.

Are the differences among belief, faith, and trust clear? Are we able to trust in His character and sovereign will during the most difficult circumstances, when our heart-wrenching prayers can really desire only one answer, but we do not see it materializing?

Church Disputes Regarding God's Truth
The Inerrancy of God's Word

2 TIM 4:3, 4

For the time will come when they will not endure sound doctrine, but according to their own desires, because they have itching ears, they will heap up for themselves teachers;

And they will turn their ears away from the truth, and be turned aside to fables.

2 TIM 3:7-9

Always learning and never able to come to the knowledge of the truth.

Now as Jannes and Jambres resisted Moses, so do these also resist the truth; men of corrupt minds, disapproved concerning the faith;

Always Ask, "What Is God's Truth?" and Stand on It Alone

> *But they will progress no further, for their folly*
> *will be manifest to all, as theirs also was.*

There will always be those in Christ's Church who resist sound doctrine and seek out "teachers" who will tell them what they wish to hear. Disputes arise and cause many to doubt the inerrancy of the Bible. Many Christians reject the inerrancy of the Bible because they have been indoctrinated to believe that today's culture and advanced knowledge are far more sophisticated than the authors of the Bible. Therefore, they teach that its words mean what they want them to mean. Most are non-Christians or Carnal Christians, and their reasoning is as misplaced as the Lord reveals it to be. The root of their error is rejection of the Bible's declaration that "all scripture is given by inspiration of God" (2 Tim 3:16). Without this, there is no ultimate source of truth. Individuals and cultures default to mankind's vacillating whims. They define truth by convenience and change it as easily as the wind molds sand dunes during a hurricane. Those who believe that the Spirit inspired the entire Bible have God's eternal foundation of truth to stand on and grow in.

Truth or Tradition

Christian denominations and even factions within denominations take different positions regarding critical areas of Bible truths. A Christian's position in these areas is to be founded on the Spirit's revelation of the Bible and not on secular and carnal reasoning or personal experience. Many areas that are simply preferences or traditions have been declared "religious law and doctrine" within churches. This brings chains in place of Christ's light and life.

We are to give grace on non-doctrinal issues but say "No" when biblical doctrine is bent or broken. We are to lovingly stand on Bible truths for issues such as the virgin birth of Christ and His dual identity as both God and man. Sadly, some individuals and churches who call themselves "Christian" do not believe in either. Some will even tell you that the "god" of all religions is the same "God" as Jehovah in the Bible. God's truths are pivotal, and we must never indicate any agreement with deception. Jesus' display of love in the gospels never included permitting individuals to accept and teach deceptions of the enemy.

God's Truth—or Tribal Beliefs?

JOSHUA 5:13, 14

And it came to pass, when Joshua was by Jericho, that he lifted his eyes and looked, and behold, a man stood opposite him with His sword drawn in His hand. And Joshua went to Him and said to Him, "Are You for us or for our adversaries?" So He said, "No, but as the Commander of the army of the Lord, I have now come."

We are not to expect God to join our side in conflicts. We are to join Him in His purposes and His methods. This takes great discernment and dependence on the Holy Spirit. It does not result from blindly following earthly leaders, churches, organizations, and cultures.

All of us grow up embracing "tribes" which shape our beliefs. These include families, race, ethnicity, economic status, church denominations, clubs, and political parties. Unless we permit God to expand our horizons, we get stuck in adopting their beliefs as truth, often at the expense of biblical truth.

Always Ask, "What Is God's Truth?" and Stand on It Alone

Our Tribal Beliefs Are Not the Embodiment of God's Truth

Many refer to tribal beliefs as "filters" through which we view life. When we primarily engage with individuals of our own or similar beliefs, all of our tribal positions are reinforced. We are in essence "speaking into an echo chamber" and feeling falsely and naively justified in our positions. The echo reinforces, but we have learned nothing. We can be deceived into thinking our beliefs best reflect God's. All cultural entities do this, both predominant culture and every subculture. Each tries to persuade others to adopt its beliefs and methods, as it resists or disparages the methods of others.

We must break out of our comfort zones and walk in Christ with others of different experiences. Only then can we grow in understanding God's truth and His differing perspectives as viewed from different journeys. We are never to condone bending God's truths, but we are to be open to His revelation that others may understand a perspective of His truth that we cannot see.

Any of us who do not believe we embrace tribal truths in place of God's truths, in some areas, are deceiving ourselves. Permit God to free you of the tribal traps that bind you. He will then be able to use you more fully in His kingdom. Good Christians on all sides are deaf and blind to God, as they seek to have their broken or bent tribal beliefs become "God's truths." We are to join God in His missions, not ask Him to embrace ours.

Politics

For many Americans, God is undeniably either Republican or Democrat. Some have even set political leaders up as idols that they follow, regardless of how ungodly these leaders behave. Christ openly corrected and confronted leaders who led their followers into untruth. God's prophets confronted their evil behaviors with great bravery. *Evil governments and religious leaders are to be held accountable by the Church, beginning with you and me.*

One of Satan's Great Deceptions

One of the enemy's great deceptions has taken root among elements of the Christian Church. It is presented by those who say, "If Jesus did not say something specifically in the Gospels, Christians do not have to accept it, regardless of how clearly it is stated in other portions of the New or Old Testaments."

Those who present this argument seemingly declare that only the specific statements of Jesus in His earthly role, "the red-letter quotes," meet the litmus test for defining truth. They discount all of the other statements of the Spirit throughout the Bible as not being the "words" of Jesus.

They are treating the scriptures with great inconsistency. Clearly, they do not believe 2 Tim 3:16: "All Scripture is given by inspiration of God." This leaves them with a conundrum they dismiss. If the Spirit did not inspire *all* of the words in Scripture, how can they trust that the words ascribed to Jesus are actually His words? What portions of the Old and New Testaments do they believe were written under the inspiration of the Holy Spirit, and what portions were merely written by men? When did they or their church gain the enlightenment and authority from God to cast off the Bible's truth that all scripture is by the inspiration of God? Once they set that foundation aside, Christianity becomes merely a philosophy, generated by the best efforts of humans.

Mysteriously, the quotes of Jesus become their sole gospel, even as they pridefully interpret them based on their personal beliefs. They have set themselves and their values and concepts above those of God. The enemy knows how to deceive even the elect.

Additional Scripture Truths

JOHN 16:13

However, when He, the Spirit of truth, has come, He will guide you into all truth; for He will not speak on His own authority, but whatever He hears He will speak, and He will tell you things to come.

ROM 1:18

For the wrath of God is revealed from heaven against all ungodliness and unrighteousness of men, who suppress the truth in unrighteousness.

2 THES 2:9-11

The coming of the lawless one is according to the working of Satan, with all power, signs, and lying wonders,

And with all unrighteous deception among those who perish because they did not receive the love of the truth, that they might be saved.

And for this reason God will send them strong delusion, that they should believe the lie,

that they all may be condemned who did not believe the truth but had pleasure in unrighteousness.

The Truth About Yourself

We are to know and stand on not only the Bible truths about God and His promises but also on the truths that God reveals about ourselves. These include our identity in Christ, our gifts, and our kingdom roles and missions. They also include knowing the "roots" of the brokenness and dysfunction in our lives. These roots often become strongholds that result in our operating in the flesh instead of the Spirit. We are to face these with honesty and find Christ's victory over them. Accordingly, we become stronger tools in Christ's hands. (We discuss this in Chapter 21.)

God will transform our lives into His by providing healing at the roots of our strongholds. He replaces brokenness with His truth. We are to take responsibility for unhealthy behaviors by bringing them to our loving Father.

Application

What does God's Spirit have for you?

- What is He saying/revealing about your daily walk? Do you stand on His truths, or do you let haunting lies misdirect you?

- Where are you in your intentional walk with the Spirit? Do you hear the Spirit and obey or do you ignore and block Him?

- What has He revealed about belief, faith, and trust? Do you really trust God, or do you grasp hold of every prayer and basically demand that your own desires be accomplished, in your way and in your time?

+ Are you maturing in Christ by letting Him replace your tribal beliefs with His all-encompassing truth?

+ What are His next steps for your journey? How are you going to get intentional about these steps?

CHAPTER 15

IF WE LIVE IN THE SPIRIT, LET US ALSO WALK IN THE SPIRIT

GAL 5:16-25

I say then: Walk in the Spirit, and you shall not fulfill the lust of the flesh.

For the flesh lusts against the Spirit and the Spirit against the flesh; and these are contrary to one another, so that you do not do the things that you wish . . .

If we live in the Spirit, let us also walk in the Spirit.

Our Masterpiece Lives Result Only from Walking in the Spirit

Of all the things that we are to learn as Christians, *next to salvation, "walking in the Spirit" is the most crucial.* It is life as God designed and commanded it, and we either join Him in this walk or forfeit the masterpiece lives that are His gifts. However, *walking in the Spirit requires growing our roots deeply into Christ through an ever-developing personal relationship, Bible study, and learning to abide in Him. Thus, everything we have studied from Chapter 3 until now is foundational for engaging in the maturing process and journey of learning to "walk in the Spirit."* We are to know the difference between "walking in the Spirit" and "living in the Spirit," and to understand how significantly "walking in the Spirit" surpasses the life of average Christians. We are to learn to permit the Spirit to reveal when we are and are not walking in the Spirit, as He calls us to Him.

Living in the Spirit means that we have become spiritually alive through salvation in Christ. However, if that is where our spiritual life stops, we live as Carnal Christians.

Walking in the Spirit is living under the authority and in the power of God's Spirit. He is in charge as He communicates through our spirit. Under the Spirit's power, we are continuously *Being and Becoming* His masterpiece. He transforms us and accomplishes all our kingdom missions both in and through us as we obey. This is the life of the Spiritual Person, discussed in Chapter 12. It is built on the biblical foundations laid in our first fourteen chapters. Its realities are developed here and in the following chapters. Non-Christians are able neither to live in nor walk in the Spirit.

Walking in the Spirit is a supernatural life, but *it is God's natural life* for His children. It is not mystical or some out-of-control emotional or flesh-sourced experience. It is life under the control of and in the power of God's Spirit.

We are to approach this life with humility, as we unwaveringly depend on the Spirit. We engage life through God's love, truth, faith, and power, and cast out fear and doubt. Some denominations teach members to avoid anyone who claims to hear from the Spirit and walk in the Spirit. They are robbing individuals and Christ's Church of the very lifestyle that God instructs. In Galatians 5, He states, "If we live in the Spirit, let us also walk in the Spirit." This is God's command, *not a suggestion*.

If We Live in the Spirit, Let Us Also Walk in the Spirit

There have been many ungodly excesses in this area. These have resulted in both confusion and rejection of this ultimate calling to God-given life. Some Christians believe they are walking in the Spirit, while they dishonor Him and sow discord as they copy His work through the expressions of their own soul (minds, wills, and emotions.) Neither they nor their churches discern the difference. Some servants of the enemy imitate the works and power of the Spirit in order to manipulate throngs of sincere and trusting people for Satan's gains. At times, innocent errors arise as immature Christians learn their way and misunderstand the Spirit's leadership; these occur because no one understands the Spirit correctly all of the time. An incredibly disruptive error arises when sincere Christians innocently follow the voice of the enemy, who has deceived them by deceptively imitating God's voice and twisting His truths. Good teaching and mentoring by the leadership of Christ's Church minimizes these errors and results in a healthy body of believers who *are living biblically by discerning and walking in the power of the Spirit.* Without walking in the Spirit, Christians are capable of living only in the futility of imitating Christ and His masterpiece life.

We are not to cast aside this incredible walk in the Spirit due to the errors and deceptions of mankind. Let the scriptures and the Spirit of God direct us, as we consider this subject and determine whether we are going to embrace the Holy Spirit in this victorious life or reject Him!

We approach this subject in the following areas: Living in the Spirit; Being Filled with the Spirit; Walking in the Spirit; and Abiding in Christ. We intentionally include repetition from earlier chapters.

Living in the Spirit

GAL 5:25
If we live in the Spirit, let us also walk in the Spirit.

This scripture (along with countless others throughout the Bible) establishes God's truth that living in and walking in the Spirit are two distinct situations. Living in the Spirit speaks of coming alive through salvation. When individuals receive Christ, they are forever indwelt by the Holy Spirit, and their spirit becomes alive to God's Spirit. Their spirit spends eternity with the Father.

Many in the Church stop at this salvation level of the Christian life. They then attempt to live "like" Christ as they religiously seek to obey the Bible, keep the rules, and be good people, all through efforts of their flesh. They do not submit fully to the authority of the Spirit. They are sincere, and they will go to heaven, but they have stopped at the threshold of Christ's life for them. There is so much more. The Bible commands us to move forward to be "filled with the Spirit" and "walk in the Spirit." Some Christians equate these commands. We present them as separate but fully interdependent.

Be Filled with the Spirit
Be Baptized with the Holy Spirit

I believe that "being filled with the Spirit" and "being baptized with the Spirit" refer to the same encounter with God. Some will view this differently.

Being Filled with the Spirit

EPH 5:18

*And do not be drunk with wine, in which is
excess, but be filled with the Spirit.*

Ephesians 5:18 instructs Christians that being filled with the Spirit is a command, not an option. It goes beyond receiving Christ and knowing that the Holy Spirit indwells us. The filling of the Spirit results from absolute surrender of every portion of our life and heart's desires to the Spirit's authority and control, followed by inviting Him to fill every corner of our being. Nothing is to be withheld from His sovereignty. No dark corner is barricaded. Our lives are Christ's, and we know we can do absolutely nothing of kingdom value without Him.

This life depends on asking the Spirit to fill us and is then dependent on moment-by-moment intentionality. God has given mankind free will. We are free every moment to take back control, ignore the Spirit, and return to walking in the flesh. It is out of our love for Him that we come willingly under His authority.

As we do this, whether we realize it or not, we are also beginning the life where it is "no longer I who live but Christ who lives in me," Galatians 2:20. These transformations result only through revelation of the Spirit. Imitating this through head knowledge, because our churches teach it or because all our friends are doing it, does not result in filling or transformation. Just as in salvation, the Spirit must lead and call us for this decision to be real. When we engage with the Spirit's revelation in this way, and embrace it by the faith that God provides, we know that we are filled. *Being filled by the Spirit is a continuous process of surrender and filling, not a once-and-done interaction with the Spirit.*

Baptized with the Spirit

Some of the many scripture reasons to consider that being filled with and baptized by the Spirit are equivalent. (Disagreements exist but must not separate us.)

> **ACTS 1:5, 8 (JESUS IS SPEAKING ABOUT PENTECOST.)**
> *For John baptized with water, but you shall be baptized with the Holy Spirit not many days from now*
>
> *But you shall receive power when the Holy Spirit has come upon you;*
>
> **ACTS 2:4A (PENTECOST THAT JESUS HAD REFERRED TO.)**
> *And they were all filled with the Holy Spirit*

First, Jesus speaks of Pentecost as "you shall be baptized with the Holy Spirit." Then in Acts 2, the Spirit states that "they were all filled with the Holy Spirit." Two words but one experience.

(If you have scriptural reasons to view this differently, not your personal or church's experience, then be blessed, but please don't let our differences distract you or anyone else from the wonder of this command and blessing of God.)

In Acts 2, the apostles were together and of one accord, when the Spirit came upon them and filled them. They began to show signs of the power and manifestations of the Spirit, from that time forward. They had experienced some of this before, as Christ sent them out.

When we are filled with the Holy Spirit and obeying Him, we cannot avoid power. He is power. Importantly, *that power is not ours and is not wielded by us*. It is His, and it flows both in and through us for His purposes and the glory of the Father. *We are to live and walk in the power of the Spirit, not the struggles of attempting to be religious or of "acting" like Christ through our flesh.*

The reality of the "filling of the Spirit/Baptized with the Spirit" is related in other places in the Bible. In Acts 8:5-17, Philip, one of the twelve apostles, presented Christ in Samaria, and many individuals were baptized in Christ's name; they were saved. Peter and John came and found that the new believers had not yet received the Holy Spirit. "They had only been baptized in the name of the Lord Jesus." Peter and John laid hands on them and prayed, and they received the Holy Spirit. I do not understand why these converts did not receive the Spirit's filling as Phillip prayed for them. He was an apostle and carried all of the authority, power, and knowledge of Peter and John. He was filled and must have known God's filling is for every Christian. However, I embrace this scripture as truth. These disciples were saved but not filled. It indicates there is a receiving of the Spirit that goes beyond the indwelling at salvation.

This subject has been argued for centuries. Each of us is to seek counsel and ultimately the Spirit's revelation of scripture instead of holding blindly to our tribal beliefs. Unfortunately, many individuals and some denominations equate their personal experience to scripture. When their experience does not align with scripture, they create a theology that supports experience and leaves those scriptures discarded as "not for our time."

There are many differing beliefs about the baptism of the Spirit and being filled with the Spirit. Some have become divisive. We are not to let God's blessings and commandments divide His Church. Neither are we to ignore the truth that being filled with the Spirit is a commandment of God. We are to study the Bible under the revelation of God's Spirit to find His truth for all issues. Here are a few beliefs that you may choose to evaluate.

- The Spirit indwells all believers at salvation. Being filled/baptized with the Spirit follows our response to the Spirit's call to completely surrender our lives to Him and place them under the control of His Spirit. Living under the Spirit's control requires continuous surrender and filling, also called *the Baptism of the Spirit*.

- Filling and Baptism of the Spirit occur at salvation when the Holy Spirit enters the person. I honor this belief and believe that it has happened. I do not find biblical support that it is the "norm."

- Filling and Baptism of the Spirit is like club membership, a "rite-of-passage." Some churches do not wait for the Spirit to draw individuals through His revelation. They think Baptism in the Spirit can be gifted any time a person's head knowledge has them request it. This is not consistent with God's statements that it is the Spirit who draws believers to Him in all steps of the Christian journey.

How God does this for each person is His business, but He will do this according to Bible truths, not according to mankind's traditions, experience, and pride. Just as faith is the cornerstone of all aspects of our walk with Christ, being filled with the Spirit/Baptized in the Spirit also requires faith, and it is the gift of God. It does not result from our self-generated faith. Also, we grieve the Spirit and block His filling when we remove ourselves from under His authority.

Walking in the Spirit

Once we are filled with the Spirit, walking in the Spirit is to follow. It is not guaranteed. Walking in the Spirit requires surrender and obedience to the control and authority of the Holy Spirit. It is then the Spirit's life and power moving in and through us, not our flesh activities. (It is no longer I who live but Christ who dwells in me.) Many Christians reject His authority and deceive themselves. They believe that salvation or one experience of "filling" qualifies them for all time, to do whatever feels Christian and call it, "Walking in the Spirit." They dishonor God. As Paul teaches in 1 Cor, he had to die daily to his flesh, and we must do the same, often many times. Whenever our flesh takes charge, we are to place it again on the cross with Christ, seek forgiveness, and again request His filling, as we surrender control to Him. Thus, walking in the Spirit results from a continuous, lifelong, and wonderful journey of learning to follow His voice as we surrender control. It requires moment-by-moment intentionality. Otherwise, often unknowingly, we take control back from the Spirit and walk in our flesh. This is Carnal Christianity, which does not contain the power of God. Many Christians are blind to the fact that they walk in this condition while they declare they walk in the Spirit.

We walk in the Spirit when we surrender all of ourselves for His filling, listen to His every word, and obey by releasing Him to transform us and operate in and through us. We are beloved "tools" in the hands of the Master, and He is to be the source of all words, actions, and power. This is the life that God designed for us. It bears fruit and glorifies the Father.

Being filled with the Spirit cannot be experienced when Christians choose to walk in the flesh. Gal 5 states that Spirit and flesh "are contrary to one another." When our flesh takes control, the Spirit is grieved, and His filling/anointing is withheld as He seeks to draw us back to Him. He will not force Himself on believers. He immediately communicates that we are choosing to walk in our flesh. Then, we again have a choice. We may continue to break fellowship and act in our own power, and we do not glorify God. (Once we realize our sin, we repent, seek forgiveness, surrender anew, and request the Spirit's filling.) Or we listen to Him and stop before we sin; we remain under His authority.

Please do not brush these distinctions aside as semantics. We are to pay attention to both our own actions and the actions of others. Few Christians walk in God's Spirit through every portion of each day. Some act in-the-flesh all the time, while they mistakenly think they are Christ's instruments, filled with the Spirit. *When we walk in the flesh, much damage is done, and God and His kingdom are dishonored.*

Consider the following examples to discern between activities in the Spirit and activities in the flesh. How many Christians consistently know whether they are walking in the Spirit or walking in the flesh? Being unaware of the Spirit's voice leads to walking in the flesh. We are to be aware of our walk, to know the difference, and to return control when we stray.

- How many of our Christian acquaintances are naturally and actively "listening to the Holy Spirit" continuously, as they walk through life? Are we? We live His masterpiece life when we are listening to Him and obeying.

- When we are engaged in meaningful conversation with an individual who is seeking the Lord's guidance or peace, do we immediately ask the Spirit to be our source and then actively listen and obey? Or do we depend on our scripture knowledge, education, and experience, so that we "just" speak what we think God would speak or blithely quote scripture?

- At all times, do we actually listen to individuals and "hear what they are saying and feeling" as we concurrently listen to the Spirit for revelation? Do we then draw them out as we follow the Spirit's guidance? Are we able to be silent and truly listen to both the individual and God? One sure sign that *we are not listening to either* is that we are on the edge of our seats, just waiting for them to stop so that we can share our own experiences and knowledge. We are then working out of our flesh (mind and emotions.) .

- Similarly, do we validate and honor individuals who share from their hearts, by letting the Spirit guide us in restating both the facts and feelings that were shared? Sharing one's heart is risky and needs to be embraced and honored. The Spirit does this. Christians who are in the flesh generally do not, as they jump into sharing their own experiences, instead of validating the speaker.

- In meaningful discussions, do we share every thought that comes to us, or do we first check with the Spirit?
- Do we always present ourself as an authority who has God's answer?

Embrace the Spirit's revelation of Gal 2:20, "I have been crucified with Christ; it is no longer I who live, but Christ lives in me; and the life which I know lives in the flesh I live by faith in the Son of God, who loved me and gave Himself for me." Only then can we walk in the Spirit.

No Christian is perfect in this walk. All slip into the flesh. When our hearts are right, we permit God to draw us back and lead us onward and upward. We are to focus not on our own failures but on Him and His wonderful forgiveness, transformation, and love.

Only Our Spiritual Walk Pleases God

Consider Paul's teaching. "Walk in the Spirit, and you shall not fulfill the lust of the flesh. For the flesh lusts against the Spirit and the Spirit against the flesh; and *these are contrary to one another, so that you do not do the things you wish*." Christians who are not walking in the Spirit are in a carnal state. Their flesh is in charge, whether this is for a few minutes or an extended period. The actions and works of the flesh never honor or please God, because the flesh and the Spirit "are contrary to one another." *Acts done in the flesh by Christians who claim they are the works of Christ are detrimental to God's kingdom and are stumbling blocks for both believers and non-believers.*

If We Live in the Spirit, Let Us Also Walk in the Spirit

Don't Be Governed by Good Intentions; Follow the Spirit

As Christians, we are to always listen to the Holy Spirit and follow His commands. He knows what He is working on in each situation, and He knows what, if any, role He has for us. We are not to rush in and do or pray what we "think" our Father would want, instead of waiting on the Spirit for His direction. When we act on our own, we are probably operating in the flesh and may be in opposition to the will of God. When we do *nice* Christian things without confirming with the Spirit, we may be out of His will. When we are not operating in the Spirit, we will hurt others, as we claim to be doing what Christ would do.

Abiding in Christ

JOHN 15:1-11

4 Abide in Me and I in you. As the branch cannot bear fruit of itself, unless it abides in the vine, neither can you, unless you abide in Me.

5 I am the vine, you are the branches. He who abides in me, and I in him, bears much fruit; for without me, you can do nothing.

9 As the Father loved Me, I also have loved you; abide in my love.

These verses provide a visual and powerful analogy demonstrating the incredible truth that living in Christ and walking in the Spirit is abiding in Christ. We are a part of Him, and He is a part of us. When we are surrendered to His Spirit, His very life and power flow through us. We never stand alone or depend on our own strength and understanding. He is the source of our very life-flow and of the fruit that *He produces* in and through us. We are blessed beyond our understanding as we abide in Him through this incredible living relationship. It is to be our "all the time" connection. This is life that is like no other. Why accept anything less?

Responding to the Spirit's Voice

The more I learn to listen to the Spirit, the more often I am made aware that my flesh is taking control. At first this felt defeating. I had thought I was walking closer to Him and His will. Even now, I get frustrated as I see how often I take charge. In the past, I unknowingly marched on in my own power, thinking that I was serving Him. Now I am gratefully humble as He lovingly calls me back to Him through confession, repentance, surrender, faith, and filling. This life is a journey of sanctification, not a once-and-done answer to prayer.

God's design for a life of listening and obedience to the Spirit is not to be some "religious" requirement that you and I seek to follow. That would be unbelievably futile. It is a natural result of living, obeying, and abiding in oneness with the Spirit.

This Life Is Natural but Not Easy

As we stated, remaining filled with the Spirit and walking in the Spirit both require our intentionality and will. When I am tired, feeling down, or get too engaged in what "I" am doing, I easily slide into the position of letting my flesh be in charge. Then my anger, impatience, frustration, flesh-excitement, or lack of faith will raise their ugly heads. *At these times, the Spirit always gives* me the awareness that *I need to turn back to Him. There is always that "millisecond" when I can say "Yes" to Him and His authority or choose my own flesh and therefore sin.* Many times, I listen, and He stays in charge. Other times, I do not, and I take over and sin. It is always heartbreaking to disappoint and grieve the Trinity in these ways that are, *in reality, intentional sins.* It is also very humbling. Afterwards, I confess my intentional sin, repent, receive forgiveness and filling, and know that He embraces me fully. I start again, under His authority.

Before I wrote this last paragraph, I chose to sin. I ignored His voice and took over from the Holy Spirit. Although I was ashamed by my failure, especially while I was asking the Spirit to write this section, I returned to Him for forgiveness, placed my flesh on the cross, and asked for His filling. I received it and then knew that He had not only provided forgiveness but had also embraced writing His thoughts through me once again. I am constantly amazed at the total forgiveness and embracing love of our Father.

Analogy: Walking in the Spirit
Pride vs. Humility: Tools in the Hands of the Creator—The Gardener of Life

We repeat the shortened analogy of living as beloved tools in the Master Gardener's hands. We may be shovels, rakes, hoes, plows, or discs, but He designed us. He built us. He is also the one who designed and planned the gardens where He utilizes us. When we are not held in His hands, we can do nothing. As His special and loved tools, we have choices regarding how we look at life.

- Some tools choose to say, "Look at me. I'm the most important. I plowed the garden, and, without me, the rest of your efforts would be in vain. I did this!" Pride has robbed these tools of their kingdom usefulness.

- Wiser tools will say, "The Gardener made me. He designed the garden, and He picked me up, along with the rest of you, and utilized all of us to accomplish His plan, by the strength and skill of His own hands. Finally, He lovingly cleaned and sharpened us as He prepared us for His next work. He did everything. I am so humbled that He created and included me, along with all of you." Love, humility, surrender, and obedience bring these tools true joy and usefulness in the hands of the Gardener.

Identifying the Works of the Spirit or of the Flesh in Our Lives

Paul clearly set up the distinction between works of the flesh and works of the Spirit.

- Works of the flesh: adultery, fornication, uncleanness, lewdness, idolatry, sorcery, hatred, contentions, jealousies, outbursts of wrath, selfish ambitions, dissensions, heresies, envy, murders, drunkenness, revelries, and the like

- Fruit of the Spirit: love, joy, peace, longsuffering (patience), kindness, goodness, faithfulness, gentleness, self-control

I had always thought I was to fight in my own power against the works of the flesh, to try my best to live like Christ, and to display the fruit of the Spirit by *acts of willpower*. I misunderstood and thought I was to defeat my sins. *What a lie of the enemy and a life of frustration.* As I grew in Christ, the Spirit revealed that I was not to fight but to stand on His truths and enjoy experiencing Christ and His victories in me. He expresses the fruit of the Spirit through us. They never result from the efforts of our flesh. We create only powerless imitations.

Where Are You in This Wonderful Journey?

This is an important time to stop and ask the Holy Spirit what He wants you to learn and do. Please do not rush your time with Him. Some starter thoughts are:

- What parts of this chapter do you agree with, question, or reject? Why? Is it hard for you to believe and trust the scriptures if you or your church have not experienced them?

- If your experiences are not found in and supported by scripture, what do you choose to believe?

- Do you have scripture verses to support your beliefs in, or rejection of, conclusions in this chapter? Are your Bible references single verses that are interpreted in ways that align with your desired conclusions, or are your interpretations supported by the full context and body of scripture, including Christ's life?

- Chapters 12 through 15 are closely connected, as they lead to the ultimate life of "Walking in the Spirit." Ask God for His complete revelation of their truths and interdependence.

- What is the Holy Spirit communicating to you about your walk with Him?
- What is the enemy saying?
- What transformations are you and the Spirit going to pursue?

CHAPTER 16

THE FRUIT OF THE SPIRIT AND THE GIFTS OF THE SPIRIT

How will our lives be different as we walk in the Spirit and experience His life flowing in and through us? We will demonstrate the strengths and attributes of Christ in ever-increasing ways as He transforms us into His image. His character will express itself through us as the Fruit of the Spirit. He will accomplish His will and our missions by releasing His Gifts of the Spirit. We will become more of Him and less of our old natures as we enjoy the wonder of becoming His masterpieces.

This chapter is presented in three sections: The Fruit of the Spirit; The Gifts of the Spirit; and Divisions within the Church.

The Fruit of the Spirit

GAL 5:22-23

But the fruit of the Spirit is love, joy, peace, patience, kindness, goodness, faithfulness, gentleness, self-control. Against such there is no law.

GAL 5:19-21

Now the works of the flesh are evident, which are: adultery, fornication, uncleanness, lewdness, idolatry, sorcery, hatred, contentions, jealousies, outburst of wrath, selfish ambitions, dissensions, heresies, envy, murders, drunkenness, revelries, and the like;

At all times, Christ's life demonstrated each of the Fruits of the Spirit. We are to release His Spirit to do the same in and through our lives, as He expresses Himself as both the Lion of Judah and the Lamb of God. We are not to limit or copy Him. Acting "like" Him in our flesh does not result in His Fruit. Walk intimately with Him in His Spirit and experience His life as He develops His Fruits in us and expresses them through us. He is to be their source, not our mind, will, or emotions, as He transforms us from the inside, and the Fruit of the Spirit becomes His expression of life through us.

Many in the Church seek to limit acceptable "Christian behavior" to expressions evidenced by how *they view* Christ as the Lamb of God, while they exclude actions of the Lion of Judah. Permit the fullness of Christ's character to live in and through you.

Humans can and do demonstrate the behaviors that seem like the fruit of the Spirit, even if they are not Christ-followers. God may have wired them to naturally exhibit some of these characteristics. They may generally be joyful, patient, gentle, or loving, without having any relationship with Christ. These expressions, as nice as they are, emanate from their flesh and are not Fruit of the Spirit. They do not glorify God, because they do not arise from His Spirit. Christians who are walking in the flesh may also display characteristics of whatever fruit is wired in them, without these characteristics being of the Spirit. They are then often praised for being wonderful "Christians," just because they attend church and display many of these characteristics, even though they are in the flesh. We are not to judge people, but we are to be discerning. The church is damaging individuals' walks with Christ when it praises them for actions of their flesh.

Past hurts and sinful lifestyles will need to be placed fully under God's healing power, love, and forgiveness. One way to determine areas of life and past hurts that are unhealed is to write down each fruit. To the side, document each sin of the flesh and each emotion/action that are active in your life but are opposites of the fruit. Evaluate the opposites to see which are dominant in you. Take each of these to God for revelation, surrender, and direction for His journey of healing and replacing them with Christ's characteristics. Some of this healing will take extensive time, prayer, trust, and professional Christian assistance.

The Gifts of the Spirit

ROM 12:6-8 (NIV)

We have different gifts, according to the grace given to each of us. If your gift is prophesying, then prophesy in accordance with your faith; if it is serving, then serve; if it is teaching, then teach; if it is to encourage (exhort), then give encouragement; if it is giving, then give generously; if it is to lead, do it diligently; if it is to show mercy, do it cheerfully.

1 COR 12:7-11

But the manifestation of the Spirit is given to each one for the profit of all:

for to one is given the word of wisdom through the Spirit, to another the word of knowledge through the Spirit, to another faith

> *by the same Spirit, to another the gifts of healings by the same Spirit, to another the working of miracles, to another prophecy, to another discerning of spirits, to another different kinds of tongues, to another the interpretation of tongues. But the same Spirit works in all these things, distributing to each one individually as He wills.*

> **EPH 4:11-12**
> *And He Himself gave some to be apostles, some prophets, some evangelists, and some pastors and teachers, for the equipping of the saints for the work of ministry, for the edifying of the body of Christ*

Spiritual gifts are given by the Spirit for the accomplishment of God's purpose in the world and for the edification and unification of His church. *It is critical to remember that they belong to God. They bring glory to Him and accomplish His purposes only when they are executed in the power of the Holy Spirit.* Christians who attempt to "own" them and exercise them in their flesh's power are destructive to God's kingdom purposes and bring dishonor to Christ.

I grew up in churches that did not provide teaching and mentoring regarding spiritual gifts. I thought some of them (specifically word of wisdom, word of knowledge, and faith) were simply strong natural gifts that Christians could utilize for the purposes of God. I didn't understand many of the rest but believed that "especially gifted Christians" might be able to demonstrate these. Later, God taught me that *there is an absolute distinction between spiritual gifts and natural gifts in all areas. His gifts are available to all Christians.*

Each Christian has at least one predominant spiritual gift. *However, the Holy Spirit can, and at His discretion does, operate in all of His gifts through all obedient, Spirit-filled Christians.* He is not limited in what He can do through a surrendered believer. We are *not to block any of His expression* of these gifts through us, though many of us do so all the time. We are to *permit Him to operate freely in His full identity through us.*

The Source and Power Behind Spiritual Gifts

This analogy, shared earlier, portrays how God utilizes spiritual gifts through His children. We portrayed Christians as tools in the hands of God, who is preparing one of His gardens. One Christian is a rake; another is a shovel, and so on. In our Master's hands, each has an important role in digging up, breaking up, and leveling the garden in preparation for planting. When the job is finished, the Master stands, resting on His tools. He admires the finished work with satisfaction, as a labor of love. He greatly values the tools and the roles that they played, but they did not do the work. He designed and fashioned them and was the source of the vision, planning, energy, and skill that resulted in their use to make the garden. Finally, He lovingly cleans, sharpens, and improves each tool so that they are prepared for the next mission.

Confused and pride-filled tools might be heard saying:

+ I did this.

+ I was the most important.

+ My gifts are superior, and I should get more recognition.

+ Yes, the Master was holding me, but He couldn't have done it without me.

Tools with healthy identities would be heard saying:

+ Isn't it amazing how the Master created us and used us all to accomplish His will?

+ He is always lovingly sharpening, cleaning, and improving us for His next work.

+ Although it is His plan, energy, and power, He always blesses us by permitting us to be important parts of His kingdom work.

+ Aren't we blessed to belong to Him, to be deeply loved, and to be held in His hands?

+ Without Him, we can do nothing.

The second set of thoughts represent the truth for Christians. Without the Holy Spirit, we are like garden tools lying rusting on the ground or hanging uselessly in a shed. Yes, we are different from inanimate tools in that we can initiate action and not wait for our Master, but when we do, we are living in the foolishness of operating in the flesh instead of the Spirit, and we do not glorify our Father.

Definitions: Spiritual Gifts

(The list from Rom 12:6-8)

+ Prophecy: the inspired declaration of divine will and purpose; an inspired utterance of a prophet; a declaration of something to come.

+ Prophesy: to utter by divine inspiration; to give instruction in religious matters; to make a prediction)

- Serving: to perform services for; to furnish or supply something needed or required. (Many people who are not Christ-followers are wonderful at serving. There is, however, a great difference between one, Christian or not, who serves out of their flesh and the Christian who serves in the power of the Spirit.)

- Teaching: to cause to know a subject; to cause to know how and/or to be accustomed to; to guide; to impart knowledge; to instruct by precept, example, or experience.

- Exhortation: to excite or encourage; to incite by argument or advice; to give warnings or advice;

- Giving: to put into the possession of another for their use; to utilize what you have for the benefit of others.

- Leadership: providing authority or influence for the benefit of all; one who exercises responsible authority over some group or organization.

- Mercy: compassion or forbearance shown to another; relief of distress; compassion shown to victims.

The list from 1 Cor 12:7-11

- Word of Wisdom: God's wisdom that is revealed through the Spirit and reflects the truths of the Bible to provide insight, revelation, and understanding.

- Word of Knowledge: Spirit-given information about a subject, a person, or a situation that could not have been known by the recipient. (This one really shocked me.

I grew up believing that this portion of the verse referred to individuals who had the ability to accumulate and process worldly knowledge.)

+ Faith: Spirit-given absolute conviction, trust, and confidence that a word of God is true, or a work of God is going to happen.

+ True Christian faith is a gift of the Spirit. Eph 2:8, "For by grace you have been saved by faith. And that not of yourselves: it is the gift of God," (This is a transformational truth that, although initially it is hard to understand, is life-giving and powerful. It directly contradicts the false teaching that an individual can stand on human faith that is generated by their own will and desires, and therefore move the hand of God. They are responsible for being intentional about standing on God's truth in His faith. Faith is not passive.)

+ Healings: The supernatural restoring to health of mind, body, and spirit for the glory of God.

+ Working of miracles, signs, and wonders: God's demonstration of His supernatural powers, in order to reveal Himself and His Son, and to transform lives. These include any and all types of God's representation of Himself in supernatural power. The Bible does not provide a specific list. Luke 10:1-24 and John 14:12, among others, reveal that these gifts are available at the discretion of the Holy Spirit to all who believe in Christ. Some believe that only the apostles exercised these gifts. I find no evidence in the Bible to support this assertion that, the Holy Spirit, who lives within believers, has limited Himself from expressing these gifts as and when He desires through believers who are open to His will and lordship. The Bible is clear that false Christs and false prophets shall also appear, as the devil seeks to mislead through "all power and signs and lying wonders." (2 Thess 2:9; Rev 16:14; Mark 13:22)

- Discerning spirits: The ability to recognize what demonic spirits are operating in any given situation. The Holy Spirit then directs the believer in how they are to proceed in His authority and power.

- Tongues: Speaking to God in a heavenly language that is generated by the Holy Spirit. Speaking in an earthly language that is unknown to the speaker but is understood by some within hearing.

- Interpretation of tongues: The Spirit's translation of a heavenly tongue into common language, through a Christian.

Spiritual-Gift Assessments

Spiritual-gift assessments help identify the gifts God has wired most strongly in us. As He utilizes us in our missions, it is helpful to recognize both the strengths and potential development areas that are associated with our predominant gifts. It is also helpful to recognize and honor the gifts of others.

Remember that, although the Spirit has given each of us one or more predominant spiritual gifts, we are not to limit Him to these. He desires to live in and through us and therefore utilize the full expression of each of the gifts through us as He desires. We are responsible for operating under His control and not blocking Him. He lives within us. He is our source. He embodies all of the gifts.

Your church or the ministries that you affiliate with may have a preferred gift assessment; if so, please utilize it. If not, there are many free and printable assessments online. Here is one option: gifttest.org/survey.

Reminders for Walking in Spiritual Gifts

It is easy to misuse the gifts God has given by taking them out of His hands and seeking to utilize them through our flesh. We may do this innocently through excitement. We are to first confirm that the specifics of the gift are from God. Then, we wait for Him to reveal how He will proceed.

Examples:
Word of Wisdom, Word of Knowledge

When the Holy Spirit provides His Word of Wisdom or Knowledge, we are not to rush in and share that information with the individual or group before checking with God. What does He desire to do through us? There are four normal approaches.

- Don't say anything. Support them in prayer and understanding.

- State the Word of Wisdom or Knowledge, and ask them if this means anything to them. If it does, help them process through this with the Spirit. Avoid accusations. Ask.

- Tell them exactly what you heard the Spirit express. Don't apologize or downplay what you heard. Many individuals are always looking for a reason to ignore the Spirit's input. If you provide any reason, they will immediately discount God's gift. Share with His love and humble confidence, and help them process with Him.
- Don't do anything. The Spirit has given this to demonstrate that He is working in you, so you permit Him to develop these gifts and trust your walk to Him.

Faith

EPH 2:8-9

For by grace you have been saved through faith, and that not of yourselves; it is the gift of God, not of works lest anyone should boast.

This is a reminder from Chapter 7. Avoid the intentional or unintentional accusation that the believer did not receive their prayer request because their faith, or the faith of those praying, was not good enough. Faith is a gift of God. We stand on our faith in Him, not on faith in our faith. No amount of faith that is derived from one's efforts of the soul (mind, will, and emotions) can pretend to represent the faith of the Bible that is provided by the Spirit.

Know Whether We Are Operating in the Spirit or in the Flesh

Many churches and their members do not recognize the difference between walking in the Spirit and operating in the flesh. They often embrace Christians who are walking in the flesh as heartily as they welcome those who are walking in the Spirit. This seriously impedes the growth of individuals and the work of the kingdom of God through His fruit and gifts. Christians who do not know the difference react to their flesh (their mind, will, and emotions) as though these were the Holy Spirit and never stop to listen to the Spirit. Decisions and actions then result from worldly knowledge, wisdom, or feelings instead of interacting with the Spirit. We honor and serve Christ only as we permit Him to be in charge.

Division in Mankind's Church Over Spiritual Gifts

There are significant divisions within and among Christian churches regarding Spiritual Gifts. We highlight a few, not expecting to bring resolution but to direct our attention to God's word. Each of us is to find our answers through study and the Spirit's revelation of God's word, as we evaluate doctrines of mankind.

We believe all Spiritual Gifts are biblically accurate manifestations of the Holy Spirit and are all valid in this Church age. Accordingly, they must follow scripture. We are not to set aside Bible truths in order to explain away what we do not understand or to create doctrines that support our experiences and tribal beliefs. Neither are we to elevate and emphasize certain spiritual gifts in manners that displace our focus on Christ or are evidenced without the order that is insisted on by the Holy Spirit. We also caution that the enemy is a master at attempting to copy and emulate God's blessings. Satan has led some astray with his counterfeits of God's spiritual gifts. Finally, a few individuals knowingly counterfeit these gifts for personal gain while they are walking in the flesh. Study the Bible and listen to the Spirit at all times—and avoid human error. We are not to be distracted from the reality of spiritual gifts by the divisiveness that humans have created.

The Gifts of Tongues and Interpretation of Tongues

Some of the strongest disagreements within the Church concern these gifts. They range from denominations that believe tongues are not of this Church age and are the work of the devil to others who declare the gift of tongues is the "turning point" on which a powerful spiritual life must be based. Some teach that believers who do not express this gift cannot be filled with and walking in the Spirit.

We must always check scripture as we ask, "When did the Father give humans the right to build doctrine on their personal experience, or on a few scripture passages, instead of on His entire, unchanging Word? When did He change the Bible with regard to spiritual gifts?"

Spirit-filled Christians are not to seek the approval of mankind. They are to seek only God's biblical revelation and His approval, as they honor the counsel of others but live solely for Christ.

Is it possible that tongues are both valid and a gift that is not for all? Let us compare the work of the Spirit through three effective servants of Christ. The identities of the first and third individuals have been withheld for personal or security reasons.

The first has conducted evangelical crusades for decades in some of the toughest portions of the world (including Africa, India, and South America.) Muslims and Hindus make up a significant portion of his audiences. Through this ministry, God has drawn an average of more than one million individuals annually to choose salvation through Christ in response to the Spirit's call. This Ministry organizes follow-up resources to teach and mentor individuals in how to live and grow in Christ under incredibly difficult circumstances. The Holy Spirit expresses Himself through many signs and wonders at each crusade, including miraculous healings of physically and spiritually broken lives. The gift of tongues is given to many. The Spirit operates in all spiritual gifts through this ministry, including tongues. However, the absolute focus of this evangelist's life, preaching, and teaching is Jesus Christ, the same yesterday, today, and forever. He states that his role is to introduce people to Jesus Christ. Jesus does the rest! He acknowledges and praises Christ as the source of all that He does in the lives of millions. If, as some insist, the source of anyone's (this evangelist's) gift of tongues is the devil, they must also conclude that the devil is the source of this ministry's God-provided salvations, healings, and transformations. The Bible says "No" to this type of thinking. Jesus was accused of having demons operate through Him and responded with the truth that a house divided against itself cannot stand (Mark 3:25.) He also taught that denying the works of the Holy Spirit is a great sin. Jesus' scriptural truth is also true for this ministry. This humble and gifted man of God operates in the Spirit of God, for the glory of God, and through the Spirit's power. He takes no credit for anything and lifts up Christ at all times. Because of tongues and miracles, some denominations and individuals teach a doctrine that concludes this servant does not walk in the Spirit, and they are in tragic error.

The second evangelist is Billy Graham. If what I have read is correct, Billy Graham did not embrace the gift of tongues.

The Fruit of the Spirit and the Gifts of the Spirit

The Lord brought millions to Himself through His call on Billy Graham. Some doctrines would state that Dr. Graham was not filled or baptized with the Spirit, as he did not have or embrace the gift of tongues. This would be a tragic error and denial of the Spirit. Would Dr. Graham have been used so mightily for the kingdom without the power of the Holy Spirit working in and through him? If he were not filled with the Spirit and under the Spirit's control (much of the time as he journeyed), would his ministry have borne the fruit of the Spirit so consistently to the glory of God? Works of the flesh cannot glorify God. Is there any other realistic conclusion than that it was the Spirit that indwelt, empowered, and lived through him to result in the salvation and spiritual growth of millions?

Our final example involves a gifted pastor who sought the gift of tongues but was not granted it. Throughout his life, God worked through him to reach hundreds of lives for Christ and to steward them in walking in Christ. Through him, numbers of additional evangelicals entered the ministry, and no doubt reached many hundreds more for salvation and fruitful lives in Christ. He lifted up and praised Jesus as the source of all that the Spirit of God accomplished through him. The doctrines that would deny the work of the Spirit and the power of the Spirit living in and through this servant of God would be incorrect and accountable to God for denying the work of the Spirit.

Although I have this gift, God uses it at His discretion, not at mine, and I am blessed when He does. However, He has not made it a cornerstone of my Christianity. Learning to Walk in the Spirit is God's cornerstone in my life. I respect the many wonderful and effective Christians who stand on the gift of tongues as a centrally important blessing from the Spirit. I also respect those powerful individuals who serve in the Spirit without evidencing this gift. Conversely, whenever I observe any "spiritual" activity, such as tongues, being expressed without biblically required order in the assembly, I believe that its source is probably not of God.

Lack of Order in the Church
The Holy Spirit Works Within the Will of Christians:
The Devil Seeks to Control

1 COR 14:26, 32, 33

How is it then, brethren? Whenever you come together, each of you has a psalm, has a teaching, has a tongue, has a revelation, has an interpretation. Let all things be done for edification.

And the spirits of the prophets are subject to the prophets

For God is not the author of confusion but of peace, as in all the churches of the saints.

Individuals who operate under the control of the Holy Spirit are always able to take control of their actions. Why? Because "the spirits of the prophets are subject to prophets." In other words, *the Spirit will never override a human's free will.* As an example, the Bible instructs that, if one prophetic word is being given, and God brings a second word to another, the first is to stop. They are fully able to do so. At any time, a Christian has the freedom to either stop what the Spirit is doing in them or, unfortunately, block any movement the Spirit desires to express through them. Conversely, Satan (and all who follow him) seeks to gain ever-increasing levels of control over individuals and situations. When Satan has control of an individual, they do not have the ability to discontinue his actions through them, without the intervention of God.

When individuals claim to be operating in the Spirit but are "unable to stop themselves," they are deluded by the enemy and are operating under his authority. Consider this example regarding an activity that some call a gift of the Spirit, though it is not listed in the Bible. This is the "supposed" gift of laughing in the Spirit. Some believe that the joy of the Spirit becomes so wonderful that an individual experiences incredible laughter. In one instance, individuals who were laughing uncontrollably had to be removed from the service. They were out of control and disrupting God's service. Scripturally, this is an undeniable indication that the actions were, at best, of the flesh and, at worst, of the devil. Those who say they cannot block or stop the expression of the Holy Spirit through them, are operating in deception and are not honoring God or the Spirit.

Signs and Wonders

Disagreements, denials, and excesses exist around the gifts of Healings, Working of Miracles, and Prophecy. Man's doctrines, not God's, range from the "Name It and Claim It" churches to those that stand firmly on "Not of This Age" thinking. How sad that humans have decided they can define doctrine based on their experiences and desires instead of on the word of God. Individuals who lead people away from the truth of the Bible hold great responsibility before God, no matter how well intended their motives.

How many individuals who deny spiritual gifts such as miracles, signs, and wonders have traveled the world with an open mind to seek God and His truths with all their heart? Have they taken the risk of spending meaningful God-led time with believers who experience God's power in biblical forms they deny?

We are each responsible for seeking out the truth through our own Bible study and following the Spirit's guidance, even if this takes us to many parts of the world or to diverse church cultures in our own country. We are responsible if we accept any teaching (including mine) that we do not validate through the Bible and time with the Lord and His Spirit.

The American Gospel

The American gospel is not God's inerrant interpretation of His gospel. It is simply a perspective that has morphed out of a unique and positive culture of self-reliance and defining success through position, power, possessions, and wealth. It embraces errant beliefs like, "Obedient and faithful Christians will never go wanting financially. All they have to do to be blessed with good jobs, health, and material things is to follow Christ and believe." It increasingly supports the self-deceived notion that, "We can redefine the meaning of the Bible due to our knowledge and sophistication."

Identifing Pervasive Roots of Division Within the Church

Consider the following roots of division and deception in mankind's imitation of God's Church.

First Root
Deception: The Bible is not the inerrant word of God.
This opportunity was discussed in Chapter 4.

Second Root:
Deception: "My experience determines what I will believe!"
Individuals, organizations, and denominations determine that their experiences are the ultimate test of truth and doctrine. Thus, if we have "experienced" something, it is truth. If we have not, then it is not truth or is not for this Church Age. This is deceptive thinking!

Experience may play a validating role, but it must never override the scriptures. God will not be manipulated by selfish prayers that insist He give us a spiritual gift or answer our prayers according to our desires in order to prove Himself or validate a spiritual gift. Also, Satan will distractively emulate gifts of God in his attempt to deceive many. Please consider the following examples.

Example:

This is the story of a committed Christian woman who would not tolerate anyone who spoke in tongues. She was unrelenting in pursuing this goal, even to the point of deeply hurting individuals through her leadership positions. When asked why she was so certain that tongues were not a gift for this age, her response was, "I wanted to know whether this gift was active or not, so I said to the Lord, 'If this is a real gift, then give it to me.' He did not, so I know that it is not real!" As far as she was concerned, her experience trumped all of scripture. She did not understand that God answers prayers in a manner that is determined by His sovereign will. He is not manipulated when we set conditions that He "must meet" in order to prove His word or His character.

Example:

Individuals and churches develop their own private beliefs that provide comfort about either themselves or loved ones who are not saved. They reject the biblical requirement of salvation through Christ and replace it with something that makes them comfortable. They seek spiritual-sounding worldly perspectives that permit them to believe that the unsaved individual, normally a "good" person in their eyes, will be with them in eternity. Unfortunately, there is no shortage of churches and organizations that call themselves "Christian" who both accept and encourage non-biblical beliefs that comfort their attendees.

Example:
Apostles—Either Believing That Apostles Are Not of This Age or Identifying Leaders as Apostles without Biblical Criteria.

This example involves the consideration of whether the position of apostle is of this age. There are excesses on both sides. Many, including my wife and I, are/were taught that the office of Apostle is not for this church age, and only applied to the first apostles, including Paul. Criteria that are frequently associated with receiving this designation are that the individual personally walked with Christ, and their ministry was accompanied by signs and wonders. We believe both of those qualifiers but have since met at least one individual who qualifies. Our subsequent biblical study validated his position as an apostle. We are reasonably certain that there are a few others (not many) like him among the billions of Christians on this planet. He is an individual through whom the Lord has transformed a country for Christ and has performed many miracles, including raising individuals from the dead. This man is a channel for Christ's immense power and yet is exceedingly humble. He does not claim titles or present himself as an apostle. He simply obeys Christ and walks in all of the truths and power of the Bible. I am not asking you to embrace this, but I'm suggesting that you ask the Lord to teach you His truths through the Bible, instead of blindly following textbook or church doctrine that negates the Bible by honoring human experience, philosophy, and questionable theology above it.

Sadly, there are many who carelessly claim the title of apostle. My wife and I are deeply saddened when we meet Christians who are self-described apostles, yet do not demonstrate biblical criteria. Some even place this on their business cards because they oversee (administrate) some network that impresses them or others. They are using a different metric than what we believe is biblical. However, we leave the judging to our Lord and choose to fellowship with others.

Third Root
Deception: Making Doctrines from Individual Ministries
This root is illustrated by the example of a pastor who unquestionably had an extraordinary gift of healing. The Spirit used it powerfully throughout his life.

With sincere intentions, he became convinced that what the Spirit had made real in his life was available in the same expression through every church and believer. He created a Bible School and a church network that was strongly biblically based but included a "doctrine" reflecting his personal experiences with this gift. Many in the organization seemed to teach that, if a Christian could not be healed or heal others in the same way this Pastor was gifted, the reason reflected a weakness in their personal "faith." (As we have discussed, we believe it is destructive and unbiblical to lay this false guilt on believers.) Healings occurred, as they do at God's discretion in all Bible-believing churches, but few experienced the results the Lord had extended through this man.

We are not to take our personal experiences and missions in God, no matter how valid, and attempt to make them into doctrine. We must hold to biblical doctrines.

Fourth Root
Deception: Christians Who Believe What They Are Taught, Without Studying the Bible
This is really the easiest to deal with logically but one of the hardest areas to break. It especially happens to individuals who have stayed within one or two denominations or Christian organizations all of their lives. They generally have not been directly exposed to how differently and biblically the Lord works in various areas of the world. They may read, but they do not go and see or interact in depth with those who do. There are two concepts that are important in responding to this mindset.

The first is promoted by all excellent Bible teachers, preachers, and leaders. Each of them will say, "I am teaching you what I believe, but don't take my word for it or some theologian's study of it. Get into the word of God, and test this out for yourself through the revelation of His Spirit. Be sure that the teaching stands under the scrutiny of study in both the Old and New Testaments." Individuals who do not explore the accuracy of the studies of their pastors and teachers, or the books they read, are prone to great error. So are individuals who ignore the words of pastors and teachers.

The second is to encourage all Christians to expand their world. Teach them to ask the Lord what He has for them to see and do and to be sure they accept His invitations to stretch themselves. Consider traveling to Africa, India, or South America with an evangelist whom God uses mightily. Spend time with Spirit-filled Christians from other "tribes." Take mission trips to work with solid ministries that approach things differently than your comfort zone. God will lead if you ask.

The Lord placed my wife and me in different denominations, as He moved us around the eastern portion of the United States. This proved to be a great blessing. In each location, we asked Him, "Which church do you want our family to attend?" as we followed criteria that He presented. We ended up in four different denominations of Protestantism and in two different non-denominational churches. Our experiences were invaluable. In each church, the core Christian beliefs were consistent. However, we learned that there were both little and big differences, not only between denominations but also within each denomination. These "little" things were very important to them and got a lot of attention, sometimes to the point of driving wedges.

The two of us had grown up with basically the same beliefs on many of these issues. As He expanded our horizons, we were (are) led by God, forced by experiences, to study both the Bible and the teachings of respected individuals. We also explored how our God was touching lives in cultures other than the United States. We found that there was indeed a U.S. "gospel" that included "beliefs" that wouldn't stand inspection through Bible study and God's validation of His truths as they were expressed by Him in other areas of the world.

In comparison, we know individuals who move throughout the country and feel compelled to stay in the same denomination or in the same non-denominational churches. If they are asking God, "Where do You want to utilize us?" and are following His leadership, fantastic. If they are determining that their denomination is the only one with the "Truth!" and are dogmatically staying in that denomination without asking God, one must wonder whether they are led by the Spirit or the flesh. Anyone who is not Spirit-led in the paths they choose is taking great risks.

Making Our Decision about Spiritual Fruit and Gifts
Embrace the Works of God's Spirit—Be Free to Live

Do you desire to live as the masterpiece God created? God has specific kingdom missions for you that are equal in importance to every other Christian's. Consider the example above, where the Lord has utilized one 21st-century Christian to build a ministry thru which God has brought significant kingdom-of-God changes into an entire country. His missions and roles for you are just as important to His kingdom plans.

God's Plan for Your Life Includes His Power

The power of God is real, and it is there for His use in and through *your life*. It is there in the Fruit of the Spirit. It is there in the Gifts of the Spirit. It is there as He calls you to kingdom missions and accomplishes them through you. Only He can determine what His power will accomplish through you. What will you gain by denying the spiritual gifts and the calling that God has for you? What do you gain by rejecting His command to walk in the spirit? Only those who walk in the Spirit and His power receive all God has for them.

Stay the Course. Don't Let Divisions and Divisiveness Hinder God's Design

COL 2:8 (AS IT IMPACTS THE CHURCH)
Beware lest anyone cheat you through philosophy and empty deceit, according to the tradition of men, according to the basic principles of the world, and not according to Christ.

The above scripture is always helpful to me when I face the huge dichotomy between the wisdom of God and the pervasive thinking of the secular, "sophisticated" world and "church." Christians are seduced into feeling they need to look "enlightened" to the world. They forget that the wisdom we are to compare ourselves to is God's. Defining wisdom, sophistication, and enlightenment according to the shifting and anchorless mores of secular society, including broken churches, has always been a favorite deception of the devil.

Application
How Are You Going to Live in the Fruit and Gifts of the Spirit?

The Fruit of the Spirit and your Spiritual Gifts are one portion of the unique masterpiece that you are as God's creation. Embrace them and the Spirit, and let Him bring life and light through you to the world!

- Is your view of Christ's use of Spiritual Gifts in His Church during this church age biblical and personally studied from a global perspective? Or are you embracing the beliefs of some local gospel, secularly compromised church or denomination, or your own experience?

- Are you Spirit-led or one who walks in the flesh?

- Do you wish to explore the Bible for God's doctrines, or are you uncomfortable questioning your own beliefs and those of your family, culture, or church?

- Are you willing to have God confirm or redefine your view of Bible truth by asking Him to take you out of your safety zone and provide additional revelation by actually walking with individuals whose lives yield great fruit for Christ's glory?

- God cannot be put into a box by individuals or denominations. Neither can He be described outside of what He has revealed Himself to be in the Bible. The Bible trumps all experience or lack of experience in spiritual matters.

CHAPTER 17

THE SPIRITUAL REALM AND SPIRITUAL WARFARE

EPH 6:12
For we do not wrestle against flesh and blood, but against principalities, against powers, against rulers of the darkness of this age, against spiritual forces of wickedness in heavenly places.

Do we understand how, as maturing Christians, we are to embrace the Spirit's revelations regarding the reality of the spirit realm, the ever-present dynamic of spiritual warfare, and our active roles in it? As God's soldiers, we are called to move from training to battle. (There are no peacetime assignments in spiritual warfare.) Our eyes are to be opened, and we are to view life and purpose from God's expanded perspective. Walking in His Spirit takes on deeper meaning as He accomplishes ever-expanding dimensions of Christian life in and through us. Are you willing to live in these realities as a normal part of Christian life?

The Spiritual Realm

Scripture is filled with the reality and even the preeminence of the spirit realm. We are to embrace this truth and learn to deal first in the spiritual realm before we engage the natural. It is not some "Oh-by-the-way" parallel realm, as many consider it. God teaches us what we are to know about this realm (including about the enemy) according to His designs for our missions and our journeys. We are not to be naive and innocent, deny its reality, or feel pressured to operate in any manner other than God's unique missions for our masterpiece lives. Neither are we to make Satan's realm or even God's angels our focus. Many have been deceived into misrepresenting God by doing both. Consider these biblical truths.

Not Against Flesh and Blood but Spiritual Forces of Wickedness

EPH 6:10-12

Finally, my brethren, be strong in the Lord and in the power of His might . . . that you may be able to stand against the wiles of the devil. For we do not wrestle against flesh and blood, but against principalities, against powers, against the rulers of darkness of this age, against spiritual hosts of wickedness in the heavenly places.

What is God's truth? We wrestle against spiritual hosts of wickedness in the heavenly realms, not flesh and blood. When we view individuals and earthly organizations as our enemies, we have been deceived. Their broken activities begin in the spirit realm. We are to permit the Spirit to reveal what God is doing in the spirit realm and then pray and engage as He directs. We are not to be deceived by false teachers who seek to convince us that principalities, powers, and rulers of darkness are all in the earthly realm. Ephesians is describing the spirit realm. It is real, primary battles occur there, and God utilizes us in these battles under the leadership of His Spirit.

2 COR 10:3-5

For though we walk in the flesh (the realm where we live), we do not war against the flesh,

For the weapons of our warfare are not carnal but mighty in God for pulling down strongholds, bringing every thought into captivity to the obedience of Christ.

We are not to war against the flesh, and our weapons are not of our flesh. There is a spirit realm, and warfare is active.

Elisha's Protection

2 KINGS 6:15-18
(THE KING OF SYRIA SEEKS TO CAPTURE ELISHA.)

And when the servant of the man of God arose early and went out, there was an army, surrounding the city with horses and chariots. And his servant said to him, "Alas, my master. What shall we do?"

So he answered him, "Do not fear, for those who are with us are more than those who are with them."

And Elisha prayed and said, "Lord, I pray, open his eyes that he may see." Then the Lord opened the eyes of the young man, and he saw ... the mountain was full of horses and chariots of fire all around Elisha ... Elisha prayed to the Lord, and

> he said, "Strike these people, I pray, with blindness." And he struck them with blindness according to the word of Elisha.

Elisha is again demonstrating that spiritual forces are real, and primary battles and victories are accomplished in the spirit realm.

God, Satan, and Job

JOB 1:6-22

> Then the Lord said to Satan, "Have you considered my servant Job, that there is none like him on the earth... who fears God and shuns evil?" So Satan answered... "Does Job fear God for nothing? Have you not made a hedge around him, around his household, and around all that he has on every side? You have blessed the work of his hands, and his possessions have increased in the land. But now stretch out your hand and touch all that he has, and he will surely curse You to Your face."
>
> And the Lord said to Satan, "Behold, all that he has is in your power; only do not lay a hand on his person."

Verses 13-22 demonstrate that only after receiving God's permission, may Satan cause calamity to Job's family and possessions. Job remains faithful to the Lord.

JOB 2:1-6

Satan again asks for permission to trouble Job further. The Lord grants permission, short of taking Job's life. Job never curses God.

These interactions demonstrate truths that govern the enemy in the spirit realm and in the natural realm. Satan does have temporary reign over the earth. Here he walks back and forth, seeking whom he may destroy. Satan has *no right* to touch any of *the Lord's people, without God's consent*. Satan needs God's permission, and this occurs first in the spiritual realm. However, because we live in a fallen world, God's sovereignty and gift of free will to each of us permit things that cannot be understood by our natural senses.

Daniel, the Angel Warrior, and Spiritual Warfare

DANIEL 10:1-21
(DANIEL HAS BEEN PRAYING MOURNFULLY FOR THREE WEEKS. HE SEES AN ANGELIC VISION.)

And he said to me, "... I have been sent to you ... for from the first day that you set your heart to understand, and to humble yourself before God, your words were heard; and I have come because of your words. But the prince of the kingdom of Persia withstood me twenty-one days; and behold, Michael, one of the chief princes, came to help me, for I had been left alone there with the kings of Persia. Now I have come to... Then again, the one having a likeness of a man touched me and strengthened me. And he said, '... And now I must return to fight with the prince of Persia; and when I have gone forth, indeed the Prince of Greece will come. But I will tell you what is noted in the Scripture of Truth. (No one upholds me against these, except Michael your prince...')"

Once again, we see the spirit realm is real and that battles rage there. The spiritual forces of God and Satan are shown to have a hierarchy of power, possibly comparable to military structure. God's servant was immediately dispatched to answer Daniel's prayer and strengthen Daniel. Warfare in the spirit realm stopped Him, and the angel could not fulfill his role, until Michael joined the battle. Spiritual warfare plays the primary role for what occurs on Earth. We have all experienced it, knowingly or not. *God has honored us by giving our Spirit-led prayers and actions important influence in the spirit realm.*

Given the references to the enemy's princes of both Persia and Greece, it is likely that demonic princes have authority over geographic regions. Indeed, majorities of some towns, regions, and countries have surrendered themselves to the power of the enemy and turned their backs on God. God's remaining faithful then play a significant but difficult role.

Jesus with the Seventy

Luke 10:17-18
Then the seventy returned with joy, saying, "Lord, even the demons are subject to us in Your name." And He said to them, "I saw Satan fall like lightning from heaven. Behold, I give you authority to trample on serpents and scorpions, and *over all the power of the enemy*, and nothing shall by any means hurt you. Nevertheless *do not rejoice in this, that the spirits are subject to you, but rather rejoice because your names are written in heaven.*"

Through His Spirit, Christ's power flows through all Christians, to achieve His will in both the spirit realm and the natural. Nothing, including Satan and his demons, has any power to restrict God's will, unless humans yield authority through fear or ignorance of God's word. Warfare is clearly involved. We can be hurt or even die in His service, but only if that serves God's purposes.

Everything we do must be in obedience to Christ's direction, not fleshly whims. We are not to step forward in our own will and pride. In John 4:6-7, Jesus could have accepted Satan's taunt and thrown Himself from the temple. It was not His Father's will, and Jesus was not on an ego trip. Neither are we to tempt our Father in heaven by "picking up (actual or the equivalent of) serpents and trampling on scorpions," unless He specifically instructs us to do so.

Spiritual Warfare

Spiritual warfare is a part of life in Christ. We see the evidence in the broken lives of individuals and the ungodly actions of governments, cultures, and organizations. We also learn to recognize the enemy's subtle and direct attacks against ourselves and our families. As we mature, we learn to no longer battle flesh and blood (individuals, organizations, and governments). How are we to live amidst the realities and warfare of the spirit realm? God has delegated an empowered role to His people. Ephesians provides specific instructions that we are to live daily.

EPH 6:10-18

*Finally, my brethren, be strong in the Lord
and in the power of His might.*

*Put on the whole armor of God, that you may be
able to stand against the wiles of the devil.*

*... Therefore, take up the whole armor of God, that you may be
able to withstand in the evil day, and having done all, to stand.*

*Stand therefore, having girded your waist with truth,
having put on the breastplate of righteousness,*

> *and having shod your feet with preparation*
> *of the gospel of peace:*
>
> *above all, taking the shield of faith with which you will be*
> *able to quench all the fiery darts of the wicked one.*
>
> *And take the helmet of salvation, and the sword*
> *of the Spirit, which is the word of God:*
>
> *praying always with all prayer and supplication*
> *in the Spirit, being watchful to this end with all*
> *perseverance and supplications for the saints*

Be Strong in the Lord

We are to be strong in the Lord and His power. We are to take up the whole armor of God. Having done all He commands, we stand in Christ against the enemy's wiles.

The Armor of God

Because spiritual warfare is always active against obedient Christians, we are to wear God's full armor and stand in His power at all times. Accordingly, we experience God's protection and victory. Every piece of the armor of God is indispensable.

Belt of Truth

Our Father's armor begins with the *belt of Truth*, which secures our body armor. We will not be led astray when we stand in God's truths as presented in the Old and New Testaments. If we veer off course, He draws us back and resets our foundation through personal time with Him. When churches and Christians deny or modify biblical truth to fit their contemporary beliefs and desires, they enter a path of deception that easily progresses from wayward to an abyss of untruths and defeat.

Breastplate of Righteousness

The *breastplate of righteousness* provides protection for our hearts and vital organs, the core of Christian life. This occurs through the irreplaceable knowledge that we are righteous in Christ and only in Christ. There is nothing that we can do to be righteous before God. Good works do not affect Christ's righteousness in us, and neither do failures. Our Father always sees saved individuals as righteous through the blood of Christ.

Covering for Our Feet

Having our *feet shod* with the preparation of the gospel of peace gives us His solid footing for living the great commission. We are blessed to walk this life with Christ as His ambassadors, sharing His love, life, and word.

Shield of Faith

We take up His *shield of faith*, with which we are able *"to quench all the fiery darts of the wicked one."* God's faith embraced by us provides an impenetrable defense against Satan's pervasive forms of personal attack. This scripture declares the Lord's absolute victory and dominion over the enemy. The fiery darts of accusation and temptation that are central to the enemy's warfare strategy are not simply deflected but are "quenched" by the shield of faith. Thus, we are permitted to understand how impotent the enemy is, when we stand on God's truths and utilize His armor. This battle is not easy, especially in areas of life where deep-seated temptations, habits, and strongholds have not been fully healed. However, the stronger the enemy attacks us, and the weaker we become, the more we draw closer to God and learn to stand in Him as He produces His victories. We stand in the supernatural faith that God provides.

In my experience, the enemy starts with small and almost imperceptible darts. If my armor is down, these find their mark. I become encumbered by their wounds and do not notice the increased number and size of the darts of assault. Finally, as he hurls huge darts, I may find myself grappling with wounds of depression and doubt. If he'd hurled these large darts first, I would recognize them and immediately bring all of God's armor into play. Armor is for all day, every day, regardless of the deceptive subtleties of the enemy.

Helmet of Salvation

God's *helmet of salvation* protects our minds from all of the enemy's wiles. Regardless of what is happening, including failures and stumbles, the Lord draws us back to bathe in the truth that our salvation is secure in Christ and that He who began a good work in us will complete it (Philippians 1:6: "being confident of this very thing, that he who has begun a good work in you will complete it until the day of Jesus Christ"). We go to the Spirit to renew our minds.

Sword of the Spirit

The *sword of the Spirit*, the Word of God, is alive and powerful and sharper than any two-edged sword (Heb 4:12). His Word carries His power. Just as Christ teaches, we are to utilize it as the Spirit reveals in all areas of life, including warfare. As we speak and stand on God's truth, it is then His role to both establish His victory in the spirit realm and guide and convict individuals. It is not ours. We are to live and love by walking in the Spirit.

Pray Over All of Life

Paul concludes by exhorting us to live with all prayer and supplication in the Spirit. Prayer is to be God's umbrella over all of life. It aligns us with His will and faith and releases His power in the spirit realm and in the natural realm.

EXAMPLES OF SPIRITUAL WARFARE TODAY

Angelic Protection

YWAM friends were staying with us when their five-months-pregnant daughter-in-law started labor. At the emergency room, we approached the Lord for His will and favor. He provided an image of the hospital room. An immense and powerful warrior angel bent to fill the room. In God's authority, his presence conveyed that this couple and this child *belonged to the Lord*. No enemy could enter.

I wondered why there was no need for his sword and no attempted attack by the enemy. The Spirit revealed the couple was steadfast in their obedience and walk with God. There was no weak point in their armor. They and the child were covered by God's protection and purpose.

God's spiritual cover and warfare clearly take different forms. He is not formulaic. Even in similar situations, He will act differently, according to His sovereign will. Our experience is to not define doctrine that we are to expect in like situations.

Hundreds of Christians were praying, and through many miracles, over many months, this child not only survived but is thriving as he learns to know the Lord. The Lord later showed me an image of this boy and his older brother, in their twenties. They walked together with purpose and jostled each other in brotherly competition. The Spirit conveyed that they have a role in His kingdom similar to the "Sons of Thunder," James and John. I responded that if I were to know this image was from Him, I would need Him to grant me life for another 20 years. His loving response was, "If I am the one who showed this to you, you have already seen it." (I know that I Have.)

Responding to Demonic Outbreaks

I was providing business consulting for a couple who were also receiving individual and marriage counseling. As I drove into their parking lot, God revealed strong demonic activity. He directed me to take authority over all demonic spirits and silence them during the opening prayer. The couple gave me this authority before every meeting. Everything went well for many meetings. Once I arrived first, and the conference room was empty. I went ahead and took spiritual authority. Later, during a difficult interaction, one of the individuals exploded, switching uncontrollably between violent anger and hysterical crying. As I watched, I asked the Spirit what He wanted me to do, and He told me to calmly speak, "I do not know what spirit is in control right now, but in the name of Jesus, I command you to be silent." The individual immediately became composed, exhibited no resentment or anger, and engaged constructively from that point on. As I drove away, I asked the Lord what had happened. He explained I had taken authority over an empty room. The demons entered later with the individuals. They were not placed under Christ's authority until they were addressed directly.

Application

- What do you accept and reject? What scriptures are the foundation for your positions? If you cannot substantiate your positions scripturally, why are you willing to embrace them?
- Are you feeling faith, peace, fear, or denial? Why?
- What does the Holy Spirit have as next steps for you? Remember, your warfare role is unique. You are not to copy anyone, although God may mentor you through specific situations.
- Are you willing to become a maturing warrior in Christ's kingdom, or will you avoid the incredible life that He has for you?

CHAPTER 18

THE KINGDOM OF GOD IS NOT IN WORD BUT IN POWER

1 COR 2:4-5, 20

And my speech and my preaching were not with persuasive words of human wisdom, but in demonstrations of the Spirit and of power.

That your faith should not be in the wisdom of men but the power of God.

For the kingdom of God is not in word but in power

JOHN 14:12

Most assuredly, I say to you, he who believes in Me, the works that I do he will do also, and greater works than these will he do, because I go to the Father.

2 TIM 3:2-5

For men will be lovers of themselves, lovers of money, boasters, proud ... unholy ... lovers of pleasure rather than lovers of God,

having a form of godliness but denying its power. And from such people turn away!

What would it mean if we received these scriptures seriously and asked God to transform our lives so that we continuously lived and walked in His power, for His glory? Can you imagine speaking and walking "in demonstrations of the Spirit and of power" instead of depending on your flesh for wisdom, persuasion, and impact? What would our lives and His Church be like if we lived as citizens of the kingdom of God who walked in His power instead of being characterized by words and actions of our flesh? What would God do through us if we believed and permitted Him, through His Spirit, to do the works He did and even greater? He would express Himself and His power *uniquely* through each of us, but every aspect of our lives and the lives of all we know would be touched by His power through us. His body, the Church, would present all the fruit and gifts of Christ, instead of the efforts of the flesh. We would each *Be and Become* His masterpieces as we thrived in Christ and our Father was glorified.

God calls us to walk in the power of His Spirit. These scriptures call us to His reality for this life. Paul lived this way, and we are to do the same. Does your life reflect the first two scriptures or the last? What about your church? Sadly, a significant number of us, Christians and churches "have a form of godliness but deny its power." Be the masterpiece He created. You are a child of the King, not an impoverished victim and slave to this world's religious and secular ideologies. Only those who "walk in the Spirit" can live this life.

Your Choice

We each have a choice to make. Will we walk in God's Spirit and permit His power to flow through us to accomplish His kingdom purposes, or will we walk in the safe and comfortable style of Club Christianity? The truth about Christ's power both in and through us (and His Church) has been lost to many, as it has been denied and is not recognized as God's design for the normal Christian life. Much influence and ground has been ceded to the enemy, who is, therefore, very pleased. God's truth is to be revitalized and embraced. You are to be a thriving part of God's kingdom, and His kingdom is not in word but in power. As the Spirit fills you, and you choose to walk in Him, you cannot avoid walking in His power. You are His conduit. This is Christ's plan for each of us and His Church.

If the power of the Holy Spirit is not evident in and through an individual, a ministry, or a church, each must ask, "Whose Life Am I Living?" Identify God's unique missions and obey the Spirit as He expresses His life and power through you according to His sovereignty. Learn from others, but do not copy anyone. You are unique in Christ.

The Spirit releases His power through the lives of those who actively choose to walk in the Spirit. It is not available through those who walk in their flesh. Consider these scriptures.

ZACH 4:6B

*Not by might nor by power, but by My Spirit,
Says the Lord of hosts.*

2 COR 12:9-10

*And He said to me, "My grace is sufficient for you,
for My strength is made perfect in weakness."*

WHOSE LIFE ARE YOU LIVING?

Therefore most gladly I (Paul) will rather boast in my infirmities, that the power of Christ may rest upon me... For when I am weak, then I am strong.

Living in the Power of God

What does it take for Christians to live with the power of God flowing in and through them? Life in the power of God, following salvation, rests on four pillars.

- Knowing the word of God
- Believing the word of God
- Walking in the Spirit—being continuously under His authority
- Speaking the word, the promises of God, and the name of Jesus, in God's gift of faith.

Knowing the Word of God

JOHN 1:1-4

In the beginning was the Word, and the Word was with God, and the Word was God

He was in the beginning with God.

All things were made through Him, and without Him nothing was made that was made.

In Him was life and the life was the light of men.

Jesus is the Word, and the entire Bible reveals Him, His truth, and His life. In order to serve Him and grow in His Spirit, we must spend time in the Bible, permitting Him to fill us with His revelation and faith. The growth and effectiveness of Christian life is directly related to how much time we spend with Him and in His word. His revelation makes scripture a dynamic part of our being so that we are able to stand on His truths and live in His power. Scripture becomes alive. It is impossible to live the life that Christ has for us if we do not know His word. When Jesus confronted Satan, He did so with the word of God, and we are to do the same. (Luke 4:1-13)

Believing the Word

JOHN 8:31-32

Then Jesus said to those Jews who believed Him, "If you abide in My word, you are my disciples indeed.

And you shall know the truth and the truth shall make you free."

There is a huge difference between being *familiar with* the word of God and *believing* it in your very being. Non-Christians can know it and value it, but they cannot believe it as the living truth of God. Some Christians know what it says and in their own way "believe" it is true, because they were taught that it is, but this is not the revelation "belief" that Jesus is speaking of.

Jesus refers to belief/faith that is a gift of God. It fills the follower of Christ with the very life and truth of every statement in His word. This is not self-generated belief; the Spirit sources it. It is not hoping or thinking that the word is true but knowing in our very being that it is true. God has revealed its truths to us. We are accountable for being intentional about standing on them.

Walking in the Spirit—Led by the Holy Spirit

This subject is covered in Chapter 15. All of God's power, both in and through an individual's life, resides in the Holy Spirit. It flows in and through us only when we are walking in the Spirit. Otherwise, we are in the flesh, and the flesh results in no good thing.

Speaking the Word and the Name of Jesus
The Word

JER 1:12
Then the Lord said to me, "That's right, and it means that I am watching over my word to perform it."

The word of God and the name of Jesus carry the power of God, especially when they are spoken in God-given faith under the direction of the Holy Spirit. The truth of Jeremiah 1:12 is incredible. God takes His word seriously. It is true, and He will perform it, according to His sovereign plan. He is always "watching over it" to ensure that it is performed when we speak it under the direction of the Spirit and not for our selfish purposes. God's power resides in His word, and it will be accomplished in His way and in His time!

JER 9:23
O, Lord, I know the way of man is not in himself; it is not in a man who walks to direct his own steps.

We are to seek and walk in the leadership of the Lord, by His Spirit, or we will miss His paths and His purpose. We do not find God's direction by looking within ourselves, depending on our desires, or complying with the instruction of others.

The Name of Jesus

JOHN 14:13

And whatever you ask for in My name, that I will do, that the Father may be glorified in the Son.

The name of Jesus is to be spoken with great reverence. It is never to be used lightly or as the repetitious babblings of the heathen. When we ask in the name of Jesus, we are to be asking for what we know or believe is His will, based on scripture and our walk with the Spirit. Then we ask in His gift of faith.

God's Flow of Power Through You and His Church

The source of God's power flowing through Christians and the Church is the Holy Spirit. It flows in many ways. including:

- The Fruit of the Spirit
- The Gifts of the Spirit
- His word, as He is "watching over His word" to bring it to completion.
- Salvation, transformation, freedom to the oppressed, and masterpiece lives.

- Accomplishing God's Kingdom Purposes, Missions, and Plans
- Transformation in both the spiritual realm and the natural realm
- Spiritual warfare

Christ Loves His Church

Regardless of the strengths and brokenness that are present in today's Church, Christ's Church is His chosen instrument on this Earth, and we are to be part of it, and honor and uplift it. He is and will operate through it, and "The gates of hell will not prevail against it." Both the organized Church and Christian individuals misstep and get swept up and absorbed into so-called "enlightened" thinking. Both face the temptations to be comfortable and acceptable to an ever-dominating pluralistic society. Therefore the character and power of Christ often get lost. Accordingly, all need to be continuously purified and return to God's calling. We are to be the Spirit's instruments of His life, love, and power.

When churches and individuals walk in Christ, they will both evidence His character and His power. Yet these are missing in many. Since His Spirit is the source of God's life and power, these individuals and churches are living a shadow of the life that Christ has designed for them. Love and honor God's church and His children, but do not follow error. Be the masterpiece that He created and determine to permit God's power to flow in and through your life (your church) as you live under the control of the Holy Spirit!

What Will God's Power Look Like in Your Life?

JOSHUA 1:9

Have I not commanded you? Be Strong and of Good courage; do not be afraid nor dismayed, for the Lord your God is with you wherever you go.

JER 1:17B, 19

*Do not be dismayed before their faces,
Lest I dismay you before them.*

They will fight against you, but they shall not prevail against you. For I am with you, says the Lord, to deliver you.

God's power in our lives will look as it did in Christ's life and the lives of His obedient followers. It will be unique to each person and situation, as we walk in God's Spirit. God's purpose and the results of His power through us may not be easily seen, but we are to walk in absolute faith and trust as we humbly obey and permit His Spirit to accomplish His work. We are not to carry the burden of achieving the results that God is accomplishing through us. As we walk in His faith and power, we know that even if it is not until years after our deaths, His Spirit is accomplishing His will through our lives.

What if Joshua led His people by saying, "God told us to do this, but I do not think it will do any good"? Instead, he walked each successful step of his leadership journey by seeking God's will and leading in the faith and power of God. When he assumed he knew what God would do and led without seeking God, both he and Israel failed.

Live by always seeking God's will, obeying, and walking in His Spirit. You will know the faith, confidence, and power of God's Spirit.

Summary

- The kingdom of God is not in word but in power. Christians who do not walk under the authority of the Holy Spirit have a form of godliness but deny its power.

- All of God's power, both in and through our lives, belongs to Him.

- It is also to be His power that operates through your natural gifts if you are living for Him.

- Only when our lives are under the control of the Holy Spirit will His power flow in and through us for God's glory. When we operate in the flesh, our actions are in conflict with the Spirit.

- We must decide whose life we are going to live. His life in His power, or some copy played on a stage to please other audiences.

- How God displays His power through us is dependent on His purpose and missions for each unique masterpiece life. Don't compare or try to copy others.

- *He keeps and watches over His word, to perform it.* Walk in and share His word as He directs, and *He will perform it*, in His manner and time.

- Walk through life under the control of the Holy Spirit. Believe and live in the truth and dynamic kingdom promise of John 14:12.

Application

- What do you agree with and what do you challenge from this chapter? What scripture verses form the basis for your beliefs?
- How has the Spirit challenged you? Are you willing to pursue His thoughts, or will you insist on keeping to long-held beliefs?
- Are you willing to walk with godly Christians whose life in Christ's power will challenge your self-imposed limitations on the power of God through you and His Church?
- Do you want to live God's full and spiritually empowered life—or something less?
- Think about the following verse. Micah reveals that, when he is walking in the Lord, seeking to obey Him, and doing what the Lord has directed, he knows it is done in the power of the Lord. This verse is also true for us when we walk in the Spirit.

Micah 3:8
But truly I am full of power by the Lord.
And of justice and might,
To declare to Jacob his transgression
And to Israel his sin.

- What steps is the Spirit guiding you to take right now?

CHAPTER 19

OUR KINGDOM MISSIONS DEFINE OUR SPIRITUAL-WARFARE ROLES

Once we recognize the reality and priority of the spirit realm and spiritual warfare, how might we live differently, and what might our lives be like? We would engage life in God's priorities with spiritual awareness and in His power that is fully dependent on His Spirit. We would not be deceived into battling the flesh. Instead, we would join God's forces as they engage in the spirit realm, where victories are won. We would be free to fully engage difficult individuals and organizations with God's love instead of viewing them as enemies. The Spirit would utilize all scripture through us with greater focus and in His power. We would specifically live in the truths of the four primary warfare verses noted below. Every relationship and every God-given area of influence would reflect more of the presence, purpose, power, and touch of God.

In this chapter, we first consider the four primary verses for engaging in spiritual warfare, including application. Then we present examples of daily warfare for understanding and application in everyday reality.

Spiritual Warfare:
We Do Not Wrestle Against Flesh and Blood. We put on the Armor of God

EPH 6:10-18

*Put on the whole armor of God that you may
stand against the wiles of the devil.*

*For we do not wrestle against flesh and blood, but
against principalities, against powers, against the
rulers of darkness of this age, against spiritual hosts
of wickedness in the heavenly places....*

In the last chapter, we established that the foundation for spiritual success is recognizing that we are to direct our activities first toward principalities and powers . . . spiritual hosts of wickedness in heavenly places as God directs. We stand in the armor of God as it is presented in Eph 6.

In Our Areas of Influence (Jeremiah)

All Christians, not just leaders, are to understand the spiritual dimensions of the tasks that the Lord is accomplishing through them. They have missed the true work of God when their primary focus is on the natural. All of us are responsible to God for being leaders in the areas where He has given us influence, and this begins with our families.

Do Not Be Dismayed (Obey the Lord)

JER 1:17-19

*Therefore prepare yourself and arise,
And speak to them all that I command you.*

Our Kingdom Missions Define Our Spiritual-Warfare Roles

> *Do not be dismayed before their faces,*
> *Lest I dismay you before them.*
> *For behold, I have made you this day*
> *A fortified city and an iron pillar,*
> *And bronze walls against the whole land.*
> *They will fight against you,*
> *But they shall not prevail against you.*
> *For I am with you, says the Lord, to deliver you.*

Each of our kingdom missions will push against Satan's purposes, secular and religious culture, and church traditions. We will actively encounter spiritual warfare as we humbly obey God's Spirit and press forward without withdrawing or quailing due to reactions in the spirit realm or through mankind. We are to accept the reality that none of us will be understood all of the time, even when we are accurately obeying the Spirit. God's words to Jeremiah, "Do not be dismayed" are for each of us. We are to prepare for resistance and walk in His Spirit. If we shift our eyes off of Him, we will focus on others' "faces" and lose His effectiveness. When we are operating in His will through His Spirit, He fortifies us, and, regardless of how others come against us, they will not prevail. He achieves His purposes and delivers us.

I served Him for five years in a situation where He wanted significant change. Death threats were common against me and occasionally my family. Neither the organization nor the company understood what God was directing me to do, so there was little support. I made mistakes, but I sought to follow God at every step. I served Him, and He made impacts spiritually and culturally. Few, from an earthly perspective, would ever see it, and I paid a great professional price. That price was insignificant compared to what God taught my wife and me, and to what He was accomplishing in the spirit realm through the many resources He utilized in that situation.

Our Commissions and Spiritual Warfare

> **JER 1:10**
> *See, I have this day set you over the*
> *nations and over the kingdoms.*
> *To root out and to pull down,*
> *To destroy and to throw down,*
> *To build and to plant.*

God's format for commissioning Jeremiah is also for each of us. Achieving our unique missions through spiritual warfare follows these steps. We are commissioned to carry out our unique kingdom responsibilities in specific areas of influence. We are to follow three steps that result in spiritual victory. Ignoring them due to resistance may result in worldly popularity, but it will leave God's purpose unfulfilled, until obedient servants step in.

Apply the above verses to your unique commission in Christ. Insert your name in the first sentence. God set Jeremiah "over nations and over kingdoms." He has this day set "you" over (fill in what the Spirit reveals.) These will be areas where He has given you spiritual influence and authority. Your family is one area, and there are many more. Christians are to live their commissions humbly in God's power, anticipating pushback from the enemy, yet living according to Jer 1:17-19. We are not to be deluded into seeking and living a "soft and comfortable" Christian life, waiting for others to tell us what to do.

In the last three lines of this verse, God directs how Christians are to permit Him to bring spiritual and natural transformation. As we watch over our areas of responsibility, we do so lovingly, but *our missions are not passive and gentle assignments, especially in the spirit realm. They resemble preparing fields for planting.* There is continuous work to be done, regardless of the current condition of the field. Christ will accomplish the following steps through us, and they are not linear.

Root Out and Pull Down

Before we are to "To build and to plant," we are to remove the weeds, trash, rocks, and roots from the field. These are akin to all the things in the spirit and natural realms that impede or replace the Father in our lives, the lives of our families, and in other areas of influence. Weeds must not be just cut off at the surface. The roots must be killed, and preventive treatments kept in place. All of this begins with our own lives. We cannot experience the Spirit's power and authority fully through us if we have not let Him have *all* of us. This process is "to root out and pull down."

To Destroy and to Throw Down

Next, before we are "To build and to plant," we are "To destroy and to throw down" all of the strongholds, all of the addictions, and all of the bondages that hold us back from full and total surrender to the leadership of the Holy Spirit. The roots of these are in the enemy's spiritual realm. We are all broken and are to permit God's work in these areas. Some of these require a lifetime of surrender and healing in Christ. However, we are not to ignore them and seek to build and plant over them. Some strongholds are revealed when we ask, "Whose life am I living?" God then illuminates destructive forces and misplaced priorities that are to be corrected through His Spirit.

Are you carrying wounds that Christ wishes to heal? These include all manner of addictions, abuse in many forms, and intentional and unintentional exposure to the occult. Be certain that yours are identified and that you are committed to God's healing process. Remember this: No matter what stage of brokenness we are experiencing, God will be effective through us, if our hearts are committed to Him.

To Build and to Plant

Now come the steps of building and planting. The "ground" has been and is continuously being prepared and restored by God. We build and plant, according to God's design, so that His garden grows and blooms. Because we have worked first in the spirit realm, lives and kingdom purposes begin to flourish.

Through Jer 1:10, God conveys the extraordinary spiritual-warfare role and power that He has invested in believers. Permit Him to live in this power through you. Accordingly, His commission shall be fulfilled in and through you.

Weapons of Spiritual Warfare (In Addition to Ephesians 6)

2 COR 10:3-5

For though we walk in the flesh, we do not war according to the flesh.

Our Kingdom Missions Define Our Spiritual-Warfare Roles

For the weapons of our warfare are not carnal but mighty in God for the pulling down of strongholds,

casting down arguments and every high thing that exalts itself against the knowledge of God, bringing every thought into captivity to the obedience of Christ.

Do we and our churches follow these verses as we stand against all that opposes Christ? For many, the answer is "No," and the enemy is greatly pleased. Let's embrace His Word and become more effective members of the Body of Christ.

We do not war according to the flesh. Our weapons are not carnal. Warring according to the flesh leads us to focus on things we can see, including what we dislike about situations or people. Individuals and organizations that disturb us or stand against the things of God are viewed as the problems or our enemies, so we focus our energies against them. We think we can "win for Jesus" by utilizing earthly wisdom, power, influence, money, and sometimes anger to carry the day. The world works and wins for the enemy this way, but God does not.

What are the weapons of Christians which are mighty in God, and how are they utilized? They are presented in scripture and are to be utilized under the control and authority of the Holy Spirit. Only when we are walking in the Spirit will we be of use in spiritual warfare. God then directs our actions, and His power flows through us and His weapons. Consider the following warfare weapons that are taught by scripture and are to be wielded by the Spirit in and through Christians.

The Armor of God

In the last chapter, we established that God designed effective warfare to begin with the armor of God. We are to make His armor an integral part of our lives as we intentionally put it on and utilize each piece daily, in the Spirit. Without it, we are always vulnerable. Review these and ask the Spirit to bring them alive during each moment of the remainder of life. Remember the foundational role of prayer.

The Word of God

> **HEB 4:12**
>
> *For the word of God is living and powerful, and sharper than any two-edged sword, piercing even to the division of soul and spirit, and of joint and marrow, and is the discerner of the thoughts and intents of the heart.*

> **EPH 6:17**
>
> *And take ... the sword of the Spirit, which is the word of God:*

Direct Warfare

The word of God (and the name of Jesus) is our most powerful weapon for spiritual warfare and for blessing. Jesus is our mentor and example for appropriating God's victory over the spirit realm through the word of God. He never engaged in power struggles with either the devil or his demons. He stood confidently on the word, the truths of God, and His authority in/as God. We are to permit Him to do the same through us as we speak His word and stand in His authority (the authority He has given to us in His name), under the leadership of the Spirit.

When God has me exercise His authority over the enemy, He has me speak only as He guides and always by stating that I speak not in my authority but Christ's through His blood. I have no personal authority but am confident in His authority expressed obediently through me. When He has me pray into the spirit realm for what He is doing, the prayers are interestingly much different than I would expect.

What we are to do in every situation is totally dependent on the Holy Spirit. We are to listen and trust. He reveals when the activity is demonic. He reveals whether or not He wants to deal with the enemy through us. He reveals how He wishes to do so. He then operates in and through us.

Resisting Temptations

The first three Gospels share accounts of how Jesus resisted the temptations of the devil. Jesus did not fight or argue. He stood on the truth of scripture and silenced the enemy by quoting it. One of Satan's prevalent tactics is to misuse the word of God. Satan depends on Christians being unfamiliar with scripture. He deceives by isolating scripture verses and planting temptations that have a "core" of truth. Confused by the misuse of elements of truth, many fall prey. Those who are familiar with all of scripture and walk in the Spirit escape these temptations, as Christ did. Consider the following, where Satan misused scripture to tempt Jesus, and Jesus disarmed him through scripture. Notice the specific types of temptations that Satan still uses against us.

Temptation: To Use God's Power for Selfish Purposes

In Matt 4:3-5, Satan tempted Christ to turn the stones into bread, but Jesus answered, "It is written, Man shall not live by bread alone, but by every word that proceeds from the mouth of God."

Temptation: To Challenge Him to Prove Himself (or God)

In verses 5-7, Satan used scripture to tempt Jesus to throw Himself from the pinnacle of the temple because it is written that, "He shall give His angels charge over you." And "In their hands they shall bear you up Lest you dash your foot against a stone."

Jesus responded, "It is written again, 'You shall not tempt the Lord your God.'"

Temptation: To Put Anything or Anyone Above God for Personal Gain

In verses 8-11, the devil offered Jesus the kingdoms of the world if He would fall down and worship him. Jesus responded, "Away with you, Satan! For it is written, 'You shall worship the Lord your God and Him only you shall serve.'"

After this, the devil left Him.

Jesus established our model for engaging with the enemy. We are not to fight Satan. The battle is already won. As James 4:7 instructs, we resist, according to Christ's model, "Therefore submit to God, resist the devil and he will flee from you."

How can we be sure that scripture is available to us when we need it? We are assured in Matt 10:19-20 that the Holy Spirit will give us what we should speak. "Do not worry about how or what you should speak, for it will be given to you in that hour . . . for it is not you who speak, but the Spirit of your Father who speaks in you." Although this scripture refers to one specific situation, we will find it to be true in every situation, spiritual or natural, where we are representing Christ and obeying His Spirit. Importantly, we are responsible for maintaining our intimate relationship with Christ and His word.

Renewing Our Minds Is Spiritual Warfare

ROM 12:2

And do not be conformed to this world, but be transformed by the renewing of your mind, that you may prove what is that good and acceptable and perfect will of God.

Renewing our minds is a significant battleground of spiritual warfare. If we are not intentional about our beliefs and thoughts, we easily conform to popular worldviews, without realizing we have placed them ahead of God's truths and life. This type of warfare is utilized both in preparation for warfare and in standing against the enemy. Renewing our minds is permitting the Spirit to align our thoughts and desires with God's truth and will. This is accomplished primarily through four interactions with God:

- Spending time with the Lord in prayer, worship, praise, and fellowship.
- Spending time in the scriptures seeking the revelation and application of the Spirit.

- Listening to the Holy Spirit and enjoying His presence every minute of the day. Learning to discern His voice, to obey, and to never "block" Him.

- Taking every thought captive (2 Cor 10:5), by letting the Holy Spirit reveal when thoughts are ours, when they are the enemy's, and when they are the Spirit's. Act accordingly.

Prayer in Spiritual Warfare

Refer to Chapter 8 for the importance, purpose, and principles of prayer in the life of every Christian. This includes spiritual warfare. Prayer is central to the very life of Christians, and God has made it a critical element for bringing His kingdom plans into being. Notice how God ended His spiritual-warfare instructions in Eph 6 with the exhortation of verse 18, "praying always with all prayer and supplication in the Spirit, being watchful to this end with all perseverance and supplication for all the saints."

Prayers Regarding His Actions in the Spirit Realm

In recent years, the Father instructed me in two areas of prayer regarding the spirit realm. Permit Him to incorporate them in your life.

Spiritual Cover for Areas of Influence

Christian organizations and individuals are responsible for stepping into powerful leadership roles in the spirit realm. Through prayer, they are to provide specific spiritual cover for all under their commissioned areas of influence. They are also to pray as He directs for what He is accomplishing in the spirit realm in those areas. These prayers are a higher priority than those focused first on specific, earthly results.

He communicated this by showing me an image of the world. Expanding from a central location was a network of tight connections that covered only specific areas and, therefore, took a unique shape as it extended over parts of the globe. This network represented areas of influence, with the central area indicating the "home" of leadership. There are millions of these within His kingdom. Families are part of your networks.

Prayers for Geographic Areas and Individuals Within Them:

God has changed the way that He has me pray over spiritually oppressed areas when He has given me related responsibilities. He now has me ask Him, "What are You doing in the spiritual realm covering the area, and what are Your prayers?" I then join Him first in His prayers for impacting the spirit realm. Prayers for His will in the natural realm come after He releases me from this focus. He has taught me that He has designed His kingdom system so that our prayers are critically impactful elements for releasing His purposes and power in both the spirit realm and subsequently in the natural. This is demonstrated in many places in the Bible. He has continued to teach me to pray in this manner for all areas of life. Sometimes the answer comes clearly. Sometimes it is more challenging, and I must wait. Either way, we are then privileged to be a part of His active role and influence, in the most significant realm of prayer warfare. The spirit realm is the first place where God's victories take shape.

We Each Have Different Roles and Journeys in Spiritual Warfare

As unique individuals in Christ's kingdom, we have different roles and journeys in the area of spiritual warfare. Not all of us are led by the Spirit to confront demons, though all have His authority. Not all have the specific gift of "discerning of spirits," but it is always available through the Spirit when needed.

Our Father will teach and lead us in the unique role(s) He designed in this area. Always remember that our focus is Christ and not the enemy's actions. We are able to engage effectively in spiritual warfare only as we walk in the Spirit. *He* is then our guide and revealer, not our minds or emotions.

My Spiritual-Warfare Journey

We can fully trust God to teach us everything we need to know about spiritual warfare at appropriate times in our journey, if we are open and seek all He has for us. Each of our journeys is different, and our roles in spiritual warfare vary accordingly. *However, daily warfare in our lives and over the areas we influence is to be an active part of every Christian's life.* It is to be acknowledged and lived in Christ's victory. An abbreviated summary of my journey is shared as an encouragement.

Even though I grew up in church, I knew nothing about the Holy Spirit other than His existence, until I recommitted my life at 26. He then introduced Himself as He began transforming me through personal and spiritual battles. I grew in relationship with Him over the next years but knew little of spiritual warfare.

During my thirties, He began to inform me of the reality of demonic attacks in daily life and Christ's victory. He demonstrated how not only intentional exposure to the occult but also "innocent" exposures such as Ouija Boards and visiting fortune tellers open doors for potential demonic access to our lives. He utilized Neil Anderson's book *The Bondage Breaker* to provide insight into realities of the spirit realm and protecting myself, our family, and others. He also taught us about the deceptions of New Age "spirituality" that were infiltrating the church. This included the deception of receding deep into one's being to connect with one's "spirit guide," which usually disguises itself as an angel but is actually a demon. This all came together just before we needed it. Our two daughters were exposed to the effects of a demonic "spirit guide" through an acquaintance. One of our daughters innocently attempted to mimic the situation. Joanne and I knew what had happened and how dangerous it was spiritually. We were able to take authority and protect both children, as God had taught us.

The Lord continued to teach us, but only what we would need to know as His vessels in our specific missions. He always reminded us that He was to be our focus, regardless of what He taught about the demonic realm. We were to avoid the excesses that imprison Christians who "see demons behind every tree" and credit the devil with power that he does not have. God put all of this into practice, in incremental steps, as He developed us for each succeeding mission.

God then moved us to a new assignment. We were in for an experience that, in our flesh, was horrible, and in our spirits, was "almost" beyond endurance, but for God. In the spirit realm, we had limited understanding of what was going on until after our mission was completed, and we had left the area. Importantly, He was faithful. He had taught us the spiritual foundation that we needed, and He worked in and through us to achieve His will. He drew Joanne and me ever closer to Him and each other and prepared us for the future. We had a specific role in a community that was under deep spiritual oppression. At first, I wondered if my spiritual experiences were real or imagined. However, pastors shared that they, too, experienced spiritual darkness and oppression. A common description was, "When you fly out, you just feel the spiritual darkness and oppression fall away, and when you fly back in, the darkness envelops you!" Our role was significant spiritually, and we, therefore, experienced many attacks that were rooted in the enemy. My wife received a macabre death-threat the week after she arrived. Death threats to me were common over the five years of our service there. God supported us, and we learned, but He accomplished His will through us even as we (especially I) were frequently barely able to stand. He provided me with my own pastor, who understood what was going on spiritually in the community and in our lives. He helped me learn and stood with me as a friend whom I cherish. The oppression was constant, and God was my only refuge, true to His word. One night (described below), He revealed a powerful figure that was directing oppression toward us from the demonic realm. Christ had me resist and stand in His victory. Without these times of challenge and standing on His truths and in His faith, our spiritual growth would be limited.

Through these and subsequent experiences in my walk with God, I know that practical and powerful spiritual development and effectiveness results only from learning under fire. He prepares us for what we are to face in His missions, but boot camp only gets us so far. We truly grow in our masterpiece role and relationship with God as we engage on the battlefield of the spirit realm.

God's mentoring continues. I permit Him to connect me with individuals who experience His spiritual realm in different ways. I continuously "relearn" to walk where He wants and how He wants instead of insisting on my desired missions. In addition to my wife, He has always provided a few spiritual mentors to support my journey.

Breaking Spiritual Strongholds

Because specifics convey more than summaries, I am to provide more detail regarding the last interaction, and the importance of recognizing and breaking strongholds. God gains the victory, but we have important roles and are not merely puppets. We had been through months of spiritual attacks that we did not always recognize. I was totally drained to the point where I would come home and just drop onto our bed. Threatening and evil calls were coming in so often that we unplugged the phones. Friends warned that death threats were serious.

One night, I was unable to sleep due to tremendous oppression. I moved to another bedroom. After praying and wrestling with great anxiety for some time, two images appeared. The one at the foot of my bed was clearly a large demon. I had never seen one before and haven't since. The other was Christ standing at my head. He had taught me what to do. So, in His name, His authority, and the power of His blood, I commanded the demon to leave and not return. It did not leave and continued to threaten. Not unexpectedly, I was frightened. In Christ, I again commanded the demon to leave; it did not. I stood firm and repeated the process. The third time, the demon left and never returned. I had appropriated Christ's victory. I did not fight this demon but stood on the truths of God and the name of Christ.

The Holy Spirit then took me downstairs. For several hours, He revealed all of the sins, both forgiven and not, that I had been carrying. We dealt with each one in the blood of Christ. He took an extraordinary weight from me, much of which I could have put down years ago. Memories and guilt still attempt to slip back in to distract me, but I stand on the truth of God's forgiveness. I am not to pick them up or ask again for forgiveness. Christ took all of this. When painful memories return, I tell the source of accusation and guilt to take them to Jesus for Him to handle, because "I am free" in Christ.

I had three major questions resulting from the incident. Why did the demon not leave immediately? Why did Christ not intervene and execute His power? Why were both Christ and the demon visible to me only as representative figures? God provided answers. The demon was a powerful one and knew that the only authority I had emanated from Christ and my faith and trust in Him. When my faith was weak, the demon could withstand. As I stood firm on my belief in Christ's authority and mine in Him, my faith strengthened and matured under fire. The demon had to depart under the authority of Christ and His name. Second, Christ did not intervene, because He desires for each Christian to mature and to learn that the Christian life is totally different from the life of the unsaved. It includes and requires spiritual warfare. He had taught me what I needed to know, and He wanted me to learn to walk in active faith as I obey His teaching. He did not leave my side and made sure that I knew He was with me and would always be there. Importantly, I had roles to fulfill and missions for Him to accomplish. Maturing into them comes through obedience and faith. Finally, I do not know why this experience included me seeing both Christ and the demon as less than full-bodied. Beginning immediately, I became at peace with this and never felt the need to seriously inquire.

Spiritual Warfare Examples from the Lives of Others

As regular Christ-followers step out, take risks, and live in the reality of the spirit realm, Christ claims victory through them. Warfare is part of daily life.

There's Too Much "Light" About You

A young missionary couple served Christ with the indigenous population of Papua New Guinea. Their three children were born there, miles and miles from the nearest medical support. They lived in huts, where they would protect themselves and their infants daily from snakes and other threats. They loved and served the people with a passion.

The local religion revolved around powerful witch doctors. They openly operated in the demonic, whose forces were clearly expressed in the lives of the natives. A witch doctor invited the husband to attend a session where demons were called forth to display their power. The pastor was familiar with these events and knew actions demons had previously taken. The Lord wanted him to attend, so he went in the Spirit's protection. The procedures began and advanced to the point where the demons were summoned to appear. The witch doctors summoned and summoned, but the spirits did not come forth. Eventually, a witch doctor approached the missionary and said, "Will you please leave? There is too much 'light' about you, and the demons will not come." The light was the presence of the Holy Spirit.

"I'm Trying, but I Can't"

Remember the true story about a demon-plagued son who could not enter the property of his parents because they had fully claimed house and land for Christ, had cleansed both of all demon presence, and then had established Christ's bloodline boundaries. We are to spiritually protect ourselves and property as the Spirit leads. Warfare in the spirit realm is real.

Final Thoughts

The spirit realm and warfare are a natural part of God's missions and victories in every Christian's life. To be uninformed about or to ignore the enemy's tactics disarms and impedes the life of Christians. To focus on the enemy instead of Christ is a destructive deception. Also, we are never to fear the enemy. Unless God permits, he has no power over us unless we surrender it to him. If we deny spiritual truths and warfare and live as Carnal Christians, we are like caterpillars who bind themselves in cocoons and have the power to stay within and define the cocoon as "life," and God's masterpiece lives are then forfeited.

Come forth in Christ. Focus on Him, His plans for our lives, His Church, and His victory. Embrace Christ, and "walk in the Spirit" with all of your being, and you will experience life as He designed it. Never block Him. Know "Whose Life You Are Living."

Application

- What do you agree with, what challenges you, what threatens you, and what do you reject? What scriptural truths will help you in each area?

- Surrender to the Spirit and ask Him to actively begin teaching you what He wants you to know about walking in the specific journey of spiritual warfare that God has designed for you. Trust Him, and let Him give you the faith and confidence to move forward in His timing and His methods. Learn from, but do not copy, the spiritual lives of others.

- Determine to walk in the Spirit and truly live.

CHAPTER 20

THE RESURRECTION OF THE LION OF JUDAH IN CHRIST'S CHURCH

REV 5:5-6
But one of the elders said to me, "Do not weep. Behold, the Lion of the tribe of Judah, the Root of David, has prevailed to open the scroll and to loose His seven seals."

And I looked, and, in the midst of the throne and the four living creatures, and in the midst of the elders, stood a Lamb as though it had been slain, . . .

GAL 2:20
I have been crucified with Christ; it is no longer I who live, but Christ lives in me;

What would change in our lives and the life of the Church if we permitted the Spirit to live in and through us as not only the Lamb of God but also the Lion of Judah? We would no longer limit Christ's expression of Himself through us to the "approved" expressions of *The Lamb* that mankind's church has limited itself to and seeks to emulate. We and the Church would experience and reveal the full identity, love, and power of the Christ of the

Gospels and Revelation. Through us, Christ would impact our families and all other areas of our influence as His masterpieces, in the fullness of His identity, instead of well-intended imitators.

The Christian culture has embraced the Lamb of God, as the world defines Him, but it has effectively eliminated much of Christ's expression of Himself as the Lion of Judah. It has defined Christ's love, mercy, and compassion in this one-sided manner, which does not fully reflect the Christ of the Gospels. Permit the Spirit to awaken and express the full identity of Christ, both Lion and Lamb, in and through your life.

Christ's actions, and, therefore, "Spirit-led Christians" actions, as the Lion of Judah, express every characteristic of the fruit of the Spirit just as effectively as those we attribute to the Lamb. As Revelations demonstrates, Christ, the Lion of Judah *and* the Lamb of God, is one being who consists of and displays both expressions of His identity. He does not swap hats as He decides to be Lion or Lamb. The heavens called Him the Lion even as He stood as the Lamb. He is both, all the time, not one or the other at differentiated times. Through both expressions, Christ extends love, grace, and mercy all the time to every individual. When He wishes to engage someone through us with His Lion characteristics, and we do not let Him, we are causing harm. Permitting the Spirit, not our flesh, to express Himself through us as the loving and exhorting Lion of Judah does not hurt people; it strengthens them.

Christ's Life in the Gospels

In the Gospels, Christ demonstrates the full expression of His identity that He desires to live in and through us. His characteristics are not to be defined by religious traditions, secular invasion of the Church, and often one-sided representations of Him as the Lamb.

In order to explore the Lion characteristics of Christ, we look prayerfully at the specifics of Christ's relationships with individuals in the four Gospels. Every aspect of His encounters reveals the spectrum of how we are to walk daily in the Spirit and the truth that, "it is no longer I who live, but Christ lives in me." If Christ's words and actions in the Gospels do not seem "loving or gentle" to us, we are the one who needs to receive new revelation. This is also true when the words and actions He relays through *obedient, Spirit-filled followers* do not match our paradigms of love, mercy, patience, and gentleness. Christ delivers His messages to and through us with His expression of patience and loving exhortation necessary to transform lives. Sometimes, His interactions hurt, and that is not a bad thing. When they do, they are never destructive. He disciplines and exhorts us with love. Permit Him the freedom to approach you, and others through you, in all expressions of His being.

As we proceed, determine to have Christ become your ultimate and final role model. Learn from others, and walk in unity with and under the authority of His Church, but religious and other tribal cultures are not to dictate how you act and live as a Christian. You are ultimately responsible only to Christ. Live in the fullness of who He is and who you are meant to be in Him, as you walk in His Spirit. *You can do this only when you walk in the Spirit.*

Christ, the Lion of Judah, in the Gospels
He Is Our Example, Instructor, Mentor, and Life

The Spirit provided the following process for restoring the expression of Christ as the Lion of Judah into His individuals and church. We are to engage it with the Spirit as we request His revelation and transformation and permit Him to replace tradition and tribal beliefs with the full expression of Christ.

Background

I was asked to help strengthen a ministry's effectiveness. They had a great heart but did not understand how to provide God's excellence in their processes and the performance of staff. Their prevailing culture valued avoidance of conflict, replaced by *reconciliation at all costs*. Over several years, a leadership team worked to move the culture from being satisfied with doing "their" best to permit the Spirit to provide Christ's best. The president and director blocked appropriate changes. The ministry continued to achieve minimal success. Ultimately, an important local authority would no longer utilize them.

At one point, I again described necessary process and personnel improvements that all but one on the Leadership Team supported. The President then said, "If you were really a Christian, you would not be so direct." I was stunned but did not respond. We were facing tribal paradigms.

God has taught me to listen to all input, whether it seems appropriate or not. I am to ask Him, "What do you want me to learn from this? How much of this statement do you want me to integrate?" I went home and prayed from that perspective.

God's Process

The Holy Spirit directed, "Go to the Gospels" with His revelation, "and look at *Christ's words, purposes, attitudes, and actions in every interaction with individuals. They reveal how He walked then and desires to act and walk through you (all Christians) today."*

He communicated, "Christ, by His very nature and identity, embodies every aspect of the Fruit of the Spirit. He did not sin. He cannot act outside of who He is. Everything He did reflected all of the Fruit of the Spirit. His life in the Gospels demonstrates all of the acceptable ways that His loving character is to be lived in and through the lives of His followers. Mankind and the church have sought to 'define and control' how Christ-followers live by placing their cultural- and personal-value descriptions into church doctrine and tradition regarding behavior. *Christ in the Gospels is to be the only standard that Christians follow.* No Christian leader is to take Christ's place in directing how Christ is to live through you or the Church." Christ delivers His messages to each of us with the combination of mercy, gentleness, and directness that is necessary for giving Him the best opportunity to truly accomplish His will.

He concluded by sharing the following requirement. "Although Christ never sinned, *even the most mature Christians do when we operate in our flesh.* Therefore, *Christians are able to represent Christ and serve His kingdom only when they are walking in the Spirit.* Then, it is Christ's Spirit living in and through us. When we are not in the Spirit, even when we are "acting like Jesus," *we are in the flesh which wars against the Spirit.* We will hurt people. We will never be perfect, but when our hearts are right, the Spirit will achieve His will, as we listen and obey.

My Actions

I prayerfully read through each of the Gospels and documented all of Christ's interactions. Some of the scriptures are presented below. An additional 75 Bible passages and more than 200 scriptures which present the same truths of how Christ interacted were not included, due to space limitations. We suggest you follow this process to identify them all, if you think the scriptures presented here are exceptions. It is clear that Christ's loving approach includes more exhortation and patient-but-direct challenge than religion teaches. There are more incidents of this type of individual interaction than those behaviors that have been idolized by some Christian and secular cultures. (Where the same incident is included in more than one of the gospels, I have presented only one.)

Through this process and much prayer, the Spirit led me to embrace and then share the truths expressed in the introduction to the chapter.

Your Opportunity

Proceed by evaluating the scriptures below and repeating the process that the Spirit revealed. Permit Him to transform the ways that you permit Him to express Christ's life in and through you. We summarize but do not prescribe directive conclusions. That is up to the Spirit and your openness and obedience to Him. He individualizes His impact on each of us based on our unique missions and the stages of our walks with Him. This process should take an extended amount of time. It is a journey of revelation and transformation, not memorization. The balance of this chapter is predominantly scripture, without significant comment. Scripture carries the message God has for you.

Christ, the Lion of Judah, in the Gospels

Christ's interactions are presented in categories. They are Christ's interactions with:

- Spiritual Leaders
- Disciples
- Those Involved in His Trials and Crucifixion
- Others

At the end of each category, you are asked to work through revelation, evaluation, and application.

Christ with Spiritual Leaders

Matt 9:2-8 (Mk 2:1-12, Lk 5:17-26)
Jesus told the paralytic that " . . . your sins are forgiven you."

Some of the scribes said within themselves, "This man blasphemes!"

Jesus said, "Why do *you think evil in your hearts*? For which is easier, to say . . . "

Matt 9:10-13
(Pharisees said, *Why does your Teacher eat with tax collectors and sinners?*)

Jesus said, "But *go and learn what this means: 'I desire mercy and not sacrifice*. For I did not come to call the righteous but sinners to repentance."

Matt 12:22-37 (Mark 3:28-29)
(The Pharisees blaspheme the Holy Spirit by saying that Jesus cast out demons by authority of the demon-himself, Beelzebub.)

Jesus corrects them. "If Satan casts out Satan, he is divided against himself. Will his kingdom stand? And if I cast out demons by Beelzebub, *by whom do your sons cast them out? Let them be your judges.* But if I cast out demons by the Spirit of God, surely the kingdom of God has come upon you."

Vs 32: "Anyone who speaks against the Son of man, it will be forgiven him; *but whoever speaks against the Holy Spirit, it will not be forgiven him . . .*

Vs 34: *Brood of vipers! How can you, being evil, speak good things? For out of the abundance of the heart the mouth speaks.*

Vs 37: *For by your words you will be justified, and by your words you will be condemned.*

Matt 12:38-45 (Lk 11:24-26, 29-32)
(The Pharisees demand a sign.)

Jesus responds:

Vs 38: *"An evil and adulterous generation seeks after a sign and no sign . . .*

Vs 45: *". . . so shall it be with this wicked generation."*

Matt 15:1-9 (Mk 7:1-23) (*Debate over tradition*)
Pharisees ask, "Why do your disciples transgress the tradition of the elders? . . ."

Jesus answers:

Vs 3: *"Why do you also transgress the commandment of God because of your tradition?"*

Vs 4-6: (He discusses their disobedience of God's command to honor your father and your mother as they replace it with their religious traditions.)

Vs 6-7:*"Thus you have made the commandment of God of no effect by your tradition.*

Hypocrites. Well did Isaiah prophesy about you saying:

Vs 8-9: *These people draw near to me with their mouth, and honor me with their lips, but their heart is far from Me, teaching as doctrines the commandments of men."*

Matt 15:12-20

(His disciples come to warn Him that the Pharisees were offended. He responds.)

Vs 13: "Every plant which my heavenly Father has not planted will be uprooted.

Vs 14: *Let them alone, they are the blind leaders of the blind. And if the blind leads the blind, both will fall into a ditch."*

Matt 12:12-13 (Mk 11:15-17; Lk 19:45, 46)

(Jesus cleanses the temple)

Vs 12: *Then Jesus went into the temple of God and drove out all those who bought and sold in the temple and overturned the tables of the moneychangers and the seats of those who sold doves.*

Vs 13: And He said to them, "It is written, 'My house shall be called a house of prayer, *but you have made it a den of thieves.'"*

Matt 21:28-32

Jesus speaks the parable about obedience/disobedience of two sons to the priests and elders in the temple. He then asks, "Which of the two did the will of his father?" Following their answer, He says, *"Assuredly, I say to you that tax collectors and harlots enter the kingdom of God before you. For John came to you in the way of righteousness and you did not believe him; but tax collectors and harlots believed him; and when you saw it, you did not afterward relent and believe him."*

Matt 21:43 (Mk 12:1-12; Lk 20:9-19)
(*At the end of the parable of the landowner, Jesus tells the priests and elders*) *"Therefore I say to you, the* kingdom of God will be taken from you and given to a nation bearing the fruits of it:"

Matt 22:15-22
(*Pharisees seek to trap Him in discussion about taxes.*)
   Vs 18: But Jesus *perceived their wickedness*, and said to them, *"Why do you test me, you hypocrites?"*

Matt 22:23-33
(*Sadducees test Jesus regarding the Resurrection by asking Him about whose wife a woman would be in heaven, since she had been married seven times.*)
   Vs 29 Jesus answered and said to them, *"You are mistaken, not knowing the Scriptures nor the power of God . . . have you not read what was spoken to you by God, saying . . ."*

Luke 20:45-47
Then, in the hearing of all the people, He said to His disciples, *"Beware of the scribes, who* desire to go around in long robes, love greetings in the marketplace, the best seats in the synagogues, and the best places at feasts, who devour widows' houses, and for a pretense make long prayers. *These will receive greater condemnation.*

Luke 11:37-44

(*Jesus is asked to dine with a Pharisee. He went in without first washing, and the Pharisees were offended by His disregard of their tradition. Jesus responded.*)

"Now you Pharisees make the outside of the cup and dish clean, but your inward part is full of greed and wickedness. Foolish ones. . . . But woe to you Pharisees. For you tithe *mint and rue and all manner of herbs and pass by justice and the love of God.* These you ought to have done, without leaving the others undone. *Woe to you Pharisees. For you love* the best seats in the synagogues and greetings in the marketplaces. *Woe to you scribes and Pharisees, hypocrites. For you are like graves which are not seen, and the men who walk over them are not aware of them* . . .

Luke 11:45-52

The lawyers tell Him, "Teacher, by saying these things, You reproach us also."

And He said,

"*Woe to you also lawyers! For you load men with burdens hard to bear, and you yourselves do not touch the burdens with one of your fingers.*

. . . For you build the tombs of the prophets, and your fathers killed them . . . *For you have taken away the key of knowledge. You did not enter in yourselves, and those who were entering, you hindered.*

Luke 13:10-16

(*Jesus was teaching in the synagogue on Sabbath and healed a woman. The ruler of the synagogue was indignant.*)

Jesus answered, "*Hypocrite. Does not each one of you on the Sabbath* loose his ox or donkey from the stall, and lead it away to water it? So ought not this woman . . . be loosed from this bond on the Sabbath?

Luke 16:1-15
Parable of the unjust servant

(Jesus has just told this parable, and the Pharisees deride Him for it.)

He said to them, *"You are those who justify yourselves before men, but God knows your hearts. For what is highly esteemed among men is an abomination in the sight of God."*

John 3:9-12

(Jesus has discussed being born of both the water and the Spirit, and the difference between the flesh and the Spirit.) Nicodemus says, "How can these things be?"

Jesus answers, *"Are you the teacher of Israel, and do not know these things?* Most assuredly, I say to you, We speak what We know and testify what We have seen, and you do not receive our witness. *If I have told you earthly things and you do not believe, how will you believe if I tell you heavenly things?"*

John 8:12-47

(The Pharisees challenged Jesus for giving testimony about Himself. During the response, Jesus said, [vs 38]): "I speak what I have seen with My Father, *and you do what you have seen with your father. If you were Abraham's children, you would do the works of Abraham. . . . You do the deeds of your father . . . If God were your father, you would love Me, for I proceeded forth and came from God . . . You are of your father the devil, and the desires of your father you want to do . . . therefore, you do not hear, because you are not of God.*

Matt 23:13-33
(Jesus Condemns the Pharisees)

13: But *woe to you, scribes and Pharisees, hypocrites. For* you shut up the kingdom of heaven against men: for *you neither go in yourselves, nor do you allow those who are entering, to go in.*

14: *Woe to you, scribes and Pharisees, hypocrites. For you devour widows' houses and for a pretense make long prayers. Therefore, you will receive greater condemnation.*

15: *Woe to you, scribes and Pharisees, hypocrites. For you* travel land and sea to win one proselyte, and when he is won, *you make him twice as much a son of hell as yourselves.*

16: *Woe to you, blind guide, who says,* 'Whoever swears by the temple, it is nothing; but whoever swears by the gold of the temple, he is obliged to perform it'

17: *Fools and blind!* For which is greater, the gold or the temple that sanctifies the gold?

19: *Fools and blind. For which is greater—the gift or the altar that sanctifies the gift?*

23: *Woe to you, scribes and Pharisees, hypocrites. For you* pay tithe of mint and anise and cumin, and *neglect the weight of matters of the law; justice and mercy and faith. These you ought to have done, without having the others undone.*

24: *Blind guides, who strain out a gnat and swallow a camel!*

25: *Woe to you, scribes and Pharisees, hypocrites. For you* cleanse the outside of the cup and dish, but *inside they are full of extortion and self-indulgence.*

27: *Woe to you scribes and Pharisees, hypocrites. For you are like whitewashed tombs which indeed appear beautiful outwardly, but inside are full of dead men's bones and all uncleanness.*

28: *Even so you also outwardly appear righteous to men, but inside you are full of hypocrisy and lawlessness.*

33: *Serpents, brood of vipers! How can you escape the condemnation of hell?*

Section Application

- What has the Spirit revealed to you?
- Document principles that Christ used with Spiritual leaders.
- Why do you think that He held leaders accountable in public? (When leaders display and teach error, whether by actions or words, many followers will be led astray. Therefore, the truth must be stated at the time the error is demonstrated.)
- How did He deal with pride and conceit in leaders?
- What did He do about their lack of knowledge and wisdom or their misuse of it?
- How does the Spirit want you to permit Him to live through you in similar interactions? How are you and He going to approach this?

Christ with His Disciples

Jesus always edified and exhorted His apostles/disciples, both to teach them and to lead them to maturity. He taught with patience but also required accountability for walking maturely. *He expected them to be responsible for living what they had been taught by Him and did not coddle them when they did not.*

Jesus Teaches His Disciples the Seriousness of Being His Followers

Matt 23 (*Jesus is unafraid to reveal the faults of religious leaders to the multitudes so that His people may find the truth.*)

3: Whatever they tell you to observe, that observe and do, *but do not do according to their works; for they say and do not do.*

4: *For they bind heavy burdens, hard to bear, and lay them on men's shoulders; but they themselves will not move them with one of their fingers.*

5: *But all their works they do to be seen by men.* They . . .

6: They love the best places at feasts, the best seats in the synagogues,

7: Greetings in the marketplaces, and to be called by men, *Rabbi, Rabbi.*

12: *And whoever exalts himself will be humbled, and he who humbles himself will be exalted*

John 15:6 (The vine and vinedresser—Jesus declares the truth with love but without apology.)

If anyone does not abide in Me, he is cast out as a branch and is withered, and they gather them and throw them into the fire, and they are burned.

Matt 10:33-34, 37-38

(*Jesus is instructing the apostles as He is sending them out*)

"Therefore, whoever confesses Me before men, him I will confess before my Father who is in heaven.

Do not think that I came to bring peace to the earth, I did not come to bring peace but a sword. . . .

He who loves his father and mother more than me *is not worthy of me* . . . he who does not take up his cross and follow after Me *is not worthy of me.*"

Jesus' responses when apostles held onto an immature faith instead of living what He had taught them.

Matt 15:15-20
(Peter comes and asks for the meaning of the parable.)
Jesus responds, *"Are you also without understanding? Do you not yet understand . . ."*

John 14:8-10
Philip said to Him, "Lord, show us the Father, and it is sufficient for us."
Jesus said to him, *"Have I been with you so long, and yet you have not known Me, Philip?"* He who has seen Me has seen the Father; so *how can you say, 'Show us the Father?'"*
"Do you not believe that I am in the Father, and the Father in Me . . ."

John 20:27
(Christ appearing to Thomas after His resurrection.)
Then He said to Thomas, "Reach your finger here, and look at my hands; and reach your hand here and put it into My side. *Do not be unbelieving but believe."*

John 21:22 Speaking to Peter about John
Jesus said to him, *"If I will that he remains till I come, what is that to you? You follow Me."*

Mark 5:40 (Matt 8:26; Luke 8:25)
The disciples have been afraid during a storm. Jesus said,
   "Why are you so fearful? How is it that you have no faith?"

Matt 14:31 (Mk 6:45-52; John 6:14-21)
Peter panicked as he was walking on water to reach Jesus. Jesus says:
   "O you of little faith, why did you doubt?"

Matt 16:8-11 (Mark 8:13-21)
The disciples think that Jesus is talking about them having no bread. Jesus says,
   "O you of little faith, why do you . . . Do you not understand, or remember the five loaves and the five thousand . . . ? *How is it that you do not understand that* I did not speak to you concerning bread—but to beware of the leaven of the Pharisees and Sadducees?"

Matt 17:14-20 (Mk 9:14-29; Lk 9:37-42)
(The disciples could not heal a demon-possessed son. Jesus said,)
   "O faithless and perverse generation, how long shall I be with you? How long shall I bear with you? Bring him to me."

Mark 10:13-14
(People brought little children to Him, but the disciples rebuked those who brought them.)
   Vs 14: But when Jesus saw it, *He was greatly displeased.*

Matt 26:40
(Jesus was praying in Gethsemane and asked His disciples to watch with Him. He found them asleep and said to Peter) *"What? Could you not watch with Me one hour?"*

Mark 4:3-13

(Parable of the sower. When they were alone, the disciples asked Him about it.) Jesus replies, "To you it has been given to know the mystery of the kingdom of God; . . . *Do you not understand this parable? How then will you understand all the parables?*"

Mark 7:18-23

(Jesus has just confronted the Pharisees about their sin of washing clean on the outside but being defiled on the inside. His disciples ask Him about the parable He had used. He responds,)

"Are you thus without understanding also? Do you not perceive that . . . ?"

Mark 8:15, 17, 18, 21

Vs 15: He charged the disciples, saying, "Take heed, beware of the leaven of the Pharisees and the leaven of Herod."

His disciples misunderstood.

Vs 17: But Jesus, being aware of it, said to them, *"Why do you reason because you have no bread? Do you not perceive nor understand? Is your heart still hardened?*

Having eyes, do you not see? And having ears, do you not hear? And do you not remember?"

Vs 21: So He said to them, *"How is it you do not understand?"*

Note Well: Christ exhorts believers to maturity and accountability for living in the truth and faith they have been exposed to. Do we see much of this in today's church, or do we see more enabling of immaturity/lack of accountability and resultant dependence on leaders?

Jesus' Responses When Disciples Are Acting Against God's Will

Matt 16:22-23

Peter rebukes Jesus by telling Him that "this (being killed) shall not happen to You!" Jesus says to Peter,

"Get behind Me, Satan. You are an offense to Me, for you are not mindful of the things of God, but the things of men."

Luke 9:51-56

(Jesus sent messengers into a village of the Samaritans, to prepare for Him. They did not receive Him.)

When James and John, His disciples, saw this, they asked Jesus, "Lord, do You want us to command fire to come down from heaven and consume them, just as Elijah did?

But He turned and rebuked them, and said,

"You do not know what manner of spirit you are of.

"For the Son of Man did not come to destroy men's lives but to save them."

Section Application

- What has the Spirit revealed to you?
- What are the principles that Jesus utilized with His disciples? Has He changed, or has church culture misrepresented Him?

- What are His expectations for all disciples, beginning with you? Are you accountable for walking in all He has taught you? (We are to do this in the Spirit, not our flesh.)

- Do you agree that He always develops and exhorts His disciples into the maturity of living as He had taught them? In today's church culture, would His actions be approved?

- How do you feel when He deals with you in the same ways?

- Does He want you to permit Him to act in and through you in all the ways He displayed in the Gospels, or is He limiting Himself to what mankind's church and secular cultures have declared is acceptable? Are you restricting Him?

- Are you ever bringing glory to Christ when you walk in your flesh instead of in the Spirit?

Christ's Arrest and Trials

Jesus spoke not a word *in defense of Himself* as He faced His accusers, judges, persecutors, and executioners. He, as the Lamb of God and as a lamb to the slaughter, submitted in humble obedience to the Father and to His sacrificial work for mankind. *However, He spoke directly and boldly about His identity, God's truths, and God's authority.* Have you been taught or left with the impression that, during every aspect of His trials, suffering, and crucifixion, He spoke not a word? He is both the Lamb and the Lion of Judah during these times.

Arrest

John 18:4-8
Jesus has already told the guards that He is the one they are seeking. They ask again and He says,

"I have told you that I am He. Therefore, if you seek Me, let these go on their way."

Trial Before Religious Rulers, Sanhedrin

Mark 14:62 (Matt 26: 64)
The high priest asked Him if He were the Christ.

Vs 62: Jesus said, "I am. And you will see the Son of Man sitting at the right hand of the Power and coming with the clouds in heaven."

Luke 22:67-71
The chief priests and the scribes asked Him, "If you are the Christ, tell us."

But He said to them, *"If I tell you, you will by no means believe.*

And if I also ask you, you will by no means answer Me or let Me go.

Hereafter, the Son of Man will sit on the right hand of the Power of God."

They ask, "Are You, then, the Son of God?"

He replies, *"You rightly say that I am."*

John 18:19-24
The high priest then asked Jesus about His disciples and His doctrine.

Jesus then answered him, *"I spoke openly to the world. I always taught in synagogues and in the temple, where the Jews always meet, and in secret I have said nothing.*

Why do you ask Me? Ask those who have heard Me what I said to them. Indeed, they know what I said."

An officer struck Jesus for speaking to the high priest in that manner.

Jesus answered him, *"If I have spoken evil, bear witness to the evil; but if well, why do you strike Me?"*

Trial Before Pilate

John 18:33-34
Pilate asks Him if He is the King of the Jews.

Jesus answered him, *"Are you speaking for yourself about this, or did others tell you this concerning me?"*

John 8:35-37
Pilate asks what He has done.

Jesus answered, *"My kingdom is not of this world. If My kingdom were of this world, My servants would fight, so that I should not be delivered to the Jews; but now My kingdom is not from here."*

Pilate asks if He is a king. Jesus responds, *"You say rightly that I am a king. For this cause I was born, and for this cause I have come into the world, that I should bear witness to the truth. Everyone who is of the truth hears My voice.*

John 19:9-11
(Jesus does not respond to Pilate's questions. Pilate demands) "Do you not know that I have the power to crucify you and the power to release You?"

Jesus answers, *"You could have no power at all against Me unless it had been given you from above. Therefore, the one who delivers Me to you has the greater sin."*

Section Application

- What does the Spirit reveal to you about Christ the sacrificial Lamb and Christ the Lion?
- What does the Spirit reveal that this means for your life?

Christ with the Multitudes and Other Categories of Individuals

Jesus teaches lovingly, directly, and clearly. He does not soften His message to draw people to Him in words that seek to win their emotions or step softly around their issues.

Matt 23:1-12

Jesus characterizes the Pharisees to the multitudes and His disciples.

He spoke, saying,

"The scribes and the Pharisees sit in Moses' seat.

Therefore, whatever they tell you to observe, that observe and do, *but do not do according to their works; for they say and do not do.*

For they bind heavy burdens, hard to bear, and lay them on men's shoulders, but they themselves will not move them with one of their fingers.

But all their works they do to be seen by men. . . . They love the best places at festivals, the best seats in the synagogue and to go about in long robes and being called Rabbi.

But you, do not be called Rabbi, for one is your Teacher, the Christ, and you are all brethren.

But do not call anyone on earth your father; for One is your Father, He who is in heaven."

Luke 20:44-47
Then in the hearing of all the people, He said to His disciples,

"Beware of the scribes, who desire to go around in long robes, love greetings in the marketplaces, the best seats in the synagogue, and the best places at feasts.

Who devour widows' houses, and for a pretense make long prayers. These will receive greater condemnation."

Luke 12:1
As a multitude had gathered, He began to say to His disciples,

"Beware of the leaven of the Pharisees which is hypocrisy."

Matt 5:13
"You are the salt of the earth; but if the salt loses its flavor, how shall it be seasoned? It is then good for nothing but to be thrown out and trampled underfoot by men."

Matt 5:19
"Whoever therefore breaks one of the least of these commandments, and teaches men so, shall be called the least in the kingdom of heaven; but whoever does and teaches them, he shall be called great in the kingdom of heaven."

Matt 5:20
"For I say to you, that unless your righteousness exceeds the righteousness of the scribes and Pharisees, you shall by no means enter the kingdom of heaven."

Matt 6:7
"And when you pray, do not use vain repetitions as the heathen do. For they think they will be heard for their many words."

Matt 7:1-5
Teaching about not judging
"Why do you look at the speck in your brother's eye, but do not consider the plank in your own eye? . . .
Hypocrite! First remove the plank from your own eye, and then you will see clearly to remove the speck from your brother's eye."

Matt 7:6
"Do not give what is holy to the dogs; nor cast your pearls before swine; lest they trample them under their feet and turn and tear you in pieces."

Matt 7:21-23
"Not everyone who says to Me, 'Lord, Lord,' shall enter the kingdom of heaven, but he who does the will of My Father in heaven.
Many will say to Me in that day, 'Lord, have we not prophesied in Your name, cast out demons in Your name, and done many wonders in Your name?'
And then I will declare to them, 'I never knew you; depart from Me, you who practice lawlessness!'"

John 4:7-26
(Jesus interacting with the "woman at the well")
Jesus responded, *"You have said well, 'I have no husband,' for you have had five husbands, and one whom you now have is not your husband; in that you spoke truly."*

John 4:2
"For you worship what you do not know; we know what we worship, for salvation is of the Jews."

Luke 9:62
Jesus is responding to another who says that he will follow Him but wishes to bid farewell to those in his house.

Jesus said, *"No one, having put his hand to the plow, and looking back, is fit for the kingdom of God."*

Luke 12:49-53
(Jesus is warning about the cost of discipleship.)

Vs 49: *"I came to send fire on the earth, and how I wish it were already kindled!"*

Vs 51: *"Do you suppose that I came to give peace on earth? I tell you, not at all, but rather division."*

Luke 7:40-48
(Jesus corrects and teaches His host. First, He tells a parable and then says)

"Do you see this woman? *I entered your house; you gave me no water for my feet, but she* has washed My feet . . . *You gave me no kiss, but* this woman . . . *You did not anoint my head with* oil, but this woman has . . . I say to you, her sins, which are many, are forgiven, for she loved much . . . "

Section Application

- What did the Holy Spirit reveal to you about presenting the truths of the Gospel?

- Paul was all things to all people. He respected them and related with them. Did Paul modify the message of the gospel to attract people? Did He use cultural attractiveness to draw people to his teaching, or did the Spirit draw them to Christ and the gospel?

1 Cor 2:4

And my speech and my preaching were not with persuasive words of human wisdom, but in the demonstration of the Spirit and of power.

- Are you willing to walk in the Spirit so that your life demonstrates the Spirit, His power, His truth, and His love, while simultaneously respecting the dignity of others?

Summary

Christ's life in the Gospels, as both the Lion of Judah and the Lamb of God, defines how His love, compassion, mercy, and kindness are to be lived through us. Church and secular cultures are not to redefine how we are to live. *We are not to block the Spirit-led expression of Christ through our lives.*

Will you permit the Spirit to live in and through you in all the character and manifestation of Christ as He revealed Himself, or are you mimicking an alternative image that you received from family, friends, church, or culture? *Are you willing to follow the Spirit as your mentor and Lord?*

Examples:
Lion or Lamb: What Would the Spirit Direct?
What Does Christ's Compassion Look Like?

A Christian group discussed the following. A couple had been married for a few years. Each had had a previous marriage, and both brought children with them. The husband had an adult son who had a history of broken lifestyle. The wife had younger children. The son had previously lived with them, with seriously negative impacts. She had experienced significant concerns regarding his presence. The son had declared and acted on a commitment to break up the marriage. He had been required to leave but now had no place to go. The father brought him back into the home without consulting his wife and without a developmental plan. She did not want to reintroduce the caustic situation and did not wish to enable broken behaviors.

The group aligned around two perspectives. Some believed that the wife was not showing the "compassion" of Christ and was obligated to demonstrate it by accepting the son with no mutually accepted plan. Others believed that true Christian compassion would support the son in a more constructive and disciplined manner, including utilizing professional counseling, housing, and personal accountability.

Our point is not to choose the "right" expression of compassion for this situation. It is to consider the truth that Christ's compassion, as well as all His other characteristics, takes many forms, and the Spirit is to be the source of action, not tribal bias.

The first option reflects one view of Christ's love and compassion as the Lamb. It accommodates without setting godly standards and minimizes a primary issue of the destructive communications between spouses. It prioritizes the son's immediate needs.

The alternative is willing to ask, "What does Christ's compassion look like?" It defines options utilizing a broader perspective that some define as lacking compassion and others categorize as representing the Lion of Judah.

I later presented this situation to a respected Christian psychologist. Before we got far into the details, his first comment was, "What does Christ's compassion look like? There are many constructive options. Some individuals seem to be misconstruing enabling for compassion." He suggested that one constructive and non-enabling form of compassion could be presented by saying, "We love you, and we will not abandon you. We will walk this journey with you to help you find the organizations that will guide you through this time by providing appropriate housing, supporting your recovery from addictions, and establishing healthy lifestyles. As you work with them, we will stand with you and support you. However, you may not live with us."

Christ shows love and compassion in a manner that is most helpful for each circumstance. His solutions are unique to situations and are built on His biblical principles. If we limit God to the expressions that mankind's church, cultures, and tribes have identified with the Lamb, we are not letting Christ live fully through us.

The Lion and the Lamb in Restoration: Breaking Strongholds

A gifted pastor emulates Christ's loving manner of interceding and helping individuals gain freedom from crippling strongholds. Her work includes guiding them to the truth and away from identifying themselves negatively, based on their failures, fears, and the destructive input others continuously speak over them. Following the guidance of the Spirit, she draws them to Christ's love, truths, and His healing process. She helps them accept and stand on the truths of who they are in Him, and these gradually replace lies. She engages them from a perspective of absolute belief in who they are called to be in Christ and exhorts them to begin to establish solid foundations in Him.

With love, she will stop them, even publicly, from putting on broken identities as she calls them back to the truth. Sometimes, these interventions hurt, but the individuals love her for them, and they mature through them. Most share they value a person who truly loves them and consequently will not enable them to wallow in self-pity and lie-burdened identities and behaviors. They often express how incredibly positive it is to experience her true tough love, instead of the misplaced gentleness that has haunted them through well-intended Christians. God's touch through her results in transformation.

Some would say the Pastor's Spirit-led confrontations in public are not Christ-like. They would be accepting a restricted paradigm. Look at the scriptures above. Christ often engaged this way. Are you willing to be Spirit led and faithful enough to let Christ live through you as both the Lion of Judah and the Lamb of God?

The Lion and the Lamb at the Spirit's Time

Consider again our pastor who coaches and counsels addicts through Christ's love, grace, mercy, and strength. She walks beside individuals for months, as God works. When experience and the Spirit tell her that a person is no longer engaging with either God or her for help and is choosing addiction above all else, she helps them face and own the truth about their decisions. She makes it clear that deep substance addiction will claim their lives and that, "You are currently choosing death. Until you want to live, no one can help you." Whether they choose life or death, they greatly value her love, compassion, and forthrightness. This is Christ in action.

Cultural Blindness

The general population defines "messing up" only as being too strong or confrontational. They readily embrace "avoidance of difficult approaches" and call it "Godly behavior." *Both are equally damaging if they are not God-led. We hurt others when we act in our flesh instead of walking under the authority of the Holy Spirit.*

Full Chapter Application
What Did the Holy Spirit Reveal to You?

- What truths did the Spirit reveal to you?
- Are you willing to permit Christ to live fully through you as both Lion and Lamb, or are you chained to the half-life that cultures have imposed on you?
- Do you accept the responsibility that only Christians who are committed to the journey of learning to walk under the control of the Spirit can truly live in the fullness of Christ?
- Do you understand that whenever characteristics of Christ as Lion or Lamb are portrayed through you by your

flesh, they are destructive to His kingdom purposes and dishonoring to God?

- How does the Spirit want you to begin living in His full character and actions?
- How is your walk with Him going to be different from this point forward?
- Please ask Him to provide at least one mentor for this journey.

CHAPTER 21

Breaking Free: Christ's Victory Over Strongholds and Bondages

Heb 12:1
Let us lay aside every weight, and the sin which so easily ensnares us, and let us run with endurance the race that is set before us.

John 8:36
Therefore if the Son makes you free, you shall be free indeed.

Phil 3:13-14
Brethren, I do not count myself to have apprehended, but one thing I do, forgetting those things which are behind and reaching forward to those things which are ahead,

I press toward the goal for the prize of the upward call of God in Christ Jesus

2 Cor 5:17
Therefore, if anyone is in Christ, he is a new creation; old things have passed away; behold, all things have become new.

Everyone who is in Christ is a new creation. Even so, each of us is broken in comparison with Christ and His design for our lives. We are on journeys of sanctification which involve His transformations and appropriation of His freedom.

What do we do with the scars and wounds that attempt to anchor us to the past and the sins that seem to dominate our lives? What do we do with wounds and sin habits that become strongholds and bondages? For true strongholds, efforts of our flesh are futile. Only the Spirit can free us. This is not easy and is not to be taken lightly. Although God may free us of some things instantaneously, others require daily appropriation of the work of the cross. Deep hurts, rejections, failures, abuse, addictions, and physical or mental challenges normally fit these categories. All of these seek to shout Satan's lie that we are less than *the wonderful masterpiece that we really are in Christ.* No matter what stage we are in brokenness, crisis, and healing, as we walk in His Spirit, God uses us as His masterpieces for His glory.

Difficulties are not to be minimized by attempting to deny them, hide them under a rug, or push past them by thinking we can live in false victories of self-discipline and superficial positive thinking. We cannot change the past, but we can overcome it in Christ. His journey to healing will utilize all that has happened to us, for His good. This truth does not mean, as some Christians insist, that just because we know Him and have prayed for healing, everything will magically become fantastic from earthly perspectives. One gifted mentor teaches that one of the unfortunate ways Christians deeply hurt and hinder the recovery of individuals in crisis is to basically tell them, "Take it to Christ, and get on with your life. Everything will be fine." We each need to find His freedom and healing, and that takes embracing the intentionality of walking with Him through His individualized recovery processes.

Breaking Free: Christ's Victory Over Strongholds and Bondages

This chapter presents an introduction of basic thoughts regarding strongholds and bondages. They deserve a comprehensive study that includes spiritual warfare truths that often need to be applied through Christian psychology. That is well beyond the purpose of this book. Our intent is to encourage all to understand their brokenness and find the individualized process and freedom Christ has for them. Christ does not promise a "Pollyanna recipe" for instant and easy freedom, although it may occur. His processes for overcoming some challenges may span a lifetime as He utilizes them to bring His incredible strength into our walks for His glory. Even if you find yourself in this last situation, you can live above these circumstances in the victory of Christ's life in you. Some of my challenges require moment-by-moment surrender at the cross of Christ.

Also, it is foolish to try to "forget the past" or brush aside current challenges in critical areas. We are to deal with them in Christ. Even when we have Christ's victories over these issues, it is not realistic to expect to totally "forget" them. Memories remain, but they will have constructive impacts as we convert them into "monuments to Christ." Monument memories never have a destructive hold on us. They glorify Christ.

We look at four areas and provide references to resources that may assist you in finding Christ's freedom. These are:

- Strongholds and bondages
- Opportunities for improvement
- Processes for receiving Christ's freedom
- Resources for help

> *Every Christian has areas of bondages or strongholds. If we are not aware of ours, we have been blinded by the enemy.*

Spiritual Strongholds and Bondages
Barriers to Freedom

Webster's Dictionary defines "barriers" as:

- Anything material or immaterial that separates or impedes
- A factor that tends to restrict the free movement of individuals or populations

Deep hurts, abuse, false understandings of God or our identities in Christ, addictions, experiences with the occult, and broken relationships frequently result in bondages or strongholds. These are deeply rooted in spiritual issues. These barriers do not surprise God. He created every individual. He knows what will tempt us, the mistakes we will make, the infirmities we will face, and the life journeys He has for us. Life in Christ's Spirit *will* result in victorious kingdom life. He also knows how the enemy will seek to destroy our ability to see ourselves with God's eyes and to live accordingly.

Physical or mental characteristics, limitations, and disabilities have the potential to become barriers. They were permitted for reasons that only God understands. They may at times break our hearts, as we very reasonably ask Him, "Why?" and, "Please remove these." When He does not, and the answer to "why" is left to reside in faith and trust in Him, we are faced with options. Defeat and bitterness is one path. Finding freedom and victory in the Spirit, even as we endure painful circumstances, is God's design.

Each of these challenges may become barriers to our growth if they are permitted to gain significant and destructive influence over our lives. When any of these result in extensive destruction to quality and function of life and relationships, they may be described as bondages or strongholds.

Bondages, Oppressions, and Strongholds

We describe bondages/strongholds as repeat and destructive behaviors that express themselves in people who find that they are subject to compulsions and indeed are enslaved to habits, emotions, and desires. These are present in both non-Christians and Christians, and generally result from living under the influence of severe barriers to healthy life. The enemy desires to utilize these to bring brokenness. God brings freedom and empowerment in His way and time.

Oppressions

For our purposes, oppressions are bondages that "come on a person." They are not always present, but when they appear, they may include infrequent or unusual experiences of such things as lust, fear, anger, rejection, jealousy, worry, and inferiority. All individuals experience a level of these, but oppressions come on with great force and resist our efforts to handle them constructively. When we do not find God's help, these may become strongholds. The enemy is frequently behind these seemingly outside impulses.

Strongholds

Strongholds are areas of destructive actions and attitudes that we have embraced. They now dominate our lives and are like fortresses within us. Even if we detest them, we are hardly ever able to gain victory over them. Until we are desperate, we insist on the deception that we can control them any time we wish. They include every form of destructive lifestyle and attitude, including substance addictions, sexual addictions, outbursts of anger, worry, jealousy, enabling, hatred, and seeking to control people and situations. These repeated attitudes and actions are both self-destructive and destructive to others. (Some Christians seek to "justify" them, ignoring what the Bible teaches.) They are deeply embedded, and only the Spirit can free us. Long-term commitment, persistence, and spiritual warfare are involved. Professional Christian counseling, formal-intervention processes, and active Christian support systems each play important roles. The foundation for success is found in our personal relationship with God and our surrender to walking in His Spirit. Self-discipline and determination that rely on our flesh will never result in victory. In my experience, victory from true stronghold areas is generally moment by moment in Christ.

A partial summary of stronghold areas includes:

+ Trying to control your life
+ Addictions in all forms
+ Consistent sexual problems
+ Persistent emotional challenges, including fear, anger, rejection, jealousy, worry, inferiority, and insecurity that do not result from legitimate mental illness

- Persistent mental challenges, including confusion, procrastination, compromise, rationalization, and doubt that do not result from legitimate mental illness. Causes for these differ.

- Consistent inappropriate use of the tongue, including lying, profanity, criticism, and gossip

- Consistent sins of the heart, including judgmentalism, impatience, intolerance, bitterness, unforgiveness, pride, and covetousness

Freedom from Strongholds/Bondages and Oppression

Freedom normally involves spiritual warfare, which we discussed in Chapter 17. We do not fight against flesh and blood, and we will not find victory if that is our focus. We are to root out and throw down before we build and plant.

Freedom begins with

- Total surrender to God in all aspects of life.

- Requesting that He reveal any and all areas that you have kept from His Lordship. Surrender these, and hold nothing back.

- Confession, repentance, and walking in God's forgiveness.

- Choosing to seek life and freedom.

- Christian counseling, strong programs, and support.

- Recognizing the strong resistance from within yourself and from the enemy. Deal with it immediately in Christ.

- Learning to trust Christ's love for you and His expression of His life in and through you as you *Be and Become* even in your most difficult expressions of brokenness.

- Celebrate and worship God, as a lifestyle, right where you are, as you grow in Him.

Resources

There are many excellent Christian resources that deal with bondages, oppressions, and strongholds. We recommend these be utilized in conjunction with qualified Christian counselors who understand spiritual warfare and have a demonstrated a history of success in helping others find and live in Christ's freedom and victory. Permit God to direct you. Resources include:

- The Bible
- Your Pastor
- Perish No More Ministries: Step To Freedom
- Freedom from addictive behaviors for both the individual and those connected to them.
- *The Bondage Breaker*—Neil T. Anderson
- *Victory Over the Darkness*—Neil T. Anderson (Read for what the Spirit reveals)
- Focus on the Family—Referrals to Christian counselors

Keep Our Eyes on Christ
A Hummingbird Analogy

My wife attached a hummingbird feeder to a window. The first time a hummingbird came to the feeder, it sat on a perch and looked straight ahead, didn't eat, and quickly flew away. The second visit resulted in a similar approach, until the last few seconds, when it took a quick drink. Through succeeding visits, the time spent looking ahead diminished, and the time gaining sustenance increased. Finally, it simply landed and immediately began enjoying the nectar. We realized what had occurred. Since the room behind the window is dark, the glass acted as a mirror and the hummingbird had been distracted by its own reflection. Eventually it forgot the reflection and went immediately to focusing on gaining strength.

This is much like our own lives. When we stop focusing on ourselves and feed on and trust in Christ, we are free to grow and live as His unique and wonderful creations. Trust Him to mold your life, not your earthly hopes and dreams.

Application

- What has the Spirit revealed to you?
- How is He directing you to appropriate freedom?

PART FIVE

PUTTING IT ALL TOGETHER: EMBRACING AND LIVING AS CHRIST'S MASTERPIECE

CHAPTER 22

Accepting and Embracing the Real You—God's Unique Masterpiece

Phil 1:6
Being confident of this one thing, that He who has begun a good work in you will complete it until the day of Jesus Christ.

Jer 1:17-19
Therefore prepare yourself and arise, and speak to them all that I command you. Do not be dismayed before their faces, lest I dismay you before them. For behold, I have made you this day a fortified city ... They will fight against you, but they shall not prevail against you. For I am with you, says the Lord ...

2 Cor 12:8-10
Concerning this thing (Paul's thorn in the flesh) I pleaded with the Lord three times that it might depart from me.

And He said to me, "My grace is sufficient for you, for My strength is made perfect in weakness." Therefore most gladly I will rather boast in my infirmities, that the power of Christ may rest upon me.

> *Therefore I take pleasure in infirmities, in reproaches,*
> *in needs, in persecutions, in distresses, for Christ's*
> *sake. For when I am weak, then I am strong.*

GAL 2:20A
> *I have been crucified with Christ; it is no longer*
> *I who live, but Christ lives in me;...*

JOHN 15:5
> *I am the vine, you are the branches. He who abides in Me, and*
> *I in him, bears much fruit; for without Me you can do nothing.*

Embracing the Real You

As we move through this chapter, we are to work with the Spirit to consolidate and embrace what we have learned about how God has wired us and called us to specific lives as His unique kingdom masterpieces. These are foundations upon which God works and builds. His life is about continuous growth, and He never limits us to the obvious. Why? *The Spirit of God lives within us, and it is He Who operates both in and through us in the fullness of His identity, gifts, and power. When we know we are weak, He is strong. We are most effective when we are joyfully aware that we can do nothing in our own strength and walk in wonder as we experience Him accomplishing His will in and through us.*

> *It is your joy to never trust in your own ability,*
> *so that you depend totally on God, who is the source of all*
> *true love, gifts, power, and victory.*

Accepting and Embracing the Real You—God's Unique Masterpiece

Whose Life Are You Going to Live?

Summarize what you have learned from the Spirit and what decisions you have made.

- Whose life have you been living, other than for God's? What priority have you given God's unique life and missions?
- Which of these distractions are still deeply rooted in you and will need to be replaced with Christ?
- Have you made the decision to break free and begin the journey of living solely for Christ as the Real You? If so, what is His plan, and what help do you need? If not, do you really want to accept a lesser life?
- Have you surrendered control of your life to the Holy Spirit? Do you recognize that this is a continuing lifestyle of walking in the Spirit and is the only life that results in living as Christ's masterpiece?

Consolidating to Understand the Real You

We discussed each of the following in early chapters. Document specifics for each category. Utilize this information to bring continuous focus to your journey with Christ. You are "wired" for unique kingdom life and missions.

- My primary personality characteristics are:
- My strongest natural gifts are:
- My primary spiritual gifts are:

- My life's greatest passion is:

- Christ has utilized me most effectively in the following roles and positions:

- Above all else, I would like to hear people say the following about me at my funeral:

- Fill in your answer to the following: I believe it is *God's mission to accomplish (fill in your specific answers) through me. The answers should thrill you!*

- I am committed to Walking in the Spirit instead of in my flesh. Describe what God has revealed about how you are to live and walk in the Spirit.

- Living according to the Spirit's revelations will result in the following transformations and growth in my life:

- Just as God called Jeremiah, He has called me to be (fill in your specific "who/what"), and has He given me His authority/influence over (fill in the areas He reveals. Do not limit Him.)

- Spiritual warfare will express itself through my missions according to His plan and how I permit the Spirit to lead me in utilizing His warfare scriptures. Document what He has revealed so far about how you are to walk in them.

Ask the Spirit to consolidate this, and describe/document who you believe God created you to be and what you are to do. What do you believe are your primary kingdom missions? What will embracing this life as His masterpiece look and feel like?

Accepting and Embracing the Real You—God's Unique Masterpiece

Being Transformed into the Real You

You will spend the rest of your life in God's incredible journey of following His Spirit's leadership and maturing in His masterpiece design. Old lifestyles and sin patterns will raise their heads, as will "naysayers" who believe that you should be what they want you to be. Self-doubts may assail you as you step out in faith. Like Peter walking to Christ on the water, the waves may seem too high and the opportunity too great. As you walk in the Spirit, *neither will be true*, and God's masterpiece life will be yours. Implement the following, and your life will blossom.

Your Personal Relationship with God and His Living Word, the Bible

Everything about living and walking in God's life as His "Real You" results through your deepening personal relationship with God and your commitment to "walk in His Spirit." This life is centered in your dynamic encounters with Him and His Bible. It results in stepping out by faith into your unique missions and *Being and Becoming* God's masterpiece.

Mentors

Ask God to provide appropriate mentors for each season of your life. They are to be individuals who walk in the Spirit and experience continuous spiritual growth and increased faith through their journeys with Christ. They will be able to see and believe in you with the eyes of Christ. God will provide these individuals in His time, and there may be periods where you seem to be walking with Him and Him alone. In my most recent season, God directed me to request three mentors. The third came more than three years later. All have different roles from what I expected.

Be careful about with whom you align. Can you imagine knowing that you are to be an expert mountain climber, yet surrounding yourself with individuals who can climb only small hills? Will they be able to take you higher? We must be supported by individuals who not only embrace us in our current vision/missions but also help us move beyond these into God's ever-expanding roles. Avoid all who attempt to constrain your vision to what they believe is "realistic."

Establishing and Living in Your Winning Environment

PSALMS 1:1, 2

Blessed is the man who walks not in the counsel of the ungodly, nor stands in the path of sinners, nor sits in the seat of the scornful: but his delight is in the law of the Lord.

1 COR 15:33

Do not be deceived: Evil company corrupts good habits.

> *In order to achieve your God-created purpose, you are responsible for surrounding yourself with God's winning environment.*

The environment that you live in is made up of many parts. Some of these you may have no control over, at least for a time, but many you do. The most important elements are always under your control. Those are your personal relationship with God and your intentional journey of walking in His Spirit. He is "for you and not against you."

You ultimately have final say over another. This is how you respond to all elements and circumstances in your environment, those you can change and those you can't. You can choose to pursue continuous growth and God's freedom or declare yourself a prisoner to past and current destructive decisions and influencers.

Application

Every person and activity in your life is either lifting you toward or pulling you away from God's designed life for you. Hard choices about activities, friends, and associations may be necessary. Follow the guidance of the Spirit. Be lethal in separating from the most destructive elements, and be joyous in embracing the healthy ones. What have you been giving priority ahead of God and His unique life for you?

Consider the following elements of your environment. Add others as appropriate. Prioritize them according to those that have the most positive and negative impacts relative to helping you live your calling in Christ. Identify the five that help you most, and describe how they do so. Identify the five that most significantly block your progress and describe how they do this. Work with the Spirit to establish plans for maximizing His impact through the positive elements and minimizing the impact of the most destructive. Some actions will be immediate and some delayed. Under the Spirit's constant guidance, put these plans into action.

Share these with your spouse and mentors. Establish relationships that include specific prayers, review, accountability, and celebration, first with God and then with the others. Remember, priority relationships, like those with your wife and children, are to be honored and valued according to the word of God. You cannot claim to be honoring God and simultaneously be dishonoring those around you, beginning with your spouse!

- Spouse
- Family
- Friends
- Neighborhood
- Culture
- Activities
- Vocation/Workplace
- Entertainment: Books, Movies, Music, Television, Web, Electronics, Sports, Gambling
- Hobbies and Recreation
- Church
- School
- Gangs
- Addictions: Substances, Pornography

Accepting and Embracing the Real You—God's Unique Masterpiece

+ The infatuation you have with the roles of position, power, and wealth in your life

> *Remember, you cannot accomplish meaningful changes on your own or by acts of your will. Only the Holy Spirit can transform you, and He does this from within.*

CHAPTER 23

IDENTIFY CHRIST'S VISION, MISSION, AND PLANS FOR YOUR LIFE

PROV 29:18
Where there is no vision, the people perish:

LUKE 14:28-33 (JESUS IS SPEAKING)
"For which of you, intending to build a tower, does not sit down first and count the cost, whether he has enough to finish it . . .

Or what king going to make war against another king, does not sit down first and consider whether he is able with ten thousand to meet him who comes against him with twenty thousand?

ROM 8:5, 6, 7
"For those who live according to the flesh set their minds on the things of the flesh, but those who live according to the Spirit, the things of the Spirit.

For to be carnally minded is death, but to be spiritually minded is life and peace,

Because the carnal mind is enmity against God;

ROM 8:8
So then, those who are in the flesh cannot please God.

God has unique and specific visions and missions for each of us. What will it really mean to live each day and each season of life dynamically engaged in His kingdom missions as we walk in the loving presence and authority of His Spirit? How might this life differ from the average Christian's life? We will thrive as our true identities are released and expanded and God's masterpiece designs are realized through the Spirit. Instead of having our energies diverted into the things of the flesh, we will be intentional about permitting our Father to continuously align us with His purposes according to the things of the Spirit. All other priorities will be viewed and undertaken as elements that fit effectively into God's missions instead of coming ahead of them. Instead of giving God what time is left in our lives, *all* of our time will be His. We will no longer limit our definition of successful Christian lives to fitting comfortably into church and Christian organizations and secular culture.

God accomplishes His purposes in and through the lives of those who approach their walk with Him through intentionality. This looks different for each individual because we are wired differently. However, it includes developing intimate relationships with God, living in His word, walking in His Spirit, and fully engaging in His vision, missions, and plans for each season of life.

In this chapter, we are to clarify God's vision and missions for us and to develop and implement plans for moving forward with Him. We have identified much about how He has wired us, and that plays an important role in this process. Revelations of the Spirit are to lead.

Identify Christ's Vision, Mission, and Plans for Your Life

Vision and Missions

Although there is often confusion between vision and mission, they are vastly different. Very simply, the two are defined as:

- Vision is the very reason that you exist as either an individual or organization.
- Mission consists of the "few" specific and measurable things that you will do well, in order to bring your vision into reality.

We offer the following as truths:

- Working without God's vision and mission is wasteful and ineffective.
- Pursuing a vision and mission without a meaningful, God-designed plan is unrealistic and poor stewardship. Much energy, time, and opportunity are expended with minimal impact.
- Living in God's missions, through His Spirit, results in His rewarding and abundant life.
- Walking in the Spirit is the dynamic life of victory in Christ. It always includes growth, adventure, risk, and godly fulfillment. No other life compares.
- If we are not willing to focus on living according to His unique vision and mission, "Whose life will we be living?"
- Those who do this are consistently the most successful. Which type of Christ-follower do you wish to be?

Your Vision Statement in Christ
Definition

Your vision statement expresses the very reason for your existence. Every time you think about it, you can see and feel your God-designed purpose, and you are filled with passion and the overwhelming desire and energy to bring it into being. It is so large that it can never be fully accomplished. It is understood through progressive revelation of the Spirit. It presents an image of what you are to become or create/accomplish in Christ. It is possible only as you Walk in His Spirit. It establishes your areas of influence. For example, is your ministry international, country specific, or locally specific?

Shaping Our Visions

We have many choices, and we are to find God's vision. Vision always stretches us to permit Him to accomplish more in and through us than we believe is possible. Consider a local businessperson who has the choice of many visions. None is wrong if it is God-led. Bigger/smaller is not better, unless it is God-led. A profitable and Christ-run business is a *means to achieving* God's vision—it is not the vision. God's visions are about touching lives for His kingdom, through this business. Consider the differences between the following options:

Developing a Christ-led business to achieve a fair profit, provide employees a respectful place to work, provide pastoral support to employees, and contribute financially to God's local kingdom work.

Utilizing God's business to impact the local community, including government, business, schools, employees, and their families, so that *all* individuals who either work in or are touched by this business will understand and be helped to become who they are in Christ.

OTHER EXAMPLES:

Healthy Meals

One individual has a vision that every man, woman, and child in their county has at least one healthy meal each day

Another has the vision that every child in their local school system has at least a healthy breakfast and dinner each day.

Reading Skills

One married couple has a vision that all children in their county shall be able to read at a seventh-grade level or higher.

Another has the vision that all adults in their county shall be able to read at least at a seventh-grade level

Common Errors in Vision Statements

Many Christians commit errors that place straitjackets on God's unique purpose for their lives. Normal errors include forms of the following:

- They don't even think about kingdom vision. Winning in this earthly life is their vision.
- They pursue some great passion without asking God to establish their vision.

- They haven't learned how to walk under the control of the Spirit, so they create a flesh-generated, wonderful-sounding "Christian" vision, even though they have not really sought God's input and power.
- They limit themselves and God to a "safe" vision because they are afraid to fail or can't believe that God would have such an incredibly impactful purpose for them.

Develop Your Vision Statement

While considering the above examples, develop God's vision statement for you under the leadership of the Holy Spirit. Remember your summary of how God has wired you, giving particular emphasis to the central passion of your life and the roles where you have felt most fulfilled.

1. Don't think too small. Your vision is to reflect all that God sees for your life, not just what you have learned to see.
2. Include how you would most like to be remembered.
3. Review your summary of "How You Are Wired." Refocus on:
   a. The central passion for your life.
   b. The strongest natural gifts that God has given you.
   c. The strongest spiritual gifts that God has given you.
   d. The roles where God has worked most effectively through you.
   e. The joy that you experience in certain areas as you obey and step way out of your comfort zone.
4. Write God's vision statement for your life. It should be concise and not exceed two sentences. One is normally best.

5. Let it sit for a day or two as you and the Holy Spirit consider it. Refine it as you are led.
6. Share it with your spouse and mentors. Does God's passion explode within you as you share? Do they validate it or stretch you further? If appropriate, go back to work.
7. Finalize your vision statement.

Your Mission Statement in Christ
Definition

Your Mission Statement describes the limited number of initiatives, three to five, *that you will do extremely well in order to fulfill your vision.* These actions are revealed by the Holy Spirit. Mission elements may stretch the realm of possibility. They focus on results that are specific and measurable. Wonderful-sounding *conceptual* results are not really measurable.

Examples of Mission Statements

Consider the following Mission Statement options that are built around the previous vision statements.

Pair with the above Vision Statements:
Vision: Healthy Meals

First Couple's Mission Options:
One Option: In order for this vision to be accomplished, we will *organize and fund food-distribution centers* in the *five largest cities in the county,* so that *fifty percent* of the hungry receive *at least one* nutritious meal per day.

Second Option: In order for this vision to be accomplished, we will *raise one million dollars per year* for each of the *next five years* and *distribute it* to *qualified food-distribution institutions* who serve the most critical populations in *five areas of our county*.

Vision: Reading Skills

First Couple's Mission Options:
One Option: In order for this vision to be accomplished, we will *identify all single-family units* within *five miles of our church* and ensure that each family *with a reading need* is *supported by a qualified* reading tutor.

Second Option: In order to accomplish this vision, we will *develop a group of qualified reading tutors to effectively support every child* with *reading needs* in their *local school system*.

Develop Your Mission Statement

1. Under the Spirit's leadership, specify the measurable three to five things that you are driven to do well in order to accomplish your vision statement. Document these.

    +

    +

    +

2. Let this sit for a few days, as you and the Spirit ponder and finalize them.

3. Document these in one concise sentence that impassions you.
4. Share with spouse and mentors. Are you thrilled as you share? What is their feedback?
5. Finalize your mission statement.

Finalize: Vision and Mission

Combine your Vision and Mission Statements into one single-page document that you commit to and share as appropriate.

Objectives and Action Plans

How much more effective will you be when you develop and adhere to objectives and action plans? Few individuals have written visions and missions, and fewer yet have action plans with specific objectives. An even smaller percentage follow their plans with discipline. Those who do these things are consistently the most successful by an incredible margin.

Truths about the importance of plans and follow-up:

- If "nothing" is your target, that is exactly what you will hit.
- One minute of planning saves countless minutes of effort.
- Objectives and Plans help you achieve maximum effectiveness.
- Individuals who follow the leadership of the Holy Spirit in setting objectives and action plans are the most effective in living God's masterpiece lives.

Your Life's Objectives—Reasonable and Balanced
Developing Individual and Marriage Objectives

We utilize the image and analogy of the Wheel of a Conestoga Wagon for assessing the health and balance of our godly lives. God provided me with this analogy more than forty years ago. Draw your own wheel. The center hub is Christ, and the outer rim connects all of the spokes and represents God's masterpiece design for your life. Insert nine spokes, each having ten equal demarcations. We suggest focusing on the nine areas noted below. If the hub, spokes, and rim are all healthy, your life is in balance and aligned with God's purposes. Growth takes place in a balanced manner. If any spoke is not healthy, the life you live is very bumpy, and the wheel will also not take you the full length of God's intended journey. If all spokes are at a similar length, but at a lower level of health, say, a ranking of three, things may be in balance, but opportunities to improve and live more fully and effectively are extensive. The nine spokes, listed by priority, are:

1. Spiritual Health: Personal Relationship and Maturity of walking in the Spirit

2. Marriage/Spouse

3. Family

4. Health: Physical and Emotional

5. Ministry—Your Kingdom Roles and Missions

6. Career/Vocation

7. Financial

Identify Christ's Vision, Mission, and Plans for Your Life

8. Recreation/Social/Relationships
9. Continuous Learning

Wagon-Wheel View of Individual and Family Life and Objectives Individual Lives and Marriage

We suggest that you first evaluate the balance of your life and confirm your conclusions with your spouse and/or mentors. (Your spouse will benefit from following this process.) Next, in a joint effort with your spouse, consider the health of your marriage. From this work, you will jointly set objectives and plans.

The Process

Whether you are evaluating yourself, your marriage, your family, or your kingdom missions, the process is the same. Follow the Spirit's guidance.

- Specifically define and document what a perfect rating of "ten" would look like for each spoke.

- Specifically rate and document how each area of your life/marriage/mission is currently functioning. Provide not only the number but also the specific reasons you rate it thus—strengths and development areas.

- Connect the rating marks of each spoke and sit back to view your life-wheel. Does it reflect how you experience life as stable, mature, immature, or really bumpy?

- Consider the Vision and Mission statements for your life (and marriage.)

- Determine which elements of the wheel need to become your greatest improvement priorities. You will be most successful when you work on a small number of priority items at a time. Three is generally an effective number, but one is appropriate if it is critical.

- For these priority items, determine what an appropriate improvement objective is for the upcoming time period. One year is a maximum. For example, you may desire to move your marriage relationship from a three to a six. Define the measurable characteristics of the "six" that you are envisioning. It is of limited value to set general objectives that sound like, "We will improve our marriage" or "We will treat each other with respect." Be specific about what that will look like and how you will measure that success. Remember that many of these spokes are related. If your marriage is hurting, then improving your spiritual lives will normally also be appropriate.

- Develop specific and measurable plans for accomplishing individual mission, kingdom mission, marriage objectives, etc. These are to be broken down into milestones with dates, so that you are following and celebrating incremental successes, instead of waiting to hit the final destination. Sometimes getting to your objective in the allotted time is not realistic, and you learn that achieving a lower objective is terrific for this season.

- Get help from skilled Christian counselors in every area that is critical and not making effective progress.

- Review progress, and make adjustments monthly as related to critical priority elements.
- Celebrate milestone accomplishments.

Whether you are considering your God-given missions, your marriage, or your family, this wagon-wheel analogy provides an effective image. An individual rides on a unicycle, the marriage on a two-wheel wagon, and the family on a three- or four-wheel wagon or more. If you or others in your family have short and long spokes in your wheel, functionally the entire family is being bounced all over the place. If the hub, the rim, or a couple of spokes are broken, then the wagon stops or is dragged along by horses with enough energy to pull it. The journey is not effective, and God's masterpiece destination is seemingly out of sight.

We all have "spokes" that need to be strengthened and improved. However, God's journey is not dependent on perfection and "tens." His successes are experienced through journeys of continuous growth in our relationships with Him and our steps toward maturity all along the way.

We consider Spiritual Health, Marriage/Spouse, Family, and Personal Health to be the foundation priorities. God is to be first by light years, and nothing is to compete with Him for that priority. If His "spoke" is broken, in reality, the hub and the axle do not function, and all else suffers. Spouses are to come ahead of your children, even though children are extremely important. There are broken circumstances that may seem to make improvement impossible. With professional guidance, they are to be approached in Christ instead of tolerated.

More about Action Plans

Let the Spirit guide you in establishing realistic improvement milestones and bite-sized action plans along the way to your objectives. Determine what must happen to achieve each milestone, who has specific responsibilities, and agree to completion dates. Don't use commitments and dates to beat each other over the head with. "Progress in the Spirit" is what you seek. Realignment is almost always necessary. If one of you keeps avoiding your commitments, you probably need to get pastoral or other forms of help. Celebrate each milestone.

Once your planning is complete, step back and make sure it is realistic and that you believe it is going to work. Then set up a schedule for coming together to ensure that you are on target or to recognize that plans and objectives need to be adjusted.

We suggest the following for keeping up with important commitments and objectives.

Good practices for relationships include a weekly time together to share about and celebrate successes and experiences with God. Ask for forgiveness corresponding to unresolved hurts. Take specific actions to rectify unresolved hurts and not repeat them.

Monthly time to discuss how the specific improvement areas are progressing and to celebrate and/or make adjustments and resets.

Annually, let the Spirit lead you in finding His next levels of blessing.

Application

Different personalities will respond to this chapter in ways that range from wanting to run away to being very excited. What is your response?

Identify Christ's Vision, Mission, and Plans for Your Life

+ Who do you believe is more likely to result in living God's unique life and marriage—individuals who know God's vision and missions and are following specific plans, or those who spend each day driven by outside forces and doing what makes them comfortable or puts out fires?

+ Which individual life or marriage do you want to experience?

+ If you wish to be God's masterpiece in both individual life and marriage, how is the Spirit guiding you, and what are you going to do? The full structure may be too much for you to start with. Take the one or two bites He suggests.

CHAPTER 24

THIS CHRISTIAN LIFE IS NOT A GAME

MARK 8:34B-38

He (Jesus) said to them, "Whoever desires to come after Me, let him deny himself, and take up his cross, and follow Me.

For whoever desires to save His life will lose it, but whoever loses his life for My sake and the gospel's will save it.

For what will it profit a man if he gains the whole world, but loses his soul?

Or what will a man give in exchange for his soul?

For whoever is ashamed of Me and My words in this adulterous and sinful generation, of him the Son of Man also will be ashamed when He comes in the glory of His Father with the holy angels."

REV 3:16-19

So then, because you are lukewarm, and neither cold nor hot, I will vomit you out of my mouth.

WHOSE LIFE ARE YOU LIVING?

*Because you say, 'I am rich, have become wealthy,
and have need of nothing'—and do not know that you
are wretched, miserable, poor, blind, and naked*

*I counsel you to buy from me gold refined in the fire, that you
may be rich; and white garments, that you may be clothed,
that the shame of your nakedness may not be revealed;
and anoint your eyes with eye salve, that you may see.*

*As many as I love, I rebuke and chasten.
Therefore be zealous and repent.*

MATT 7:21-23

Not everyone who says to me, 'Lord, Lord,' shall enter the kingdom
of heaven, but he who does the will of My Father in heaven.

*Many will say to Me in that day, 'Lord, Lord, have we
not prophesied in Your name, cast out demons in your
name, and done many wonders in Your name?'*

*And then I will declare to them. 'I never knew you;
depart from Me, you who practice lawlessness!*

LUKE 12:16-21

"The ground of a certain rich man yielded plentifully. And he thought to himself, saying, 'What shall I do?... So he said, 'I will do this: I will pull down my barns and build greater, and there I will store all my crops and my goods. And I will say to myself, "Soul, you have many goods laid up for many years; take ease; eat, drink, and be merry."

But God said to him, 'Fool! This night your soul will be required of you; then whose will those things be which you have provided?'

This Christian Life Is Not a Game

*So is he who lays up treasure for himself
and is not rich toward God."*

MATT 7:13-14
*"Enter by the narrow gate; for wide is the gate and broad is the
way that leads to destruction, and there are many who go in by it.
Because narrow is the gate and difficult is the way
that leads to life, and there are few who find it.*

JOHN 6:60-68 (JESUS HAS JUST DESCRIBED EATING AND DRINKING FROM HIS SACRIFICE OF HIS LIFE)
*Therefore many of His disciples, when they heard this said, "This
is a hard saying; who can understand it?" ... He said to them,
"Does this offend you?" ... From that time many of His disciples
went back and walked with Him no more. Then Jesus said to the
twelve, "Do you also want to leave?" But Simon Peter answered
Him, "Lord, to whom shall we go? ... You are the Christ ..."*

GOD DESIGNED YOUR CHRISTIAN LIFE AS AN ESSENTIAL ELEMENT IN HIS KINGDOM PLANS

Are You Living the Incredible Life Christ Designed?

Where do we find ourselves in the above scriptures? What does Jesus mean as He describes *lukewarm followers whom He will vomit out of His mouth?* And what might the life of "hot" Christians look like as it is differentiated from the lives of followers who are "lukewarm" or "cold?" Like Jesus, the lives of "hot" Christians are "all-in." They learn to hold nothing back as they surrender willingly to walk under the authority of the Spirit. Their priorities begin with God and His Spirit's accomplishment of their unique missions through them. All else aligns correctly under these and is accordingly lived more effectively in Spirit. They are far from perfect, but they are growing daily. They have not walked away from, minimized, or denied Jesus.

There are many ways that Christians walk away from Jesus, even as they claim His name. Just as in John 6, many seekers and some Christians turn away because the life He places before them requires more than they are willing to accept. Others leave Christ's calling as they stay in the church but do "Christianity" their way. If they do not like what the Bible says, they redefine its meaning and find others of like persuasion so that they all feel justified in their personal beliefs. Others stay in the Church and choose to experience only the milk of Christ. They attend (or don't), participate, and claim Christ. But they do not choose to leave this safe and limited experience of Christianity to venture with the Spirit into the wilderness, where they walk amongst Christ's soldiers, those who are focused on God's missions within their areas of influence.

We are to live His life by engaging it in all the fullness of the Spirit. His exhortation to each of us is, "This (Christian) life is not a game!" His initiation of this chapter occurred as follows.

"This Life Is Not a Game!"

I was privileged to serve with a ministry that supported God's work in a challenged area. Drug dealers, crack houses, and economic needs were prevalent. The individuals and families who lived there are incredible and loved by God; He was connecting with them and calling them to Him. One night a young man was killed in a tragic situation. I asked God for His prayers for the family and what He was doing in the spirit realm over that area. He answered, *"This life is not a game! The Christian life of every believer is not a game. The spiritual lives of many unsaved individuals and the masterpiece lives of all Christians are at stake and depend on His Church. The very lives of many people are at risk every day, and most of them do not know Jesus. Although the immediate danger of death by violence, sickness, or addiction is not as imminent in all areas of the world (as it is here), it is just as real. Whether individuals have wealthy and comfortable lives or are subject to tidal waves of danger, they are all facing spiritual death every second. This is not a game!"*

His followers are to be *fully engaged*, in the roles that He has designed. Only He can develop His Church and individual Christians into the force they are to be in His kingdom. Seek to walk every minute in His Spirit or accept the fact that we have chosen a lesser life or a lesser role as individuals and organizations. Many "talk" about the Spirit, but *few consistently walk in Him*. We are not to establish nice, safe tribal cultures, where, saved or not, most are comfortable simply being "church Christians" who fit in. He loves His church and is patient with it, but He is calling it and us to rise up and live in the fullness of His design. Discipleship merely begins with salvation. We are to intentionally and fully engage in His unique kingdom lives and missions. This is achieved only by walking in God's Spirit. Are you permitting God's Spirit, through your spirit, to live and guide your life, or is your soul/body in control?

Christ Takes Us Outside of Our Comfort Zones!

Walking in Christ continuously matures us as He leads us outside our comfort zones. Christianity is not simply about being saved and having lives and families that we feel good about, as we pridefully compare ourselves to others. It is not about giving money and volunteering a little conscience-healing time while "letting the Church do the rest." And it is not about living the "nice, safe, life of comfort" that many American churches prescribe. There is nothing wrong with being successful and wealthy, or with enjoying the blessings that God has given us. There is major error in defining the "successful Christian life" by the standards of western society instead of by God's individual call and purpose for each of us.

His life is about engaging actively in the Spirit at all times in His work with humanity. Of course, it begins with sharing the gospel, but we are also called to much more. Not everyone is to stand in dangerous situations, but merely filling safe roles within the walls of our churches or ministries is generally not all that He has for us. What about our neighbors, and who is our neighbor? What is His specific mission through us today and for this season of our life? Christ's life is about taking our next obedient step of faith into areas where we are totally dependent on Him. If we are relying on our capabilities, we are out of His will.

The Spirit once showed me a joyous family consisting of husband, wife, and two children, as they were leaving church to return home. God revealed the following. *They love the Lord, tithe, attend services, and may even serve. They are happy. God has blessed them with health, a comfortable life, and they know how much He loves them. However, God wants them, and every family, to know that He has much more for them in their kingdom identities. Clearly, no one has mentored them to view their lives as more than enjoying the fruits of church and the American dream. Therefore, they do not understand the true abundant life of letting the*

Spirit guide them into God's masterpiece lives. Do they understand the dynamic of kingdom life presented in Luke 12:48?" . . . *For everyone to whom much is given, from him much will be required; and in whom much has been committed, of him they will ask the more.*" This was not and is not a statement of condemnation and burden. It is a promise of the incredible and abundant life that flows forth from those who grow and serve in His Spirit. It is speaking first and foremost about all that God has given in spiritual knowledge, gifts, and missions. This we are to *steward above all earthly gifts.*

As we consider the above scriptures, do we understand that our Father is concerned about the self-focused and self-defined lives of Christians and Christian Churches who embrace the American and also the Western gospel and are blinded to the kingdom life and spiritual warfare? This type of church life is desensitizing Christians to the masterpiece lives that God created and robbing them from *Being and Becoming* all God designed.

THE CHRISTIAN LIFE IS REAL

God's Life for You Is a Gift
You Have Not Earned Anything

> **1 COR 4:7 (IS VERY CLEAR)**
>
> *For who makes you different from another? And what do you have that you did not receive? Now if you did indeed receive it, why do you boast as if you had not received it?*

Do we think we "earned" any of the blessings God has bestowed on us, be they good looks, natural skills, health, business ability, wealth, spiritual gifts, or His kingdom impact through us? If we do, then may God forgive us. Our very faith in God, our salvation, and every kingdom and worldly gift is from Him. We are to steward all of this, including the truths and mysteries in His Spirit, with great humility.

1 COR 4:1-2

Let a man so consider us, as servants of Christ and stewards of the mysteries of God.

Moreover it is required of stewards that they be found faithful. I used to take credit for my driven and focused personality. I thought, "Everyone can choose excellence." Ultimately, I learned I did not create either that drive and focus or the willingness to apply it; God did. I am (we are), however, responsible for intentionality in learning and living in the ways of the Lord by walking in His Spirit.

Responsibility for Lifestyle Choices

Human virtues, including love, honesty, integrity, personal discipline, stewardship, self-reliance, deferral of gratification, respect for the rights and personal worth of others, and total surrender of life to the Lord, are *"learned"* virtues. (These are different from spiritual fruit and the character of Christ evidenced by those who walk in the Spirit.) Humans do not come out of the womb as anything more than self-focused individuals. Some are blessed as these behaviors are taught by solid families or other good role models. Even so, not all choose to live by them. Others do not have this advantage. However, *all are accountable for evaluating and applying what is taught in the Bible and what they can observe in varying healthy cultures and environments.* We are accountable for our choices.

When we become Christians, God introduces the expression of His Spirit's life in and through us. From that point on, we are responsible for learning from His Spirit and permitting Him to transform us into Christlikeness. Truly saved individuals who continue to live broken lives by lying, cheating, stealing, gossiping, taking advantage of others, and dishonoring others can no longer credibly blame these actions on their background or their families. We are responsible before God for intentionality in following His Spirit in all He has revealed. These transformations are not easy, and some take lifetimes as we embrace the Spirit's transformations.

The Character and Virtues of God Work!

In all cultures, the character and virtues of God produce good for both those who evidence them and the cultures themselves, regardless of whether those living them are Christians. To the level that every dominant culture or subculture lives in God's virtues, healthy lives and cultures are an accompanying result. To the point that cultures and subcultures ignore God's principles or deceptively twist them for selfish and controlling purposes (such as political gain, justifying racism, or manipulating socio-economic/ethnic groups), these cultures decay. When God's principles are set aside, all cultures wither into broken systems. Christian cultures and subcultures also decay when they attempt to live Christ's principles in the flesh instead of the Spirit.

Regardless of race, gender, ethnicity, political party, or socio-economic status, we are to live and walk in Christ's characteristics and virtues, by the power of the Holy Spirit. No subculture is to claim our allegiance above Christ. We should appropriately embrace our heritage, as long as we are not lifting it up as preferable to others. Be careful if you or your culture is living any way other than seeking to walk in the Spirit, in the character and virtues of God. Those who justify ungodly lifestyles and brokenness as "just who we are," while they insist their broken characteristics work for them, are deceiving themselves as they attempt to avoid responsibility for destructive lifestyles. The enemy has captured and deceived them. (Only God and His word are to determine what is destructive, not other tribes.)

None of us has an excuse for blaming our broken lifestyles on anyone else, even though they may have caused them. Our Father has called us to His love and has revealed Himself. He has given us the opportunities to make choices. He will continue to do so, until—and even after—our hearts are hardened beyond hope.

What Does Living in God's Unique Missions Look Like?

The biblical truths and principles of this life are the same for all. Only you and God will know and walk your specific missions daily. We are not to envy, copy, or seek to emulate anyone else. We are to know "Whose Life We Are Living" and choose God's life for every moment. There we will find Christ's abundant life as we live in His purpose with the joy that only Christ can bring. Each of us will sometimes fail and take control, but the Spirit will call us back and return us to His journey. The purity of our faith and our hearts are loved by God, and His measure is not perfection.

This Christian Life Is Not a Game

Let Him raise you to walking in the fullness of His masterpiece life and missions, because "This life is not a game!" *This is His abundant life for you, and it is unique and an integral part of His kingdom plan. Don't leave this earthly life with any of God's masterpiece left caged within.*

Application

- Whose life are you living?

- Are you willing to become all He created you to be as you embrace the fullness of living in your missions under the authority of the Spirit, because "This Christian life is not a game"?

- Are you committed to walking in the Spirit, and do you surrender all control to Him continuously? When your flesh takes control, do you hear Him calling you back, and do you immediately return?

- Do you want God's life for you or the one that you have chosen in response to expectations other than God's? Even if you feel successful and embraced by secular and church cultures, have you chosen God's life? If you are not walking in the Spirit's control, you are outside of His masterpiece life.

- What are your next steps with the Spirit?

CHAPTER 25

PUT ON GOD'S MANTLE, GO, AND TRULY LIVE!

Never Stop Learning and Stepping Out for Christ

2 KINGS 2:13

He (Elisha) took up the mantle of Elijah

EPH 5:14-18

Therefore He says: "Awake, you who sleep, Arise from the dead, And Christ will give you light."

See that you walk circumspectly, not as fools but as wise, redeeming the time because the days are evil.

Therefore, do not be unwise, but understand what the will of the Lord is.

And do not be drunk with wine, in which is dissipation, but be filled with the Spirit,

COLS 4:17B

Take heed to the ministry which you have received in the Lord, that you may fulfill it.

Do you know what it means to put on the "mantle" God designed for you and how living in this specific call is the only way to experience "truly living"? It means that you have set aside all else as you commit to living solely in your God-given identity for God's purpose. You say "Yes" to God's mantle that is your kingdom mission(s). You join with your Father God on your lifelong journey of serving in the power of His Spirit. All other elements of life fall under this priority. You truly live as you experience Christ living in and through you, and you delight in all that He accomplishes and reveals.

Kingdom living is not about position, prominent social influence, accumulating possessions, or even health. Secular society embraces all of these and chases after them for a lifetime. Christians often do the same, but they should know better. Although it is appropriate to enjoy God's gifts of earthly success (which He loves to provide as He chooses), these are not His measures for success in the lives of His Christian children.

Consider Joni Erickson Tada. She had a severe accident when she was a teenager and became a quadriplegic. She receives help with almost every activity, deals with nearly constant pain, and is confined to a wheelchair, although she has learned to view it as a blessing. She has fought cancer at least twice. Even so, she thrives. She is well known as an evangelical Christian author, radio host, and founder of Joni and Friends, which is a worldwide organization for providing Christian ministry to those with disabilities. Joni creates art by holding the paintbrush in her mouth. She is married. She is very truthful about the challenges of dealing with pain, disappointment, and depression,

Put on God's Mantle, Go, and Truly Live!

and she does not "fake the Christian life" by hiding from these realities. She turns to Christ to handle them, and chooses to live a victorious, Christ-honoring life. She has chosen to "Really Live" in Christ.

> *Truly living each day for Christians is living in a deep and loving personal relationship with God, while yielding control of our lives to His Spirit. God's Spirit transforms us and accomplishes His missions in and through us. Each minute is then an expression of Christ, whether it is tragic or victorious. We walk with Christ in a passion that others cannot imagine, even when we are experiencing absolute brokenness. Our lives may be very difficult, but they are filled with God's victory. As we walk in the Spirit, we are no longer "trying" to be Christ's masterpiece. We are Being and Becoming it through His power.*

Truly living as a Christian takes many forms, but it is not ever about walking through life expecting to always have a sunny day and a smooth road. Neither is it about self-focus. It is about knowing God's absolute love and walking in His Spirit as we live *"all-in"* according to His purposes/missions. His masterpiece life eclipses every other option. Embracing it requires salvation, being filled with the fullness of God (His Spirit), and walking in His Spirit. Then, we truly live.

WHOSE LIFE ARE YOU LIVING?

EPH 3:16-21

*... that he would grant you, according to the riches
of His glory, to be strengthened with might
through His Spirit in the inner man,*

*that Christ may dwell in your hearts through faith;
that you, being rooted and grounded in love,*

*may be able to comprehend with all the saints what
is the width and length and depth and height—*

*to know the love of Christ which passes knowledge;
that you may be filled with all the fullness of God.*

> *Truly living does not have anything to do with what we do in our own strength. It is all about what Christ does both in and through us. Have we given Him our all and held nothing back?*

Living every day in Christ takes intentionality. We fail when we do things in our own strength. Even as we seek to walk in His Spirit, we will sin, but with decreasing frequency. Importantly, when we do, we do not let the enemy defeat us. We listen to the Spirit, get up, repent, receive forgiveness, and move on, stronger in His unconditional love. Every day is an incredible journey with our Father, who always sees us as His finished masterpieces in Christ. He knows our hearts and understands that, just as children fall while learning to walk, we will occasionally fall as we step out in faith. *Put on your mantle, and live.*

Do Not Get Distracted

Many of us become distracted by the brokenness and continual decay of the cultures surrounding us. It is natural to be aware and even grieve, but God does not want us to be drawn away from His purposes. We are most effective when we remain laser-focused on the missions He has assigned, and on walking them in His Spirit. Doing otherwise is being drawn into the futility of walking in our flesh.

And They Truly Lived!

I have a favorite line from the movie *Secondhand Lions*. Two bachelor brothers lived much of their lives full of energy and enthusiasm. They got encumbered by age and started to give up, but then found a way to experience new things. In their nineties, they die while living a final dream of stunt flying. The movie ended with the comment that, throughout life, "They truly lived!" Extraordinary events in all of our lives are wonderful, but they normally do not make up the greatest number of our days. Even these high-octane movie characters found real meaning in the daily patterns of successfully loving and parenting their nephew.

Most of our days are to be spent finding God's joy in our daily walk with Him, as we live that day's elements of our kingdom missions. Portions are spent in finding His purpose and deep growth during days or seasons of challenge and pain. As Christians, we are to live every moment, whether they are exciting, average, or difficult, in the incredible wonder of walking in Christ. We are never to stagnate as God leads us to grow in Christ and step out for Him until the moment that He calls us to heaven.

As long as our minds are working, He has a new experience of Himself and His life for us. (He does use us even if He permits us to live with dysfunctional minds.) Each life has significant Kingdom value. This is not meaningless positive thinking; it is His truth. I am not always successful in living this way, but I am committed to His victories, including finding His growth and love during my broken times and failures. His life for us is not easy, but it is incredible as we learn to walk every step holding the hand of our Heavenly Father, who delights in us.

Decide to truly live in Christ. Choose His life and His mantle, and you will leave this Earth with all of God's purpose and power having been expressed both in and through you for His Glory. Nothing will be left caged within.

Nothing will ever be more satisfying than knowing that we are living in His Spirit as His masterpiece. We have heard God's unique calling, have obeyed the Spirit, and have permitted Him to live both in and through us to accomplish His missions through His love and power. We will be one of His children who have "Truly Lived."

Whose Life Are You Living?
Whose Life Are You Going To Live?
Walk in God's Spirit for His Purposes—and Truly Live!

JOSHUA 1:9

Have I not commanded you? Be strong and of good courage; do not be afraid, nor be dismayed, for the Lord your God is with you wherever you go.

About the Author

Curt Martin is a Christian author, speaker, and seminar leader. His kingdom mission is to help individuals and organizations thrive as the unique masterpieces God designed. He has forty-five years of experience in leading business organizations, engaging in business consulting, and participating in ministries at board and volunteer levels. He serves as a pre-marriage mentor and a facilitator of marriage development and *Whose Life* groups. Curt enjoys developing meaningful relationships with individuals of every ethnicity, socio-economic background, and journey for gaining Christ's victories over conflicting priorities, broken identities, addictions, and mental health challenges. He believes that the greatest opportunity in the Christian Church is for each Christian to learn to walk in Christ's Spirit on their journey of being and becoming the unique masterpiece He designed and ensuring that as they transition from this life to heaven nothing of Christ's identity, mission, and power for their life will be left caged within. He and his wife reside in Lancaster, PA.

Printed in Great Britain
by Amazon